UNDERSTANDING ELDER ABUSE IN
MINORITY POPULATIONS

UNDERSTANDING ELDER ABUSE IN MINORITY POPULATIONS

Edited by
Toshio Tatara, Ph.D.
Sociology Department
Shukutoku University
Chiba, Japan

USA	Publishing Office:	BRUNNER/MAZEL
		A member of the Taylor & Francis Group
		325 Chestnut Street
		Philadelphia, PA 19106
		Tel: (215) 625-8900
		Fax: (215) 625-2940
	Distribution Center:	BRUNNER/MAZEL
		A member of the Taylor & Francis Group
		47 Runway Road
		Levittown, PA 19057
		Tel: (215) 269-0400
		Fax: (215) 269-0363
UK		BRUNNER/MAZEL
		A member of the Taylor & Francis Group
		1 Gunpowder Square
		London EC4A 3DE
		Tel: +44 171 583 0490
		Fax: +44 171 583 0581

UNDERSTANDING ELDER ABUSE IN MINORITY POPULATIONS

1 2 3 4 5 6 7 8 9 0

Printed by Braun-Brumfield, Ann Arbor, MI, 1998.

A CIP catalog record for this book is available from the British Library.
∞ The paper in this publication meets the requirements of the ANSI Standard Z39.48-1984 (Permanence of Paper).

Library of Congress Cataloging-in-Publication Data

Understanding elder abuse in minority populations / edited by Toshio Tatara.
   p. cm.
Includes bibliographical references.
ISBN 0-87630-919-8 (case: alk. paper). – ISBN 0-87630-920-1 (pbk.: alk. paper)
1. Elder abuse–United States. 2. Minorities–United States. I. Tatara, Toshio.
HV6626.3.U52   1998
362.6–dc21   98-33541
                                                                                    CIP

0-87630-919-8 (case)
0-87630-920-1 (paper)

Contents

v

Contributors

DONNA M. BENTON, Ph.D., is an Assistant Research Professor of Gerontology at the University of Southern California, Andrus Gerontology Center, and is codirector of the Research, Training, and Information Transfer Core of the Alzheimer's Disease Research Center. She is also chair of the Ombudsman Blue Ribbon Committee at WISE Senior Services and has served as a consultant for the Los Angeles County Area Agency on Aging. She is the author of more than 20 articles, book chapters, and books and has presented numerous lectures, workshops, training projects, and conferences on elder abuse and neglect, including the National Conference on Understanding and Combating Elder Abuse in Minority Populations. She is currently a participant in a multicultural study on minority elders' attitudes towards elder mistreatment and reporting.

ARNOLD S. BROWN, Ph.D., is Professor Emeritus of Sociology and Gerontology in the Department of Sociology and Social Work at Northern Arizona University. In addition to his more than 20 years of teaching, he has conducted numerous research studies on Native American elderly, and he is currently a participant in a multicultural study on minority elders' attitudes towards elder mistreatment and reporting. He has also contributed to *The Gerontologist* and the *Journal of Elder Abuse & Neglect* and published a sociology-of-aging textbook, *The Social Presses of Aging and Old Age*.

JOHN R. CARLSON, M.S., is a Research Assistant Professor in the School of Nursing at the University of North Carolina at Chapel Hill, where he has been on the faculty for ten years. Since 1973, he has been involved in research in many areas of aging and elders, such as health, housing, and satisfaction in community dwelling; and factors related to and instrumentation for detecting confusion in hospitalized elders. His current research is in public definitions and perceptions of elder abuse, detection of elder abuse, and nursing screens for chronic cognitive impairment.

DAVID K. CARSON, Ph.D., is a Professor of Child and Family Studies in the Department of Family and Consumer Sciences at the University of Wyoming, and a licensed Marriage and Family Therapist. Over his 20-year career, he has worked in many countries and with numerous Native American tribes and is the recipient of several major teaching awards. He has published over 45 journal articles and reports, a recent article being on elder abuse among Native Americans in the *Journal of Elder Abuse & Neglect.*

NICOLO A. FESTA, M.S.W., has 20 years of experience working with persons who are elderly and persons with mental illness and mental retardation. He is currently employed at the Texas Department of Protective and Regulatory Services in the Adult Protective Services program, where he has been employed for 12 years.

MARY A. FLUM, M.A., was a research analyst for the National Center on Elder Abuse. Prior to her work there, she worked at the American Association of Retired Persons on preliminary research for the project, *Images of Aging in America.* Her area of interest is advocacy toward older adults vulnerable to abuse. She received her M.A. from the University of Northern Colorado in gerontology, and her B.S. in consumer economics from Indiana University in Pennsylvania.

ADRIANA C. FRANCO is a graduate of Texas Tech University at Lubbock with more than 6 years of experience in working with aged and disabled persons. While employed by the Texas Department of Protective and Regulatory Services she has worked in several areas of the Adult Protective Services Program and is currently a Program Specialist III; she is responsible for developing statewide policy.

LINNER WARD GRIFFIN, Ed.D., M.S.W., is an associate professor and the Associate Dean for Graduate Studies in the School of Social Work and Criminal Justice Program at East Carolina University at Greenville. She also serves as the Associate Director for Educational Programs for the ECU Center on Aging. She has an extensive background in social-work practice with individuals and families in geriatric, health, and mental-health settings. She has completed research that has yielded numerous articles and other publications in the areas of elder abuse and maltreatment, adult-protective services, and organ transplantation. She also has provided consultation and training in adult-protective services and about elder maltreatment in the African American community to many states' agencies and at national forums. She is a member of national and North Carolina task forces on aging-services delivery and interdisciplinary medical practice, and she is a member of a consortium of university planning boards in gerontology.

JOYCE M. HALL is Chief of the Protective Services Unit of the Rhode Island Department of Elderly Affairs. She lectures and provides in-service training on elder abuse to local agencies and at seminars and conferences, and she is a board member of the Providence Mental Health Center and the Governor's Council on Mental Health.

CAROL HAND, M.S.S.W., serves as an adjunct lecturer in Social Work for Mount Senario College and as staff for the Center for Health Policy and Program Evaluation at the University of Wisconsin, Madison. She has been involved in numerous projects that focused on elder Native Americans and the general elder population, coordinated an Administration on Aging grant intended to address elder abuse by male caregivers, and developed an assessment tool to determine the effectiveness of Wisconsin's community long-term care services from the perspective of clients.

MARGARET F. HUDSON, Ph.D., R.N., is an Associate Professor of the School of Nursing at the University of North Carolina at Chapel Hill. She recently conducted a study on elder abuse with a grant from the National Institute of Health and has published numerous reports, book chapters, and articles for the *Journal of Elder Abuse & Neglect*, among other publications, on elder abuse.

DELMA JUAREZ has over 20 years of experience working with aged and disabled persons. She served as Director of the Capital Area Planning Council, Area Agency on Aging in Austin, Texas, and also served as a supervisor with the Texas Department of Human Services Aged and Disabled Program. She is currently employed by the Texas Department of Protective and Regulatory Services as a Program Specialist III in the Adult Protective Services Program.

LISA B. KUZMESKUS, M.A., is a demographer with the U.S. Bureau of the Census, Population Division, Population Projections Branch. She works primarily on producing a series of monthly national estimates of the population and the yearly updates associated with the national estimates and the projection series. Furthermore, she assists in the production of aging-related products developed by the branch. Prior to this, Ms. Kuzmeskus was a Research Analyst with the American Public Welfare Association, spending most of her time working for the National Center on Elder Abuse and the National Elder Abuse Incidence Study. Her research interests focus on the demography of aging, the abuse of the elderly, and minority aging. Ms. Kuzmeskus has coauthored many relevant publications, including *Summaries of the Statistical Data on Elder Abuse in Domestic Settings for FY 95 and FY 96* and a series of information sheets that pertain to elder abuse.

LINDA L. LAMB, M.S.W., has worked in programs that serve persons with disabilities and the elderly for more than 22 years. In 1988, Ms. Lamb piloted the In-Home and Family Support Program, the first direct-grant program in Texas providing assistance to persons with disabilities and their families. She is currently employed by the Texas Department of Protective Services State Office as a Program Specialist in the Adult Protective Services division.

BETTYE M. MITCHELL, M.A., is Director of Adult Protective Services of the Texas Department of Protective and Regulatory Services. With 20 years of experience working with elderly persons, she is in frequent demand as a keynote speaker, group facilitator, and trainer on the topics of aging, motivation, and elder abuse. She serves on the International Advisory Committee on a project, originated in Japan, to develop and disseminate a Professional Capability Evaluation Protocol in Health and Social Services.

AILEE MOON, Ph.D., is Associate Professor in the Department of Social Welfare, School of Public Policy and Social Research, at the University of California, Los Angeles. She is active in gerontological research in the areas of elder abuse, mental health, and service utilization and is currently participating in a multicultural study on minority elders' attitudes towards elder mistreatment and reporting. She is also co-principal investigator on a 4-year study that examines social supports and long-term care use among elderly Korean Americans. She has written more than 20 articles, research reports, monographs, and book chapters, and she serves on the boards of several service agencies.

LISA NERENBERG, M.S.W., M.P.H., is Director of the San Francisco Consortium for Elder Abuse Prevention. She has authored numerous articles and training materials on elder abuse, including *Financial Abuse of the Elderly*. She is a frequent presenter at professional forums, including the National Conference on Understanding and Combating Elder Abuse in Minority Populations, and provides training and technical assistance to state and local adult-protection and aging-service providers across the United States and Canada. Her special interest is in culturally specific outreach, and she has edited and authored manuals on elder abuse in the Asian and African American communities.

MARGARET RITTMAN, M.A., was the Research Editor for the National Center on Elder Abuse (NCEA) and the Research and Demonstration Department of the American Public Welfare Association (APWA) until March 1998. She served in these positions at NCEA and APWA for about 10 years. Ms. Rittman has been the director of habilitation services for a state program on mainstreaming adult and elderly patients with developmental disabilities. She has written book chapters and publications on medicine, including technology and philosophy, and is a private consultant to the U.S. Department of Education.

CARMEN D. SÁNCHEZ, D.S.W., is Professor and Dean of Academic Affairs at the Graduate School of Social Work of the University of Puerto Rico in San Juan. She serves as consultant on aging and social-work issues for the Veterans Administration Hospital, is a member of the National Advisory Council, and has lectured all over the world. Recognized as an expert in aging affairs in Latin America, Puerto Rico, and the United States, she is the author of more than 25 articles, book chapters, and books published in three languages. She is also a participant in a multicultural study on minority elders' attitudes towards elder mistreatment and reporting.

YOLANDA M. SANCHEZ, Ph.D., is an Assistant Professor of Adult Development and Aging in the Department of Human Development and Family Studies at the University of Nevada, Reno. She has worked extensively in service delivery and program development with Latino communities in Mexico, California, and Michigan, and she has recently completed a cross-regional project examining elder abuse in two Latino communities in Nevada and Michigan. She has coauthored book chapters, is published in the *Journal of Elder Abuse & Neglect*, serves on advisory boards for several local and national organizations, and is participating in a multicultural study on minority elders' attitudes towards elder mistreatment and reporting.

TOSHIO TATARA, Ph.D., is a Professor in the Sociology Department at Shukutoku University in Chiba, Japan. From October 1977 through April 1998, he served as Director of the Research and Demonstration Department at the American Public Welfare Association (currently the American Public Human Services Association). He also directed the National Resource Center on Elder Abuse from October 1988 through September 1992 and the National Center on Elder Abuse from October 1993 through April 1998. With over 25 years of professional experience in human services, Dr. Tatara has directed nearly 50 research, demonstration, evaluation, and training projects, and he is considered one of the nation's leading experts in elder abuse and child foster-care statistics. He is the author of more than 50 articles, book chapters, and books published both in the United States and abroad. He served as Principal Investigator for the first national elder-abuse incidence study undertaken in the United States, which was completed in the summer of 1998 and sponsored by the federal government.

SUSAN K. TOMITA, Ph.D., is an Associate Director of Social Work at Harborview Medical Center in Seattle and manages the Medicine–Surgery Social Work Unit. She is also a clinical associate professor at the University of Washington School of Social Work. Specializing in the assessment and treatment of various forms of elder abuse, she developed the nationally adopted Elder Abuse Diagnosis and Intervention protocol, coauthored two editions of a book on elder mistreatment, cofounded the Greater Seattle Elder Abuse Network, and is participating in a multicultural study on minority elders' attitudes towards elder mistreatment and reporting. She lectures nationally and has extensive volunteer experience in the Asian community.

Preface

Understanding Elder Abuse in Minority Populations was born out of a desire to bring to the public perspectives and information about elder abuse that have heretofore been missing, so that many crucial elder-abuse issues related to minority communities could be examined in-depth for the first time. To date, no books addressing elder maltreatment specifically in racial and ethnic minority populations have been published in the United States or anywhere in the world.

With that in mind, researchers and practitioners with expertise concerning elder abuse in several minority populations—Black, Hispanic, Asian American, and American Indian—were asked to contribute manuscripts on their research findings or on the knowledge gained from their years of professional practice. From the start of this book project, it was the intention of this editor to recruit, to the extent possible, the researchers and practicing professionals who are members of minority groups. The result of this effort was gratifying because most of this book's chapter authors are indigenous to the culture on which they have written. In addition to 10 "culturally specific" chapters, three other chapters were added to address cross-cultural issues in elder abuse and to present an extensive review of the literature on minority elder abuse. Together, the 13 core chapters of this book hopefully will infuse new perspectives into discussions pertaining to elder abuse.

ORGANIZATION OF THE BOOK

This book is organized into five major sections on four racial/ethnic populations: Black, Hispanic, Asian American, and American Indian. The first section, elder abuse in the Black population, is addressed in three chapters. In Chapter 2, Hall provides a look at her experiences in providing services to abused elders in Rhode Island. She notes the problems and strengths of Black elders and their families and gives a framework for providing services to those who are abused. Hall's particular area of interest is examining the reasons that keep friends and neighbors of an abused Black elder from seeking help for the abused person. These reasons provide insight into how to structure outreach services to any community of elderly persons.

In Chapter 3, Griffin emphasizes the need to involve elderly persons, and not solely researchers and practitioners, when we define elder maltreatment. Mislabeling the problem and providing inappropriate interventions can occur if the elderly are not involved in this ground-level work, Griffin explains. Interestingly, the author's research shows that an area that needs to be examined in Black elder abuse situations is the extent to which perpetrators may be "involved in dependent, mutually beneficial relationships" with the elder. We need to look closely, Griffin notes, at whether these relationships involve emotional maltreatment of the adult child as a type of "encouraged" infantilism. This information is critical in addressing the elder's situation.

In Chapter 4, Benton elucidates the risk factors that may be more pronounced and others that may be less important in looking at elder abuse in the Black community. She also delineates possible ways to target outreach activities, which are an essential element for finding and helping elderly people who are being abused.

Chapters 5 through 7 address the issue of elder abuse in Hispanic communities. In Chapter 5, Yolanda Sanchez finds that the lack of elder-abuse research in the Latino community may stem from a tendency by researchers to overemphasize family solidarity among Latino people and does not necessarily indicate an absence of elder abuse. She shows how acculturation and assimilation into the mainstream culture need to be factored in when assessing elder abuse in any Hispanic community.

In Chapter 6, Mitchell et al. examine how the Texas government is providing adult protective service workers with a basic foundation to acknowledge distinct cultural characteristics in the Mexican American community that may have a relationship to elder mistreatment and service delivery. To assess the staff's cultural sensitivity, a self-assessment questionnaire was administered, followed by discussions in focus groups of caseworkers, supervisors, and program administrators. Information gained in these efforts is being used to make improvements in the service delivery system in Texas.

Carmen Sánchez, in Chapter 7, addresses elder abuse in the Commonwealth of Puerto Rico. She describes the need for more in-home services for frail elderly, as the majority of Puerto Rican elderly are cared for at home. Sanchez also explores the insidiousness of ageism and how it manifests itself and affects the elderly in Puerto Rico.

Chapters 8 and 9 present the issue of elder abuse in the Asian population in this country. In Chapter 8, Moon concentrates on elder abuse and neglect among the Korean elderly in the United States. She identifies the most common types of elder abuse in the Korean American community: the exploitation of the labor and finances of elderly parents and neglect of their emotional, social, and functional needs. Moon recommends enlisting community organizations that Koreans frequent, along with social-service agencies, to create activities that encourage interactions and improve relationships between elderly parents and their adult children.

In Chapter 9, Tomita examines the importance of group membership in addressing how elderly Japanese individuals define themselves. She offers an in-depth look at how the elderly view abusive situations, and she also explores the cultural factors that affect elder abuse. Tomita provides practice implications for working with Japanese elder-abuse victims in the United States.

Chapters 10 and 11 concentrate on Native Americans and elder abuse. Chapter 10, by Brown, focuses on the patterns of abuse among elderly Native Americans and offers policies and corrective actions to prevent abuse. These actions center on educational efforts, one for families and another for professionals, including social workers, law-enforcement personnel, and tribal officials. Brown also looks at the lack of economic development and the cultural isolation that are important factors leading to possible elder abuse or neglect.

In Chapter 11, Carson and Hand examine the process of aging in tribal cultures and provide a conceptual structure for understanding abuse and neglect among Native Americans. The risk factors for abuse are examined and the programs, services, and changes in legislation and policy that are needed to address elder abuse and neglect also are discussed.

Cross-cultural perspectives on elder abuse, from a research standpoint and a practice approach, are presented in Chapters 12 and 13. Hudson and Carlson conducted a study on perceptions of elder abuse among Caucasians, African Americans, and Native Americans residing in North Carolina. The authors found that all three racial groups agreed with most aspects of the experts' taxonomy and definition of elder abuse. The study also found that when given specific elder-abuse scenarios, the Native Americans rated more items as abusive than African Americans and Caucasians, with African Americans rating more items as abusive than Caucasians. The possible implications of these findings are discussed.

In Chapter 13, Nerenberg looks at culturally specific outreach programs that are aimed at providing protective or preventive services to specific communities. The author's experiences in elder-abuse prevention are described and specific strategies for extending access to underserved groups are discussed. The author gives information that can serve as guidance to those interested in designing culturally specific outreach programs.

Finally, Chapter 14 presents an in-depth examination by Flum, Kuzmeskus, and Rittman of the research literature on abuse and neglect of minority elders. This chapter focuses on research in the Black, Hispanic, American Indian, and Asian American communities. Although generally there is a lack of studies on minority elder abuse, some significant studies have been done, with important supplementary research on cultural conditions and use of medical or social services by minority elderly adding much to the discussion. Several findings in the literature, including the importance of adult children tending to their parents' needs, the cultural preference to try and solve elder abuse issues within the ethnic community, and the types of abuse that most commonly surface in different ethnic communities, add a vital dimension to this book that can help shape the discussion of abuse and neglect of minority elders.

Toshio Tatara
Tokyo, Japan, July 1998

Acknowledgments

The completion of this book would not have been possible without the cooperation of the researchers and practitioners who have contributed their time and effort in writing these chapters. The editor would like to extend his deep appreciation to the chapter authors for completing their work in a timely manner. Further, the editor is greatly indebted to Ms. Bernadette Capelle, Acquisitions Editor with Brunner/Mazel Publishers, for her advice and comments on earlier drafts of the book, Ms. Catherine Kovacs, Production Editor with Brunner/Mazel Publishers, for her assistance in finalizing all the manuscripts, and Ms. Leslie Bivens, Administrative Assistant for the National Center on Elder Abuse, for typing the draft manuscripts.

Chapter 1

Introduction

Toshio Tatara

Research on elder abuse in the United States has made great strides in helping to delineate definitions of abuse, neglect, and exploitation, explore causes of various types of maltreatment, develop and implement ways to treat and prevent the problem, design tools to assess the risk factors of abuse, and evaluate and validate programs serving victims and perpetrators (Stein, 1989). Thus, a considerable amount of information is available today regarding the possible causes of elder abuse and the effect of abuse on elders and their families, as well as about ways in which the problem should be combated. Yet what is known about elder abuse today has been derived largely from studies of individuals and groups that were mostly White. It is not that minorities were excluded from studies of elder abuse, but rather that early researchers were more preoccupied with efforts to understand the nature of elder mistreatment *generally* than they were concerned with the circumstances of particular racial or ethnic minority elders. As public awareness of elder abuse gradually rose and more researchers became involved with inquiries into elder abuse, a lack of (as well as a need for) knowledge of how elder abuse is defined, identified, and treated in minority populations became apparent (Moon & Williams, 1993).

This book comes at an opportune time in history when "cultural diversity" in aging is no longer just a concept but a reality in the United States, and an "aging society" is just around the corner: There is now an urgent need for developing new approaches to address issues in such a society (Bass, Kutza, & Torres-Gil, 1990; Stanford & Torres-Gil, 1991). The main purpose of the book is to critically examine abuse and neglect in several racial and ethnic minority populations mostly from minority researchers' viewpoints and based on their empirical studies. What is offered in this book is relevant today, but the book's relevance to the field of elder abuse may increase in the future, as the nation's minority elder populations rapidly grow.

1

Table 1.1   U.S. Elder Population from 1997 Through 2030

	1997	2000	2010	2020	2030
U.S. elder population, ×1000	44,159	45,363	55,623	73,769	87,875
Percent increase from 1997	—	2.7	26.0	67.1	99.0
Total U.S. population, ×1000	267,645	274,634	297,716	322,742	346,899
Percent increase from 1997	—	2.6	11.2	20.6	29.6
Percent of elder population	16.5	16.5	18.7	22.8	25.3

Note: For the purpose of this analysis, an elder is defined as anyone who is 60 years of age or older.

Source: Day, *Population Projections of the United States by Age, Sex, Race, and Hispanic Origin: 1995 to 2050*, 1996.

DEMOGRAPHIC CHANGES AMONG THE ELDERLY IN MINORITY POPULATIONS

The elder population is growing very fast in the United States, and if current trends continue, in about another 30 years, it is expected that one out of four persons (or 25.3%) in this country will be an elder, 60 years of age or older (Day, 1996). Specifically, there will be a rise in the number of the U.S. elder population from 44,159,000 in 1997 to 87,875,000 in 2030—an increase of 99.0%. It is well accepted that this stunning rate of growth in the elder population is attributed largely to the fact that the "baby boomers" will be becoming members of the elder population in a 20- to 30-year period, right after the turn of the next century, and more people will be living longer. The U.S. Bureau of the Census predicts that during the same period, the total U.S. population will increase only by 29.6%, from 267,645,000 to 346,899,000, as shown in Table 1.1. One of the most amazing features of the current demographic changes in the U.S. population is the rapid growth of racial and ethnic minority elder populations. This phenomenon is not new and must have been in progress since the 1960s, but it has not been widely recognized or discussed (Spencer, 1988; American Society on Aging, 1992).

Table 1.2 presents the U.S. Census Bureau's projections of how the minority elder populations, as well as the White elderly population, in this country will grow in numbers from 1997 to 2030. For the purpose of this analysis, the following four groups are defined as minority elderly: Black, Hispanic, Asian/Pacific Islander, and American Indian.

As shown in Table 1.2, the White elder population will grow steadily from 37,010,000 in 1997 to 64,292,000 in 2030, resulting in an increase of 73.7%. On the other hand, projected increases in the numbers of minority elder populations over the same period are phenomenal: For example, the Black elder population will rise from 3,671,000 in 1997 to 8,484,000 in 2030 (an increase of 131.1%), while the Hispanic elder population will grow from 2,322,000 in 1997 to 10,457,000 in 2030 (an increase of 350.3%). With this rate of increase, Hispanic elders will become the largest category of minority elders in the first 30 years of the next century, surpassing Black elders. Additionally, the Asian/Pacific Islander

Table 1.2   U.S. Elder Population by Race/Ethnicity from 1997 Through 2030

	1997	2000	2010	2020	2030
Total U.S. elder population, ×1000	44,159	45,363	55,623	73,769	87,875
Black, ×1000	3,671	3,815	4,814	6,900	8,484
Percent of elder population	8.3	8.4	8.7	9.4	9.7
Percent increase from 1997	—	3.9	31.1	88.0	131.1
Hispanic, ×1000	2,322	2,627	4,135	6,858	10,457
Percent of elder population	5.3	5.8	7.4	9.3	11.9
Percent increase from 1997	—	13.1	78.1	195.3	350.3
Asian/Pacific Islander, ×1000	963	1,125	1,889	2,988	4,179
Percent of elder population	2.2	2.5	3.4	4.0	4.8
Percent increase from 1997	—	16.8	96.2	210.3	334.0
American Indian, ×1000	192	208	283	385	464
Percent of elder population	0.4	0.5	0.5	0.5	0.5
Percent increase from 1997	—	8.3	47.4	100.5	141.7
White, ×1000	37,010	37,591	44,503	56,637	64,292
Percent of elder population	83.8	82.8	80.0	76.8	73.2
Percent increase from 1997	—	1.6	20.2	53.0	73.7

Note: An elder is defined as anyone who is 60 years of age and older.
Source: Day, Population Projections of the United States by Age, Sex, Race, and Hispanic Origin: 1995 to 2050, 1996.

elder population will increase in number from 963,000 in 1997 to 4,179,000 in 2030 (an increase of 334.0%), whereas the American Indian elder population will change from 192,000 in 1997 to 464,000 in 2030 (an increase of 141.7%). Finally, all the minority elder populations combined account for 16.2% of the total U.S. elder population in 1997, but the proportion of the minority elder populations will continue to grow in the next few decades and is expected to reach 26.8% of the total U.S. elder population by 2030. In other words, by the end of the next generation, aging of this country's population will be such that one out of four will be an elderly person and one in any four elderly people will be a minority elder.

The implications of growing minority elder populations for the incidence of elder abuse among minority elders cannot be determined immediately. However, it appears reasonable to assume that unless there is significant improvement in conditions that make minority elders vulnerable to elder mistreatment, minority elders will continue to be overrepresented in the statistics for reports and victims of elder abuse. For many years, researchers argued that more minority elders were experiencing economic, social, and health conditions that were adverse to their well-being than White elders (National Indian Council on Aging, 1981; National Center for Health Statistics, 1984). It appeared that there was a great deal of agreement among experts that minority elders are much poorer, less educated, more underemployed, more prone to illness, and more likely to reside in substandard housing than White elders (U.S. Congress, 1988; Cuellar, 1990; Lopez & Aguilera, 1991; Krause & Wray, 1991; Lacayo, 1991). However, studies that examined elder abuse in minority populations were inconclusive in specifying the vulnerability of minority status as a cause of the problem (Cazenave, 1983; Hall, 1987; Williams & Griffin, 1991). Interestingly, some researchers also found from their study of a larger nationally representative sample of elders that the "rates of abuse and neglect were no higher for minority than for white elderly" (Pillemer & Finkelhor, 1988). Nonetheless, data appear to be compelling that minority elders are currently faced with more risk factors that threaten their well-being than are White elders (Manuel & Berk, 1983; American Society on Aging, 1992), and there is an immediate need for removing these risk factors, regardless of whether or not they are specifically related to elder abuse. Next, a brief examination is done to show how racial and ethnic issues have been addressed in earlier studies of elder abuse in the United States.

RACE/ETHNICITY OF ELDER-ABUSE VICTIMS IN PREVIOUS STUDIES

Researchers working on early studies of elder abuse gathered some data on race and ethnicity, but they did not extensively analyze these data to explore the effect of race/ethnicity on elder mistreatment. Thus, except for showing the fact that minority elders do become victims of elder abuse, many early studies offered little additional information about the relationship between race/ethnicity and elder abuse. Further, the numbers of elder-abuse victims examined by early studies were so small, in addition to not being chosen in a statistically sound manner, that the studies' results could not be generalized. For example, Lau and Kosberg (1979) reported that of 39 elder-abuse victims they had identified from the case records of an agency serving aged and chronically ill people, 29 were White and the remaining 10 were Black. Similarly, Block and Sinnott (1979) found 26 victims of elder mistreatment from a survey of professionals and agencies in Maryland and reported, without giving exact numbers, that 88% of them were White and 12% were Black. Gioglio and Blakemore's study in New Jersey (1982) identified a "total of 23 unduplicated incidents of various forms of elder abuse" but found that all of these abuse incidents involved White elders. Hall (1987), on the other hand, showed that 44% (or 126 people) of his sample were minority elders, and 56% (or 161 people) were nonminority. Of Hall's 126 minority elders, 81 (or 64%) were Black and 45 (or 36%) were Hispanic. The fact that Hall's study relied on the data provided by the Texas Adult Protective Services Program accounts for the presence of a large number of Hispanic elders (most of whom were assumed to be Mexican Americans or Mexicans) in the sample. Finally, Longres's data (1991) on the elderly in Milwaukee County, Wisconsin, who were referred to the state's elder-abuse reporting system revealed that Black elders were overrepresented (whereas 19.5% of the substantiated cases were Black, only 5.2% of the county's population were Black elders), and White elders were underrepresented (whereas 79.0% of the substantiated cases were White, 93.6% of the county's elders were White). Nonetheless, the researcher concluded that "black elderly were

Table 1.3 Race/Ethnicity of Domestic Elder Abuse Victims

Race/Ethnicity	Fiscal year			
	1993	1994	1995	1996
White, %	66.8	65.4	66.5	66.4
Black, %	19.3	21.4	19.3	18.7
Hispanic, %	10.8	9.6	9.9	10.4
Native American/Alaskan, %	0.5	0.5	0.6	0.7
Asian/Pacific Islander, %	0.5	0.6	0.4	0.3
Other, %	1.1	0.6	1.9	1.9
Unknown, %	1.0	1.9	1.4	1.6
No. of States Reporting	32	29	31	31

Note: All data are based on substantiated reports of domestic elder abuse.
Source: Toshio Tatara and Lisa M. Blumerman, *Summaries of the Statistical Data on Elder Abuse in Domestic Settings: An Exploratory Study of State Statistics for FY 93 and FY 94* (National Center on Elder Abuse, Washington, DC, 1996); Toshio Tatara and Lisa M. Kuzmeskus, *Summaries of the Statistical Data on Elder Abuse in Domestic Settings for FY 95 and FY 96* (National Center on Elder Abuse, Washington, DC, 1997).

no more likely than white elderly to be perceived as experiencing a form of mal-treatment."

It is only recently that states' information systems on elder abuse began col-lecting race/ethnicity data, and not all states are as yet able to generate statistics showing the racial or ethnic characteristics of elder abuse victims. Tatara, who has been collecting and analyzing data on elder-abuse reports from states since the mid-1980s, showed for the first time in 1996 that both Black and Hispanic elders were overrepresented in the state statistics for the substantiated reports of domestic elder abuse (Tatara & Blumerman, 1996; Tatara & Kuzmeskus, 1997). Table 1.3 presents that data on race/ethnicity of domestic elder-abuse victims for fiscal year 1993 through fiscal year 1996 that were gathered from states. Informa-tion about "percentage of elder population" for each racial/ethnic group presented in Table 1.2 would be useful in analyzing whether a particular group is propor-tionally overrepresented or underrepresented in the state statistics for domestic elder-abuse victims.

Table 1.3 shows that, indeed, Black and Hispanic elders were overrepresented in the state data on domestic elder abuse victims over the years. However, it is im-portant to stress that not all states are included in these data, thus making the data less than nationally representative. Additionally, the nature of these data is such that no tests of statistical significance can be performed. Therefore, these fig-ures in Table 1.3 provide only "descriptive" information about each racial/ethnic group's representation and do not say anything about the statistical significance of each figure. Nevertheless, the fact remains that roughly one of three victims of elder abuse (or 32.0%) who are known to authorities is a minority elder at least in the 31 states that provided data. If the ratio of minority elder-abuse vic-tims to White elder-abuse victims in the remaining states in the country is the same as that obtained from these 31 states, minority elders are overrepresented in the nation's elder-abuse victim population by nearly 100% because the minority elder population accounts for only 16.2% of the U.S. elder population in 1997. This information should be a source of great concern for many people, because it suggests that the rate of minority elders' representation in the elder-abuse victim population will be astoundingly high when the nation's minority elder population reaches 26.3% of the total U.S. elder population by 2030, as shown in Table 1.1.

A BRIEF DISCUSSION ON ELDER-ABUSE REPORTS AND ELDER-ABUSE INCIDENCE

The data on elder abuse victims that were used to construct Table 1.3 were derived from the aggregate statistics of substantiated reports of elder maltreatment gathered from states by the National Center on Elder Abuse (NCEA). "Substantiated reports" are counts of reports of alleged elder maltreatment for which an official determination has been made after an investigation that the alleged act of maltreatment indeed occurred. "Reports" are not exactly the same as counts of individuals. Some reports involve more than one elderly person; others are duplicated reports on one person who has been reported by more than one reporter. The NCEA's investigation shows that, generally, the count of elderly victims is slightly smaller than the count of elder abuse reports each year (Tatara & Kuzmeskus, 1997).

The national estimates of counts of reports of domestic elder abuse have been available through NCEA and its predecessor, the National Aging Resource Center on Elder Abuse (NARCEA), since 1986. Tatara (1989) attempted to generate similar estimates for fiscal years 1983, 1984, and 1985. However, because the number of states providing actual counts of reports upon which each year's national estimate was to be constructed was so small for these years, the attempt was less successful than it was for subsequent years. Table 1.4 presents the national estimates of domestic elder abuse reports from 1986 to 1996, generated by the NARCEA and NCEA (Tatara & Kuzmeskus, 1997).

The number of domestic elder abuse reports rose sharply in the United States between 1986 and 1996 and marked an increase of 150.4% during this 10-year period. It must be stressed that elder abuse is known to be very underreported, and, in fact, one study found that only 1 out of 14 cases comes to public attention (Pillemer & Finkelhor, 1988). If this finding is true, the reported cases compiled by NCEA represent only a small fraction of the true incidence of domestic elder abuse in this country.

The true incidence of elder abuse is not known and probably will never be known. To date, there have been two efforts to estimate the national prevalence or incidence of elder abuse. The first such effort was made in 1986 by two researchers, using a nationally representative sample of more than 2,000 elders chosen from the Boston Metropolitan area. This study, which was supported by a grant from the National Institute on Aging, produced an estimate of the national *prevalence* of domestic elder abuse and reported that, nationwide, between

Table 1.4 National Estimates of Domestic Elder Abuse Reports, 1986–1996

Year	Estimate	Increase from 1986, %
1986	117,000	—
1987	128,000	9.4
1988	140,000	19.7
1989[a]	—	—
1990	211,000	80.3
1991	213,000	82.1
1992[a]	—	—
1993	227,000	94.0
1994	241,000	106.0
1995	286,000	144.4
1996	293,000	150.4

Note: Reports are not counts of elders, the count of whom is smaller by 7% to 9% than the number of reports each year.
[a] Data were not collected for these years, making national estimates impossible.
Source: Toshio Tatara and Lisa M. Kuzmeskus, *Summaries of the Statistical Data on Elder Abuse in Domestic Settings for FY 95 and FY 96* (National Center on Elder Abuse, Washington, DC, 1997).

701,000 and 1,093,560 elderly people were abused or neglected in 1986 (Pillemer & Finkelhor, 1988). The second effort is a 4-year study to estimate the national *incidence* of domestic elder abuse, now being conducted by the NCEA and their contractor, Westat, Inc., a statistical consulting firm based in Rockville, Maryland. It was the U.S. Congress that directed the Department of Health and Human Services to perform the study, and the Department's Administration for Children and Families and the Administration on Aging jointly funded NCEA's study in the fall of 1994. In addition to calculating the estimated number of elderly persons mistreated in domestic settings during 1996, nationwide, the study is expected to generate information about the characteristics of domestic elder-abuse victims, as well as abusers. The race/ethnicity breakouts of abuse victims also will be among the types of information that the study will produce when its findings are finally released in the fall of 1998.

Regardless of what this national study will show statistically regarding the incidence of elder abuse among minority populations, there are few doubts that minority elders are considerably more vulnerable than White elders when it comes to domestic elder abuse, as illustrated by the authors of many chapters in this book. Further, it is also true that minority elder populations are growing very fast in this country, as described here. These being the cases, there is an urgent need now for seriously examining elder abuse among the nation's minority populations. It is safe to say that failure to do so would be costly to everyone in society.

REFERENCES

American Society on Aging (1992). *Serving elders of color: Challenges to providers and the aging network.* San Francisco: Author.

Bass, S. A., Kutza, E. A., & Torres-Gil, F. M. (Eds.). (1990). *Diversity in aging.* Glenview, IL: Scott, Foresman.

Block, M. R., & Sinnott, J. D. (Eds.). (1979). *The battered elder syndrome: An exploratory study.* College Park, MD: University of Maryland Center on Aging.

Cazenave, N. A. (1983). Elder abuse and black americans: Incidence, correlates, treatment, and prevention. In J. I. Kosberg (Ed.), *Abuse and maltreatment of the elderly. Causes and interventions* (pp. 187–203). Boston: Wright Publishing.

Cuellar, J. (1990). *Aging and Health: Hispanic American Elders.* Stanford Geriatric Education Center Working Paper, No. 5. Stanford, CA.

Day, J. C. (1996). *U.S. Bureau of the Census Current Populations Reports,* Series P-25, No. 1130. *Population projections of the United States by age, sex, race, and Hispanic origin: 1995 to 2050.* Washington, DC: U.S. Government Printing Office.

Gioglio, G. R., & Blakemore, P. (1982). *Elder abuse in New Jersey: The knowledge and experience of abuse among older New Jerseyans.* Trenton, NJ: New Jersey Department of Community Affairs.

Hall, P. A. (1987). Minority Elder Maltreatment: Ethnicity, Gender, Age, and Poverty. *Ethnicity and Gerontological Social Work, 13,* 81–93.

Krause, N., & Wray, L. A. (1991). Psychosocial correlates of health and illness among minority elders. *Generations,* Fall/Winter, 25–30.

Lacayo, C. (1991). Living arrangements and social environment among ethnic minority elderly: Current trends. *Generations,* Fall/Winter, 43–46.

Lau, E. E., & Kosberg, J. I. (1979). Abuse of the elderly by informal care providers. *Aging,* September–October, 10–15.

Longres, J. F. (1991). Black and white clients in an elder abuse system. In T. Tatara (Ed.), *Findings of five elder abuse studies: From the NARCEA program* (pp. 53–80). Washington, DC: National Aging Resource Center on Elder Abuse (NARCEA).

Lopez, C., & Aguilera, E. (1991). *On the sidelines: Hispanic elderly and the continuum of care.* Washington, DC: National Council of the Raza.

Manuel, R. C., & Berk, M. L. (1983). A look at similarities and differences in older minority populations. *Aging,* May–June, 21–29.

Moon, A., & Williams, O. (1993). Perceptions of elder abuse and help-seeking patterns among African American, Caucasian American, and Korean American elderly women. *The Gerontologist, 33,* 386–395.

National Center for Health Statistics (1984). *Health indicators for Hispanic, Black, and White Americans.* Data from the National Health Survey, Series 10, No. 148. Washington, DC: Department of Health and Human Services.

National Indian Council on Aging. (1981). *American Indian elderly: A national profile.* Albuquerque, NM: Author.

Pillemer, K., & Finkelhor, D. (1988). The prevalence of elder abuse: A random sample survey. *The Gerontologist, 28,* 52–57.

Spencer, G. (1988). *U.S. Bureau of the Census Current Populations Reports,* Series P-25, No. 995. *Projections of the hispanic populations, 1983–2080.* Washington, DC: U.S. Government Printing Office.

Stanford, E. P., & Torres-Gil, F. M. (Eds.). (1991). *Diversity: New approach to ethnic minority aging. Generations,* Fall/Winter, 1991.

Stein, K. F. (1989). *Working with abused and neglected elders in minority populations: A synthesis of research.* Washington, DC: National Aging Resource Center on Elder Abuse (NARCEA).

Tatara, T. (1989). Toward the development of estimates of the national incidence of reports of elder abuse based on currently available state data: An exploratory study. In R. Fillinson & S. Ingman (Eds.), *Elder abuse: Practice and policy.* New York: Human Sciences Press, 153–165.

Tatara, T., & Blumerman, L. M. (1996). *Summaries of the statistical data on elder abuse in domestic settings: An exploratory study of state statistics for FY 93 and FY 94.* Washington, DC: The National Center on Elder Abuse (NCEA).

Tatara, T., & Kuzmeskus, L. M. (1997). *Summaries of the statistical data on elder abuse in domestic settings for FY 95 and FY 96.* Washington, DC: The National Center on Elder Abuse (NCEA).

U.S. Congress. (1988). *Demographic characteristics of the older Hispanic population: A report by the Chairman of the Select Committee on Aging.* Washington, DC: Government Printing Office.

Williams, O. J., & Griffin, L. (1991). Elder abuse in the black family. In R. L. Hampton (Ed.) *Black family violence: current research and theory* (pp. 117–127). Lexington, MA: Lexington Books.

Part One

Elder Abuse in Black Communities

Chapter 2

Abuse of Black Elders in Rhode Island[1]

Joyce M. Hall[2]

INTRODUCTION

Case Study I

In 1978, a Black female came to see me at my office in the Department of Elderly Affairs. She lived with her husband who would not give her any money to take care of the home appropriately. He used to go to the race track and often lost all his money there. The client collected Social Security of her own but had to turn over her check to her spouse. If she complained, he would threaten to hit her in the head, which terrified her. The client had two sons who tried to help the mother, but they did not dare cross the father. To compensate for this they denied that the mother was being mistreated. The sons told me, and others, that a man's house was his castle and that he could treat his wife any way that he pleased. The father had bought and paid for her by marriage. His behavior was accepted as "his right." When word leaked out that the client had looked to an agency for help, it was a terrible affront to the community and even to her family. After many months, I finally was able to get the client to leave her abusive situation, relocate to elderly housing on her own, obtain employment as a foster grandparent, and gain back her independence and dignity.

As a Black professional, this case became my introduction to minority elder abuse, and my work with this client became the blueprint for parts of our current elder-abuse protection program in Rhode Island. This experience also gave me new insight into the phenomenon of minority elder abuse. Throughout this chapter, I use case stories of elder-abuse victims I have known to illustrate how elder-abuse problems and solutions have affected the lives of Black elderly peo-

---

[1]The views expressed in this chapter are those of the author and do not necessarily reflect the policies or opinions of any state or local agency.

[2]The author wishes to thank Margaret Rittman for her editorial assistance in completing this chapter.

ple. I am hopeful that the knowledge I have gained can be used to combat elder abuse in any ethnic group.

Rhode Island's Role in Elder-abuse Protection

Rhode Island was one of the first states to address the newly recognized problem of elder abuse. In 1981, the Department of Elderly Affairs (DEA) was awarded a 3-year discretionary grant from the Administration on Aging to study the prevalence of elder abuse, to increase awareness among the elderly and the community at large about elder abuse, and to develop modes of intervention to adequately address it. The DEA is the state agency in Rhode Island that is solely responsible for administering all resources and services and providing information for elders 60 years of age and older.

Although combating elder abuse in all racial groups is the goal of the DEA, the problem of elder abuse in the Black community appears particularly difficult to approach because it is often hidden. Black elders and their family members can go to great lengths to present to the public an image that abuse does not occur in their community, when in reality it does.

Prevalence of Elder Abuse

Approximately 180,000 residents, out of the state's total population of 1 million people, are 60 years of age or older (U.S. Bureau of the Census, 1990). Of the state's Black population of roughly 30,000 to 40,000 people, Black elderly (over 60 years of age) constitute about 3,300 people; the majority (two thirds) of elderly Blacks are female. Of the elderly population, our department estimated that 300 to 500 Black elderly people could be reported to the DEA Abuse Program. However, because of underreporting for Black elderly persons, the DEA received only 11 reports of elder abuse for Blacks, out of 900 reports for all ethnic groups for 1996 (self-neglect and institutional elder abuse are not included). Nationally, there has been an unfortunate and consistent pattern of underreporting of elder abuse among all ethnic groups, and we have seen, in particular, underreporting among Blacks in Rhode Island. The underreporting among Blacks is illustrated by a comparison with reporting of elder abuse in the Hispanic population. Although the Hispanic population is fewer in number than the Black population, each year the DEA receives 3 times the number of reports on Hispanic elders.

Public Education in Rhode Island's DEA Program

Throughout the early years of the program, a successful public-awareness campaign was implemented for the elderly, service providers, and public, private, and local agencies. To educate elderly people, a dramatization of several elder-abuse vignettes, enacted by elders, was taken to senior centers and meal sites. To educate professionals—hospital workers, police, visiting nurses, and social workers—service programs were conducted statewide by senior DEA staff indicating how to identify abuse symptoms. Most of the mandatory reports received in Rhode Island's Program come from these professionals, so an aggressive effort was made to reach as many caregivers to elders as possible.

Following our public-education initiative, we began to look at developing new intervention modes, which are addressed in the next and the final sections of this chapter. But to understand how to work with the Black community and how to develop interventions, we must first explore some of the major reasons behind elder abuse in the Black community, including a look at the profiles of those who abuse elders and their victims. How a Black community may function and barriers to elder-abuse prevention are discussed. Principles for staff training and the importance of having minority staff work on elder-abuse programs are discussed in depth in the final sections of this chapter.

UNDERSTANDING AND ADDRESSING ELDER ABUSE AMONG BLACKS

Factors that Contribute to Elder Abuse

I have observed that although elderly people in general do not openly reveal their family problems in a group setting, Black elders are more apt than seniors in many other racial groups to hide or deny any notion of abuse or maltreatment occurring in their community, whether the elder is in a group or meeting privately with a caseworker. Some of the factors that contribute to the perpetuation of Black elder abuse among the elderly victims are these strong feelings of denial, rationalization, and shame. To some degree these factors are seen in all elder-abuse cases and, it appears, are exhibited not only by the victim but by abusers and even professionals and service providers.

Elder-abuse victims have further expanded on their feelings and said that they tolerate abuse at the hands of their loved ones for several reasons: humiliation, fear of rejection or the withdrawal of love, and hopelessness. In some cases, I have found that elder-abuse victims have sought relief by adopting fatalistic viewpoints or by developing dementia. The abuser then defends his action by rationalization, shame, self-interest, drug dependency, blaming others, and justification.

Of all the possible reasons for denial of elder abuse, shame may be the primary cause in the Black community. Oddly, not only does the elder deny and hide the problem of abuse, but his or her neighbors and others who are aware of the abuse hide it also. I tend to believe that Black elders may be inclined to endure much pain and suffering in order to present a dignified face to the public. Perhaps because Black people may not be seen in a favorable light, they want to protect the family from scorn, so they are willing to suffer in silence.

In society in general, women often have not been treated well, and the Black culture has been no exception. In some homes in which a Black woman was not treated well by her spouse and the woman complained to the minister or other family members, the woman was advised that she had a responsibility to "make a go of it" and was told that it was a woman's place to keep the family together. Often verses were quoted from the Bible to support these contentions. Any problems often were kept "behind closed doors." Today we are trying to educate all ethnic groups about elder abuse so that elders no longer tolerate abuse and suffer in silence because they are embarrassed. Times, however, may be changing as the young Black female is becoming more liberated and educated and, hopefully, is beginning to question these notions.

Efforts to Overcome the Problem

In an effort to counteract the problem of hiding or denying maltreatment or abuse that occurs in the Black community, key councils were formed throughout the state composed of various public and private agencies and service providers. Members of other groups were contacted to assist in these efforts, with special emphasis placed on trying to involve the religious community and other volunteer organizations, but to little avail. During this period, it was suggested by some that perhaps elder abuse did not occur in the Black culture. I am quite confident that this is not the answer.

Profile of Victims and Abusers

The typical profile of a Black elderly victim in Rhode Island is female (99%), 75 years of age or older, physically independent, and not mentally impaired. The typical abuser of a Black elder is male (son, grandson, or husband). Often the abuser is dependent on the elder for his or her psychological, financial, and emotional sustenance. A majority of the abuse reports of Black elders involve alcohol or some type of substance abuse. Often it involves adult children who move back home without financial means to pay their own way. In many cases, single mothers with their children may move back home because of insufficient money to make ends meet.

Although Rhode Island has a very high rate of reports of physical abuse of the elderly, this is not frequently reported in the Black elder-abuse reports received thus far. When physical abuse of the Black elderly is reported, it is usually perpetrated by a spouse or by a grandchild. It is more likely that reports of exploitation, neglect, and isolation are seen in the cases of Black elders. Exploitation is examined here because it is the most frequently reported type of abuse.

Exploitation of Black Elders

Exploitation ranks first among the most common reported abuses of Black elders, followed by neglect and then physical abuse. This differs considerably from findings in the state regarding White elder-abuse cases, in which physical abuse is the most common reported abuse, followed by neglect and exploitation. Unfortunately, I have known of cases in which Black elders have had to be physically removed from their homes to prevent their Social Security checks being taken by their loved ones. The amount of the check does not have to be considerable. The fact that it comes regularly and is always on time is what matters to the exploiter. Usually the problems have been ongoing for some period of time. It is seldom a case of a one-time occurrence.

The Black victim, in most instances, is easy to work with toward goals of protection and safety except if the case involves a son or a grandson who is exploiting the elder for money. I tend to believe that the Black elder is willing to give up her meager Social Security check so her son or grandson can satisfy a drug addiction, hoping it will prevent him from stealing elsewhere and landing in jail. If there is a female abuser, there is more likely to be an element of physical abuse involved with the exploitation of the mother or grandmother. The Black male abuser often uses "threats" to intimidate the elder into believing that if she does not give up her money, the abuser will move out or withhold his love and attention from the victim.

Case Study II

The DEA received a report from a senior center that serves a mostly Black constituency, regarding a Black elderly female who resided in her own home with her unmarried daughter and seven grandchildren. She attended the center often and complained about not having medicine, clothes to wear, or money to spend, although she received about $800 a month from her Social Security check. This should have been enough for her to live on. During our investigation, it was learned that no one in the home worked and the 13-year-old grandchild was expecting a baby. The daughter was described as being somewhat mentally handicapped and was on welfare. The daughter had never been married. The home was sparsely furnished, cold, and unkept. The kitchen had bare wood floors, broken windows, and holes in the plaster.

The client was very spunky and a delight to be around. She joked and was often seen as the life of the party. However, she had great difficulty ambulating, was incontinent, and was unable to provide for her own activities of daily living. The client's daughter admitted that the elder's money was used to make ends meet. Very little was left over for her needs and she often did without. This problem had been going on for years before it was reported. A hospitalization brought it to the forefront. The agency did not report this case as neglect, exploitation, or abuse, but rather as self-neglect because the client could not care for herself. No one raised a question about what was happening in the client's home or why the client never had any money or proper clothes to wear. The house was eventually lost to back taxes, which resulted in the client's placement in a 24-hour facility, which in this instance was the best possible solution given the lack of resources or other appropriate family to assist.

Case Study III

A recent report involved an elderly Black woman who lives with one son, in his 40s, in a section of a three-story tenement house; another son, who is a drug addict, lives on a separate floor in the same house. The client is very frail, arthritic, diabetic, and on dialysis. The drug-dependent son coerces and threatens his mother for money to support his habit. Neither son works. The client has obtained several restraining orders against the son on the second floor, but to no avail, as he ignores them and comes into her living area anyway. The client lives in a declining neighborhood. Agency personnel, such as visiting nurses, social workers, or even police, often are reluctant to provide services to clients who live in this area. Many times the client has been asked to leave her apartment and community to go elsewhere for services. No one, friend or neighbor, wants to "tell" or report any problem for fear that the police would come and institutionalize her son. If the client breaks an appointment, it is assumed that she is noncompliant, when in fact, she is often prevented from keeping her appointments by her son.

The client's home is in dire need of repair. The toilet leaks from the upper floor and drips down into the cupboards below that contain her food and dishes. Although her home is sparsely outfitted, it appears to be neat and kept up. Roaches are very evident throughout the home. The house would be nice if it had been kept up and repair work done. No one has provided services for the client in many years. Neighbors are well aware of this elderly woman's situation yet do not call or ask for help. This neighborhood fears social-service agencies and dreads the police. They fear calling attention to the "goings on," which are often illegal, because of their fear of maltreatment from the police or authorities. They are all too familiar with the lack of respect, rough harsh treatment, and worse, lack of concern or belief shown by those who are supposed to help them. The community members then become part of the problem by covering up or not reporting wrongdoings that occur where they live. This problem is perpetuated over and over, which leads to blight and benign neglect and eventually the breakdown of the neighborhood into slums and ghettos.

Overall, our experience in elder-abuse cases has shown that there seems to be much less contact with Black abusers than with their White counterparts. It may be that the Black perpetrator is afraid to be in contact with what they perceive to be the "authority" as much as the "authority" may fear confronting the Black abuser in the Black community. Conversely, Black abusers are usually more apt to agree to a plan of care for the elder, in word at least, although they often fail to follow through without a lot of prompting and follow-up.

Networks in the Black Community

Even today, few minorities in Rhode Island participate in elder community programs, such as senior centers, meal sites, or adult daycare centers, which are attended mostly by White elderly in Rhode Island. Minority elders are rarely seen in nursing homes or state institutions. In one study done in the beginning of the

DEA's abuse program some reasons given by minorities as to why they did not participate were a lack of transportation, language difficulties, and cultural barriers. Privately, some added that they believed that they were treated with benign hostility or indifference by some other elders and staff members.

Black elders view the relevance of services and interventions according to their cultural mores, their personal histories, and their viewpoints about the extended family and its values and systems. Black elders appear to adhere to the cultural values associated with using the extended Black family system for help rather than using nursing homes or outside living arrangements. This may partially account for the few Black elders seen in many senior programs and for the low number of abuse reports.

The Role of Family in the Black Community

The family is sacred in nearly all African cultures. To put a member of one's family "away" because of old age is a disgrace. Thus, it has been traditional for Black people to keep the aged and the sick in the home. Ernest Cox (1981), a graduate student at Brown University, conducted a geriatric research project and found that several senior citizens he interviewed were taking care of their mothers. Although this was a hardship for them, they would not institutionalize their elderly loved ones because their mothers had taken care of them. Those interviewed believed they had done all they could do for their mothers and felt no guilt.

Years ago one of the great strengths of the Black culture was that entire communities helped each other with childcare, food, and other types of support. Churches, especially Black churches, were looked upon as havens for the oppressed and downtrodden. Fraternal orders, undertakers, and politicians were also a support to impoverished families, helping them find jobs and providing food and other necessities. In fact, within the Black culture, elders were most often looked up to, especially the elder Black female. It was unheard of in my youth in the 1930s and up to present times, and especially in my own family today, for anyone to treat their elders with anything other than respect, deserved or not. Even grown children, who were married with children of their own, would defer to the elder Black female in the home. Today, sadly, this deferential treatment of elders may be dying out in the Black community and may no longer hold true for any racial group. In the Black family, children often are being cared for by their elderly grandmothers when the children's parents leave them at the elders' homes. This is increasing at an alarming rate. Many of the reports we receive today, from all racial groups, arise from these circumstances, especially cases of financial and material exploitation by adult children and grandchildren. Although community is still important in the Black culture, the various facets of a community must again be mobilized to help care for those in need in our communities.

There is, however, an unspoken informal network of protection, real or imagined, in the Black community that functions when economic or social ills cause a breakdown in formerly well-functioning family systems. This is important because a large number of Black elders are from single-person households created by the death of a spouse or separation or divorce. The informal network, although operational, is not steady nor dependable. The elderly may not be able to depend on this network for intensive needs and thus the elders may suffer from neglect.

Black elders have always looked for comfort and support from a network of churches, service groups, lodges, and professional and fraternal organizations. In southeastern New England, churches need to play a larger role in assisting Black elders. In my experience, I have found that Black elderly here typically do not join traditional senior citizen associations, such as the local chapter of the American Association for Retired Persons, as older Whites do. Instead they typically join other groups, particularly churches. Thus, we need to work closely with churches to empower them to speak up and report elder-abuse cases when they occur, instead of ignoring the abuse.

BARRIERS TO ELDER-ABUSE PREVENTION

How the dominant culture and the Black elderly interface socially must be understood and addressed if a system of relevant coordination and services is to achieve the goal of increasing utilization by Black elders of programs or services, which include abuse interventions. Barriers often seen in the Black community are low income, high unemployment, poor communication skills, lack of accessible services, lack of transportation, and lack of long-range planning.

Cantor and Mayer (1976) showed that economic barriers prevent Blacks from securing quality services that are more accessible to White elders. They concluded that there was strong evidence to support their observations that more affluent Whites also saw doctors more often for prevention purposes.

The Black population, including Black elders, are often leery of social workers and other professionals, in particular because they see very few people of color in any of these positions. Usually if social workers come around it spells trouble for someone in the family, or their services or resources may become jeopardized. Black people, especially elderly Black persons, believe that the majority culture always views them in negative terms.

The need of service providers to gather facts and history and share information greatly impacts Blacks and their utilization of services and resources that are typically scarce. Often, the Black elder's lack of understanding of questions or misunderstandings about information from service providers leads the way to missed opportunities for services, missed appointments, and a lack of protection. Many of our older minority clients, especially our Black elders, did not receive much formal schooling. These elders were mostly self-taught and consequently are often reluctant to ask questions when they do not know about or understand an issue. Therefore, they often go without needed services or interventions that can improve their quality of life and remove them from harm. Service providers need to learn how to talk to elders in plain, clear language that is not patronizing, if they want to be effective, be understood, and benefit the client.

Transportation or the lack of transportation often impinges on the safety and well-being of all elders. The lack of transportation fosters isolation and limits access to various services and resources, which often results in more costly shopping, loss of services, and fewer choices available for needed services.

Case Study IV

This report is one of the few received from the church community. The church was prevented from seeing the parishioner and giving her Communion, which led to their request for our agency to intervene. Strict anonymity was requested and maintained in this case.

In this case, an elderly Black female had been repeatedly found by the police wandering in the street looking for her long-dead husband. The client has four children. The oldest daughter lived out-of-state. Her two sons lived in the same town and the youngest daughter lived in Massachusetts and was considered to be an outcast. The entire family was in denial about the mother's decline in mental functioning and was hostile to efforts of help from the police and the DEA. The adult children were also hostile to each other. The two sons and oldest daughter were aligned against the youngest daughter. The eldest daughter, who was happily married, was somewhat removed from the situation but responded when called upon. The two sons resided somewhat near one another. Both worked hard to support their families. The oldest son was the spokesperson for the family. The youngest daughter was deeply resented and openly hated by her siblings. She was the last to leave home and she was the only one to go to college (Brown University); she also had married a man outside her religious upbringing. She planned to move into the mother's home, with her family, to care for her mother. The other family members put all kinds of barriers in the way of this happening. Meanwhile, the mother was still wandering and it was unsafe for her to be living alone. Finally, a resolution was found through the court system. Coguardians, consisting of the oldest son and the youngest daughter, were appointed by the judge to look after the mother's health and safety needs. However, when this did not work out, the judge said he was very disappointed in the oldest son's refusal to allow the sister to move into the house to care for the mother. The judge finally ordered placement of the elderly woman in a nursing home because she was not receiving proper care.

RECOMMENDATIONS FOR WORKING WITH BLACK ELDERS

Generally, we need to improve paraprofessional and professional awareness. We must integrate an understanding of minority issues into our mainstream consciousness. We must foster interest and sensitivity towards the mistreated Black elder. We need to develop effective community service systems for the elderly.

We need to have a clearer understanding of the cultural lifestyles of various ethnic groups, particularly Black Americans. Although we have found that the basic value systems of families are the same across cultures, we need to look at the particular needs of each group, such as some elders needing help in understanding and reading forms for services, or in overcoming their reluctance to ask for help. As far back as the early 1980s, different professional groups decried the dearth of formal studies and lack of knowledge regarding the lifestyles, needs, and aspirations of the Black elder. We need to focus on these areas to better understand the diverse needs of Black senior citizens.

We must strive to educate and train professional service providers and sensitize them to elders' needs, especially those of Black elders. Cox (1981) found that the elderly gave these reasons for not using services: limited outreach to elderly, services located outside the neighborhood, limited transportation, inadequate knowledge by staff about cultural differences, and lack of familiarity by providers with traditional informal support services in the minority communities. We also must encourage personal outreach efforts rather than depend on impersonal printed information or video programs.

In Rhode Island, we need to do a better job of recruiting and hiring minority staff for elder-affairs services, from caseworkers to administrators. Not to be understated is the need for protective-services staff to represent the clients that they serve. It is evident that participation in programs is enhanced when minority staff are on board and provide services to their elders. We also need to enhance minority-student participation in gerontology programs in colleges and universities.

Professionals Need to Examine Their Belief Systems

Professionals come to the workplace carrying their own belief systems, rationalization and denial mechanisms, ageism prejudices, religious motives, or learned racism. Too often it is the professional who is the hardest to convince that elder abuse does exist. Interventions and creative problem solving are still a "works in progress:" There are few guidelines to follow; there is a serious lack of community or social-service resources; there is a lack of appropriate shelters for elders that are accessible and, worse, an apparent lack of concern or caring about abuse in the elder population. Often, there is more concern shown for a dog who is found to have been abused than for an older victim who has been enduring horrendous living conditions for many years at the hands of their families and loved ones.

Over time, it has become apparent to me that all types of professionals view the same situations very differently depending on which group of people they deal with; that is, similar situations or problems seen or heard within the Hispanic, Italian, Portuguese, Native American, Caucasian, or Black families are evaluated differently. Various acts are called abuse for one group and yet seen as something else for another. It also has become apparent to me that behavior that is unacceptable for some groups is expected and seen as natural behavior for others, particularly Black elders. Society seems to believe that spousal abuse in some minority groups is to be expected and thus is tolerated. Loved ones are viewed as chattel, often with little interference from police, courts, social workers, or the state. Practitioners should be aware that they may be potentially liable for acts of omission as well as commission.

Let us not understate how the insensitivity by some agency staff and service providers creates barriers to utilization of services by minority elderly, especially Black elders. People have a unique ability to sense how someone feels about them without being told. Being insensitive is totally unacceptable in any service that pretends to serve vulnerable older people. Black people generally have been raised to respect their elders. They are deeply offended when they are not shown the same type of respect by others. Usually, their recourse has been to not return to the program, to refuse to participate in the services they need, or to not allow a service provider to give them the care necessary to sustain their safety and well-being.

Through my casework, I have developed what I believe is an essential list of attitudes for those of us who work with elder-abuse victims from any racial/ethnic group:

1   Treat each person as an individual who is respected.
2   Allow the person to express his or her feelings in his or her own way.
3   Accept and recognize each person on his or her own merits.
4   Provide services and intervention in a nonjudgmental manner.
5   Make the client aware of his or her right to self-determination and other important issues.
6   Keep every client's case in strict confidence.
7   Ensure that the elder understands what is being proposed for him or her and why.
8   Work with the entire family when allowed by the client.
9   Provide follow-up on each case—without it the client can "fall through the cracks."
10   Continue discussions on the division of the family role versus the government role in preventing and treating elder abuse.

The Role of Government

As demographics change, government priorities must change. The fact that people are living longer will necessitate enormous shifts in how monies will be allocated and how they will be spent. The Black social structure and culture should be encouraged and supported to continue to care for elders whenever possible and feasible to do so. Yet, it is just as important to look at governmental agencies and programs and see that they have an important role to play and should be utilized when the safety and well-being of the aged Black elder is called into question. There are very definite limits to what family members can or should be expected to provide for the frail dependent elder. This must be considered with all elders, including the Black elder. The government is beginning to realize that just because there are adult family members providing care in the home, the regulations should not automatically state that all services must be discontinued. The lack of assistance places tremendous burdens on the caregiver that, if not bearable, can lead to abuse of the elder. High levels of frustration and a lack of awareness of available services may cause actions to happen in families that are not intentional abuses but are just as detrimental to the elders involved.

It is difficult to formulate coherent public policy as a basis for service delivery to this population. Societal issues of downsizing and government cutbacks do not help and often strain what little resources are available to assist this population. The passage of Social Security and Supplemental Security Income programs was a boon to Black elders who often had worked long hours all their lives but received such low wages that in retirement they could not be sustained in today's socioeconomic environment without entitlement programs. Policymakers must have a clear understanding of Black elders and their individual needs, values, and lifestyles before promulgating regulations, services, and instructions that then often go underutilized by the elderly person.

Recognition of Elder Abuse by Professionals and the Community

Hospitals, doctors, nurses, social service personnel, and other service providers should know the symptoms and signs that indicate that abuse or mistreatment may be occurring. More important is the need to confront the issue and not turn our heads the other way. We must learn how to listen to our children and our elderly and stop changing the subject when issues that are painful to hear are brought up. The denial of victimization by loved ones and family members has led to terrible mistreatment of elderly, women, and children and has even resulted in death. Obviously we need to go back to the "old time ways" of teaching our children to respect their elders, others, and themselves. This must begin at a very young age. We need to become more aware and concerned about our families, our communities, and how we treat each other collectively.

We also need to continue to educate our elders, family caregivers, and those in churches, workplaces, and schools that abuse of the elderly is "alive and well" and on the increase worldwide. Each year more and more reports are received in Rhode Island and across the nation. Protective services are the responsibility of the entire community. All agencies must band together to provide a community-wide response system. State and federal governments must increase funding to support intervention for and treatment of elderly abuse.

It has taken many years for the plight of abused children to receive a modicum of attention. Abuse of women is only now receiving a fair amount of concern and the recognition that there are serious domestic problems in our families and homes. How long must we wait before the nation wakes up to the fact that abuse between family members does happen and is occurring at an alarming rate across the age spectrum? The problems affect all races and cut across all economic and religious lines. These are problems and affairs of the heart that speak to how people treat one another. The latest statistics indicate that, nationally, we receive only one report for every 14 abuses that take place (Pillemer & Finkelhor, 1988). Will we rise to the challenge of preventing and treating elder abuse by starting to confront the economic and social problems that fuel it, along with conducting a continual public education campaign? I believe we can and we must address elder abuse more effectively and openly, and I hope to continue to be a part of that effort.

REFERENCES

Cantor, M., & Mayer, M. (1976). Health and the inner city elderly. *The Gerontologist, 16,* 17–25.

Cox, E. (1981). *Geriatric research fellowship paper.* Unpublished manuscript, Brown University, Providence, RI.

Pillemer, K., & Finkelhor, D. (1988). The prevalence of elder abuse: A random sample survey. *The Gerontologist, 28,* 51–57.

U.S. Bureau of the Census. (1990). *Federal census.* Washington, D.C.: U.S. Government Printing Office.

Chapter 3

Elder Maltreatment in the African American Community: You Just Don't Hit Your Momma!!!

Linner Ward Griffin

INTRODUCTION

Elder maltreatment has been an unfortunate manifestation of aging in American society. It is unclear, however, if the increased numbers of abused elders are due to a heightened awareness of maltreatment spurred by publicity and research, improved reporting procedures by human-service professionals, or an increase in instances of maltreatment. During the past decade, a clear definition or understanding of the phenomenon of elder maltreatment has not been forthcoming. Abuse and neglect are two facets of the term *elder maltreatment* about which most researchers agree (Crystal, 1987; Moore & Thompson, 1987; Valentine & Cash, 1986). Elder abuse has been described as physical, emotional, sexual, verbal, or financial (exploitation) harm of an older person. Neglect, when related to elder maltreatment, refers to caregiver activities or individual activities of an elder that result in the denial or absence of needed assistance (U.S. Congress, Senate Special Committee on Aging, 1977).

Both researchers and practitioners have acknowledged a lack of uniformity and clarity in the conceptualization and classification systems used to identify elder maltreatment (Griffin & Williams, 1992). Hudson (1989, 1994) and Johnson (1989) note the inconsistencies in identifying the behavioral manifestations of elderly maltreatment whether it is elder abuse (physical, emotional, verbal, sexual, spiritual, or financial exploitation) or neglect (by caregiver or self-neglect). Blanton (1989), Brown (1989a), Hall (1986), Johnson (1989), Griffin and Williams (1992), and Williams and Griffin (1991) also question the applicability of instruments used to capture and measure abuse and neglect from one region of the United States to another. Yet information from such research is used in the training of practitioners and applied in adjudication and treatment of clients despite the aforementioned gaps in knowledge.

One consequence of this vagueness could be notable differences in how social workers and adult-protective-service practitioners apply states' criteria to identify abuse cases, that is, if abuse cases are labeled as such within their communities (Moon & Williams, 1993). Although interventions provided by social workers and others within the health and social-service systems may be based on clients' needs, such interventions may not be comprehensive or responsive to clients' total needs (Griffin, 1993). For example, clients may receive a narrower range of services or workers may be less able to provide the psychological and legal protection needed by older victims if they are unclear about the parameters of maltreatment of elders.

Practice-based and Researcher-focused

Traditionally, research about elderly maltreatment is more scholarly or practitioner-centered and less focused on the aged person. Even though practitioners and researchers have sought to develop a comprehensive standard definition of elder maltreatment, one significant group usually has been omitted from the process: the elderly (Moon & Williams, 1993). Consequently, research concerning how the elderly perceive and identify an act as maltreatment and whether and to what extent their perceptions of such maltreatment are consistent with professionals' classifications of such behaviors has been unavailable. Because such gaps exist in the literature, there is a great potential to mislabel the problem and provide inappropriate interventions. Thus, it is critical that client participation be highlighted, particularly because of its empowering potential for a client group that has too often been made to feel impotent and dependent. An aged person's perception of maltreatment is a crucial element in creating better information and conceptualizations, and more uniform definitions.

Elder Maltreatment and African Americans

Traditional literature about elder maltreatment centers on the majority society's definition and experiences with abuse and neglect and surmises that the same conditions exist among minority populations or that it is not an issue in these groups (Cazenave, 1979, 1981; Hall, 1986; Brown, 1989b; Griffin & Williams, 1992). For example, much of the available research has been conducted with largely European American populations and has not included significant numbers of minority elders (Cazenave, 1981). Also, available research has not been based on issues gleaned from minority experiences, such as values, traditional behavior, or how cultural interpretations of situations may differ (Moon & Williams, 1993). The definition of elder maltreatment is very problematic within minority communities, especially within the African American community. Based on reported cases of maltreatment, researchers have described an abused elder as a post-75-year-old, middle class, widowed, White female with severe mental or physical impairment, who resides with an adult relative (Kosberg, 1988). The perpetrator, according to a preponderance of the literature, is a middle-aged adult female relative, who resides in the same home as the impaired elder. The female perpetrator may be experiencing conflicts and external stresses due to the deterioration of the older person's condition at a time when the perpetrator would choose to engage in self-enrichment activities, such as education or employment after having reared her children (Kosberg, 1988; Myers & Shelton, 1987). The applicability of such definitions to African American family situations is dubious, leading to questions about cultural interpretation of abuse or maltreatment (Griffin & Williams, 1992).

Role of Cultural Diversity

Little attention has been given to the role of cultural diversity and cultural interpretation in the definition of, assessment of, or intervention in elderly maltreatment (Cazenave, 1979; Cazenave, 1981; Williams & Griffin, 1996). For example, African American elder-maltreatment settings look markedly different from that suggested in the abuse definition. Hill and Shackleford (1975) and Billingsley (1968, 1969) completed work that confirmed the existence of the African American multigenerational family. Harper and Alexander (1990) and Hill (1971) stated that African American older people frequently live in multigenerational families but are more likely to have their children come live with them in their homes than to live in the homes of their children. Relatives who moved in with elders, ranked by incidence, included the following: (1) daughters who are divorced, widowed, or separated and their children; (2) the aged person's children and their spouses; (3) grandchildren or other relatives such as nephews, nieces, cousins, and younger siblings; and (4) other familial configurations (Harper & Alexander, 1990). Examples of "other familial configurations" included kin and nonkin families.

The definitions devised by the Senate Special Committee on Aging and used by service-delivery units are broad and offer sweeping descriptions of the categories of maltreatment. The definitions ignore issues of degree and cultural context. Specifically, there are no criteria to determine if a situation is not elder maltreatment or to explain the extent to which African Americans and European Americans differ in experience or perception of elder abuse. Attention to these items could provide more precise guidance about when maltreatment occurs and when interventions are appropriate (Williams & Griffin, 1996).

Lack of Data from Minority Elderly

However, an even deeper concern exists. Few studies have involved the elderly themselves in addressing the classification nuances of elder maltreatment, preferring instead to leave the task to professionals (Valentine & Cash, 1986). But definitions vary among professional disciplines, across cultural, ethnic, and religious groups, and by geographical locations (Valentine & Cash, 1986). Psychologists, physicians, social workers, lawyers, and other professionals have problems defining elder maltreatment. The term is "confusing because. . . there is no consensus about its parameters" (Straus & Gelles, 1986). Even fewer studies have sufficiently involved older African Americans. Cazenave (1981) encouraged researchers to explore the area of elder abuse in general, and elder abuse among African Americans in particular. Cazenave (1981) and Crystal (1987) noted that studies about elder abuse that included African Americans as a part of the samples have not had sufficient numbers of African American aged and have not explored the qualitative details of African American life or the African American elderly. "Inclusion of any specific questions about African American people in research studies has been limited and received very little attention. Indeed, research on elder abuse in the African American population is still quite sparse" (Griffin & Williams, 1992, p. 20). More studies about elder maltreatment must include African Americans as part of the samples and in sufficient numbers to explore the qualitative and quantitative details of African American life.

The role that cultural diversity plays in the definition, assessment, and intervention in elderly maltreatment has been given little attention. Although this inattention may be attributed in part to benign neglect, incorrect beliefs, and faulty theories, the complexities involved if culture is added to the mix restrict the abilities of many researchers and practitioners to consider this element fully. However, ignoring this dimension renders research misleading and treatment ineffective. As indicated previously, there is no agreement on a valid and inclusive definition of elder abuse. Furthermore, researcher and practitioner foci are more on severe cases at the expense of attention to borderline (moderate, mild, or doubtful) ones, which also has contributed to weak conceptualization.

The primary objective of this chapter is to provide information about maltreatment in African American communities and not to compare or contrast Black and White elder-maltreatment situations, although comparisons are sometimes unavoidable. The chapter, through a review of available literature and the synthesis of research conducted in North Carolina communities by this author, presents ten themes that can be identified in African American elder-maltreatment situations and relationships. Case examples and the theoretical data that support the themes also are presented. Recommendations for practitioners and researchers in elder abuse have been included at the end of the chapter.

AFRICAN AMERICAN ELDER-MALTREATMENT THEMES

Theme 1: Physically Abusing Elders Is Particularly Unacceptable Among African Americans

Unique to African Americans is the historical existence of the strong matriarch, who has been given much credit for preserving the African American family while very often maintaining employment outside the home. The struggles of the "mother who keeps things going" have caused intense feelings of loyalty and protectiveness toward her among Black children. It is not uncommon for youngsters and even adult children to experience feelings of extreme anger in response to taunts or accusations about their mothers. However, "you never hurt Momma" and "you just don't hit your momma" were heard again and again during data collection for studies of African American elder maltreatment. Elders and suspected perpetrators alike denied physically abusive or neglectful behavior. No physical or sexual abuse was noted in any of the research efforts conducted over 10 years of research in urban and rural areas. Physical maltreatment was particularly unacceptable to all parties.

> Mrs. P. is an 80-year-old widow who continues to live in the Pitt County home she shared with her husband for 59 years. Legally blind, Mrs. P. is incontinent, nonambulatory, and chair-bound. She is infirm and cannot survive without assistance from others. Her 29-year-old unemployed granddaughter and 6-year-old great-granddaughter reside with her in the evenings because she cannot live alone. Mrs. P. refuses to consider a nursing home. She insists on living and dying in [her] own home.
>
> Mrs. P.'s daughter, who lives approximately 15 miles away, is her representative payee and is responsible for her financial affairs and her overall care. Mrs. P. receives Social Security dependent's benefits on her deceased husband's account. Her income is adequate for her monthly expenses. Adult-protective services have investigated neighbor's complaints about Mrs. P.'s situation; they find evidence of self-neglect but have not insisted that Mrs. P. be removed from the home because of the interest and support provided by her daughter and granddaughter. Mrs. P.'s daughter says her mother is obstinate, uncooperative, and often combative when she does not get her way. The daughter spoke of trying to calm her mother and protect herself from thrown objects and flying canes; she insisted that she never hit back. She could never hit her mother; Mrs. P. concurred with her daughter's account of their disagreements. The daughter cried when talking about her mother's strength and determination to die in her own home.

Recognizing the social undesirability of physical abuse, several questions are raised. Was there "really" no physical maltreatment of Mrs. P. or were both victim and perpetrators simply unwilling to acknowledge it? Do members of an ethnic group that is characterized by higher rates of violence really do no physical harm to momma? Or are they physically abusive but denying it because they are aware of community sanctions—ostracism, ridicule, shame—against it. Similar fears of community reprisals and pity could cause elders like Mrs. P. to deny incidents of physical maltreatment. Findings indicated that although other types of maltreatment were present, African American perpetrators did not physically abuse their mothers (either kin or nonkin). Records from departments of social service support this finding, but future research is needed to support the reliability and generalizability of the claim. If the finding is confirmed in later studies, what then are the implications for definitions or categories of elder maltreatment in African American communities?

Theme 2: There Is a Relationship Between Social Conditioning and Abusive Behavior Among African Americans

Elder abuse among African Americans may not be simply a result of violent associations, as has been suggested throughout the Black experience in America. It may not be a result of male or female socialization to violence or long-standing familial conflicts (Myers & Shelton, 1987). Although it is believed that many of these concepts and characteristics have universal application, sociocultural influences also may contribute to abuse of the African American aged. These sociocultural influences have directed patterns of behavior among African Americans and shape the African American experience in this country. African American elders share a unique heritage that differs from other aged in the United States; it includes the anger and humiliation of a history of slavery and a geographic regional southeastern ancestry.

Historically, African Americans have been acted upon violently through racism, either personally or institutionally. Such violent social influences may predispose some persons to behave violently. Examining the etiology of African American family abuse, the societal experiences of some African Americans who abuse may be likened to those victims of abuse, who in turn become abusers themselves (Steinmetz, 1978, 1988). If victims become abusers, it has been suggested that they have undergone a social learning experience that occurs as a result of victimization. However, intergenerational transmission of violence was not found to be a significant factor by Godkin, Wolf, and Pillemer (1989).

A similar learning experience may occur in situations of financial abuse, the type of maltreatment most prevalent in African American communities (Griffin, 1994). Building upon the scenario, African American children historically have experienced poverty. Many grew up seeing adult family members rely on elders for home and food. If one uses the ideas of social-learning theory, as adults these youngsters have a higher chance of also being dependent on their elders for survival. African Americans also are subject to sociological and psychological attacks that result if victims are blamed for their own conditions (Thomas & Sillen, 1976).

Jane B., a 79-year-old African American mother of three, lives in the three bedroom "home house" with her middle child and only son, Robert, age 54. Mrs. B.'s two daughters are married with children and grandchildren of their own; both live within 50 miles of Charleston, where their mother resides. Mrs. B. suffers with hypertension and arthritis, for which she takes medication, but her physician considers her health to be good for her age and not in need of supervision. Although she has become somewhat forgetful over the past 5 years, she continues to have responsibility for her fiscal affairs.

Mrs. B.'s daughters think their brother is taking advantage of the generosity of their mother because he has not worked longer than 2 consecutive weeks since graduating from high school in 1958. Robert, a Vietnam veteran, has never married and has no children. He acknowledges that his employment record is not good but says he gets day labor when he can. He relies on his mother and her pension checks for food, shelter, spending money, etc. He explains that he is needed in the home to "look after" his mother. He gets her checks, helps her pay her bills, goes to the grocery with her, and keeps the house clean.

When her daughters and friends complain about Robert, Mrs. B. gets impatient. They stop short of accusing him of "abuse." They note that their mother allows and even encourages their brother's behavior. Mrs. B. knows Robert keeps some of the money from her monthly checks, in addition to the "spending money" she regularly gives him, because "he has to have cigarettes." Afraid to live alone, it is important to her that her son be there for her. Mrs. B. believes the money she gives Robert is a bargain because it insures that he will be there in case she gets sick. She reports that Robert can be a handful when he's had a few beers but that he has never hurt her and is generally very protective.

The situation presented in this vignette is not atypical of those faced by many social workers charged with protecting elders from harm. The adult protective service workers who investigated the home consider Robert's behavior to be abuse (financial exploitation) of his mother. Mrs. B. denies that any abuse occurs. She adamantly reminds anyone who will listen that she knows Robert "borrows" money from her, but she insists that she does not mind. She thinks the "few dollars" are a small price to pay for Robert's continued presence in her home. Her daughters believe their brother is taking advantage of their mother's generosity and "uses" her to maintain himself, instead of working. But they stop short of terming his acts "abuse"; after all, their mother allows and even encourages their brother's behavior. Such a predicament can be found in African American families. Indeed, the case situation illustrates a "gray" area that exists in many homes in minority communities across the country. It clearly raises questions about cultural interpretation of abuse or maltreatment.

Theme 3: Poverty Is Pervasive in African American Elder Maltreatment Situations

An example of the difference between the description of perpetrators and victims described earlier and the reality of the African American experience is an economic one. Pillemer and Finklehor (1989) did not find poverty to be a factor in their prevalence study in Massachusetts, but it is a recurring factor in research among African Americans. Is there more exploitation of resources among African Americans? Is exploitation more prevalent than physical abuse because of the economic status of African Americans? African Americans are still disproportionately poor and not middle class (American Association of Retired Persons–Andrus Foundation, 1987). The Center on Budget and Policy Priorities (Greenstein, Porter, Shapiro, Leonard, & Barancik, 1988) noted the following about poverty among African Americans:

The poverty rate for black Americans rose significantly in 1987, despite continued growth in the United States economy and a decline in the poverty rate for White

Americans. Poverty rates are now higher for African Americans than they were in most years in the 1970s. The black poverty rate rose from 31.1 percent in 1986 to 33.1 percent in 1987, as the number of African Americans who are poor climbed by 700,000. One of every three African Americans lived in poverty in 1987. By contrast, the White poverty rate fell from 11 percent to 10.5 percent. Poverty rates increased for many groups of African Americans: children, the elderly, young families, married-couple families, and female-headed families. (p. v)

... The number of African Americans who fall into the category that might be called the "poorest of the poor"—those with incomes below half the poverty line (below $4,528 for a family of three in 1987)—has increased 69 percent since 1978. (p. vii)

Regarding poverty, specifically among the elderly, they further state:

The gap between the poverty rates for the black and White elderly has widened. In 1978, a black elderly person was 2.8 times more likely to be poor than a White elderly person. By 1987, a black elderly person was 3.4 times as likely to live in poverty than his or her White counterpart.... The poverty rate for black Americans aged 65 and over was 33.9 percent in 1987—a third of all black elderly people were poor.... [In contrast,] the poverty rate for White elderly was 10.1 percent. (p. 9)

Poverty fosters frustration and anger about one's circumstances, increasing the potential for violence and abuse. It is not surprising that many adult African American children, who live most of their lives in impoverished conditions, return to the safety of their parent's homes for protection and the security afforded by the elder's fixed income.

Theme 4: African American Perpetrators of Elder Abuse May Be Adults Involved in Dependent, Mutually Beneficial Relationships with Elders; These Relationships May Involve Emotional Maltreatment of the Adult Children in the Form of "Encouraged" Infantilism

The existence of the African American multigenerational family has been well documented (Billingsley, 1968, 1969; Hill, 1971; Hill & Shackleford, 1975). However, Black older people are more likely to have their children come live with them in their homes than live in the homes of their children (Harper & Alexander, 1990).

Mrs. J., a 66-year-old widow, is the mother of 10 adult children. She resides in a two-bedroom apartment in Lenoir County, North Carolina, with her 41-year-old daughter, Irene, her 22-year-old unemployed granddaughter Tracey, and her 5-year-old great-granddaughter Zandra. The four generations of females maintain themselves with Mrs. J.'s Social Security retirement check and her granddaughter Tracey's public assistance check. Irene worked briefly in a school library in 1979 and 1980 but did not work long enough to qualify for either disability or retirement benefits. She suffered a mild stroke 4 months ago and is unable to care for herself or her mother.

Sickly most of [her] life Mrs. J. has never lived alone. Her husband, Peter, died 25 years ago; either a child or grandchild has lived with her every day since his death. She reports that she lived with her parents until her marriage and that her children have seen to it that she is never alone. Mrs. J. worked as a domestic after her husband's death. She never seriously considered remarriage because she did not feel she was an attractive prospect with 10 dependents. She says that she never seriously considered remarriage because her six sons would never have accepted another man in her life. Instead, she labored to raise her family alone. Mrs. J. is very involved in senior activities at the Senior Center and with activities in her church. She considers herself to be an active older person.

Physically, Mrs. J. is very thin and presents an almost malnourished appearance. Both she and Irene have histories of alcohol abuse; both have been warned against future drinking for medical reasons. Both have admitted to backsliding occasionally. Irene admits to occasionally losing her temper with Mrs. J., who both agree is not an easy woman to live with. At such times, she will leave the home for 3 to 4 days rather than do something she will regret. Mrs. J. says that none of her children have ever attacked her physically and that none ever will as she recites how much she deprived herself to rear them. Irene says that Mrs. J. really upsets her sometimes, but that she would never hit her mother.

Mrs. J. has been diagnosed with hypertension and regularly takes medication to control it. She has been recommended for Section 8 housing but refuses to consider any living arrangement that would separate her from her family. (Financial exploitation; self-neglect.)

Mrs. W. at 88 years of age is considered in "good" health by her physician, although she was recently hospitalized because of a rectal discharge. This was her second hospitalization in 12 years; part of her intestine was removed in 1981. She takes a number of medications to treat various chronic illnesses, such as arthritis, high blood pressure, foot problems, and anal polyps.

Mrs. W. had a 10th-grade education that prepared her to work as an receptionist at Camp LeJuene most of her adult life. Her husband was a Marine sergeant before his death returning from World War II over 50 years ago. She receives veteran's benefits as his widow and a small federal pension from her own employment. Mrs. W. had one son, James, who has resided in a local nursing home since suffering a massive heart attack in 1982.

Mrs. W. has never lived alone. She lived with her son James after his marriage; she continued to live with him after his divorce to care for him and his son, James Jr. Mrs. W. now lives with her 45-year-old grandson, James Jr., in a two-bedroom apartment in a public housing development in Onslow County, North Carolina. James Jr., who underwent heart bypass surgery in 1991, is unemployed and recently has applied for Supplemental Security Income to supplement his grandmother's income. He has a history of substance abuse.

Among the victims, Mrs. J., Mrs. W., and Mrs. B. provide homes for their adult children. In comparison, White elderly victims may more often live with their children in the children's homes (Myers & Shelton, 1987). Although there are no census statistics available that accurately estimate the number of impaired elders residing with their adult children, Steinmetz's 1980 study of caregivers of elders in Delaware generated results that support the notion that White elderly victims more often live with their children in the children's homes. Her study involved two samples: The caregiver sample was 95% White (N = 99); the service-provider sample reported that "the predominant living arrangement (57.3%) was an elder residing in the caregiver's home" (Steinmetz, 1988, p. 267).

Some researchers support the hypothesis that stress of caring for elders is directly related to elder maltreatment, but others (Griffin & Williams, 1992; Pillemer & Finklehor, 1989; Godkin et al., 1989) propose the reverse of the caregiver-stress hypothesis. That is, the risk factor is the dependence not of the victim but of the perpetrator. Four areas of dependence have been suggested in studies of elder abuse:

1   Financial dependence has been noted by Breckman and Adelman (1988), Anetzberger (1987), Pillemer (1985), Hwalek & Sengstock (1987), and Wolf, Strugnell, and Godkin (1982).
2   Housing dependence was identified by Pillemer (1985).
3   Disabilities, in the forms of cognitive impairment and mental retardation or mental illnesses of spouses and children, were cited by Pillemer (1985).
4   Emotional problems of abusers, as evidenced by substantial psychological impairment associated with alcoholism, arrests, and other deviant behavior, were cited by Pillemer (1985).

Applying social-exchange theory to the notion of perpetrator dependence suggests that the "feeling of powerlessness experienced by an adult child is especially acute because it so strongly violates society's expectations for normal adult behavior" (Pillemer & Finklehor, 1989, p. 180). It is also possible that abusers are responding to life stresses totally unrelated to caregiving or their dependence on the older person.

Mrs. J.'s daughter, Irene, Mrs. W.'s grandson, James, and Mrs. B.'s son, Robert, represent a type of symbiotic or mutually beneficial relationship that can be found in African American communities. The elders seem to have an understanding, an unwritten contract, with their adult child or grandchild to provide financial support, housing, etc. in return for the younger person's continued presence in the home. This is especially evident in situations in which the older person has never lived alone and fears doing so. To an observer, it appears that one child, usually a "weak" or "flawed" one, has been "kept at home" while his or her siblings were encouraged to become independent and succeed. Irene, Mrs. J.'s daughter; Mrs. W.'s grandson, James; and Robert, Mrs. B.'s son, are clear examples of this phenomenon. Hence, the alcoholic or "sickly" adult child who resides with the parent is "protected out of necessity." This represents "protection from being alone" for the parent and protection from homelessness and destitution for the adult child. A power relationship, with the older person in control, may be acknowledged less frequently. This practice seems reminiscent of the behavior of European immigrants near the turn of the century, when one child was retained at home to care for the parents. Building on the adage, "If you're not part of the solution, you're part of the problem," such behavior on the part of elders does not encourage emotional independence and maturity among the younger adults. Instead, it covertly maintains dependence and encourages social and economic infantilism or childish behavior by not requiring self-sufficiency in certain adult children. Mrs. B. openly admits "giving Robert money for cigarettes" and other behaviors that encourage him to stay with her. The dependency of African American caregivers on older persons for housing and income sharing (Harper & Alexander, 1990) may be an important determinant of elder abuse among African Americans. However, there has been no research to support or refute claims of "encouraged" dependence or of the role adult dependence plays in elder maltreatment. These are issues and relationships that warrant further examination.

Mr. N. is a 68-year-old legally blind widower who lives in a brick home in rural Onslow County, North Carolina. He has lived alone since his wife's death 6 years ago. He talks longingly of the times he shared with his wife. She was a skilled pianist and he sang professionally to accompany her for over 20 years. He has become increasingly functionally impaired since her death. He does not communicate with his neighbors and reportedly has few friends.

Mr. N. receives home health services daily to help with activities of daily living and his personal care. The aide prepares a noon meal and leaves Mr. N.'s dinner each day. The personal-care aide bathes him on alternate days and cuts his shoulder length hair bimonthly. Mr. N. says that his personal-care aide, a male, is the only person who ever visits him during the week.

Problems in stabilizing his diabetic condition have ruled out surgery for cataracts on his eyes. He also has been diagnosed as clinically depressed for 5 years but refuses to take medication. His only relative, a "step-daughter," lives in Maryland and calls weekly. Mr. N. expresses pride when he talks about his experiences raising her. She and her family visit twice each year. (Self-neglect.)

Mrs. K. is a 78-year-old widow who moved into an adult foster care home 6 months ago in Lenoir County, North Carolina. Mrs. K. and her husband, who died 10 years ago, were considered to be "well off" by the African American community. They owned several real estate properties in the community, had extensive stocks and bonds, and owned a number of certificates of deposit. Most of those holdings are gone. The last parcel of land was sold recently to pay for Mrs. K.'s foster care.

Mrs. K.'s financial affairs until recently were handled by a nonkin niece, who moved her family to Lenoir County to take care of Mrs. K. after Mr. K. died. Mrs. K.'s niece made several questionable purchases (cars, jewelry, furnishings) from Mrs. K.'s bank accounts and cashed several certificates of deposit without Mrs. K.'s knowledge. She also insisted that Mrs. K. did not need to live in her home and would be more comfortable living in a trailer that Mrs. K.'s money bought and placed on Mrs. K.'s land. The niece and her family lived in Mrs. K.'s home, which was larger than the trailer. Neither the niece nor her husband were employed, but they maintained their family of five on Mrs. K.'s resources.

Mrs. K. was told that she was almost out of money; she was given no explanation about her reduced resources. The situation was aggravated because Mrs. K. has become increasingly confused and forgetful since her husband's death. Adult-protective services removed her from the trailer and placed her in the foster-care home. She says that she likes her housemate and that she enjoys the shared living arrangement much more than she liked being cared for by her nonkin "niece."

Theme 5: Nontraditional "Family" Constellations Are Common Among African Americans

Three of the cited maltreatment victims' families (Mr. N., Mrs. B., and Mrs. K.) exhibited "other familial configurations" or families composed of kin and nonkin members. Historical traditions and societal influences may predispose African Americans to arrange their familial interactions differently than Whites, especially in rural areas. Kin and nonkin families exist and elderly relatives, or in many cases nonrelatives, have reared thousands of children. Kin and nonkin families historically have been a major source of cohesiveness among Black families. The same practice exists today. In 1975, half the African American families headed by women 65 and over included children who resided with them but were not born of the elder women (Hill & Shackleford, 1975).

The various familial configurations of African American families raise interesting issues, however, when identifying a child as the perpetrator of abuse. Is he or she a biological child? A young 18- to 30-year-old relative who is a nonbiological child? A grandchild? A nonrelative? The tendency both past and present for different generations of African American family members and nonkin to live together was and continues to be a strategy to pool limited resources. Indeed, shared living arrangements have allowed many to subsist on a minimum income (Harper & Alexander, 1990).

Theme 6: Elderly Maltreatment Victims Are Geographically Isolated from Services, Medical Care, Family Members, Etc.

Myers and Shelton (1987) propose that an important ingredient in remedying the problem of elder maltreatment is increasing the services available to help primary caregivers. Social and health problems have been responsible for generating numerous services during the 1980s aimed at relieving caregivers of some of the ongoing responsibilities of providing continual care to their aged loved ones and, thereby, relieving caregivers' stress. But what kinds of services make a difference? Are there adequate services available in rural states to affect elder maltreatment? Are these services used by elderly African Americans?

Lucas (1989) suggests four strategies that affect elder maltreatment either as prevention or treatment:

    1   Social-work intervention (coordination of formal and informal systems of care, adult protective services, family support groups, direct social services).

2 Self-help programs (Alcoholics Anonymous, Al-Anon, batterers' counseling groups).
3 Home health services (nursing, dietary counseling, physical therapy/occupational therapy, homemaker/home health aid services, caregiver training).
4 Respite (adult day care, senior companion).

Getting services to and accepted by minority communities have posed a problem. Some researchers (Krischef & Yoelin, 1981) believe that Black cultural values dictate heavy reliance on the informal helping network instead of the formal service system. They suggest that many African Americans are uneasy and unsure about support offered from the traditional public or private agencies.

> Rural elderly African Americans under use available services because: (1) they are not aware of the variety of services; (2) they are not involved in the planning nor implementation of services; (3) they are powerless in the political arena out of which decisions and programs emanate; and (4) they have feelings of alienation which dissuade participation. (Carlton-LaNey, 1991, p. 12)

They may only feel comfortable utilizing informal support networks (Barresi, 1990; Taylor & Chatters, 1986; Neighbors & Jackson, 1984). The greater truth may be that African Americans rely more on family because of the historic absence of formal community services.

> Mr. D. is a 71-year-old man who was diagnosed with AIDS 1 year ago while seeking treatment for a recurring cough. Mr. D. lives with his wife, Dorothy, in Pitt County, North Carolina. They have no children. Both receive a retirement check from his former employer. Mr. D. was a pharmaceutical salesman until 1988, when he retired. The D.s consider themselves to be a comfortable, middle-class family. Their neighbors know that Mr. D. is ill; they are unaware of his diagnosis. Mrs. D. has chosen to keep details of his illness very confidential.
> Mrs. D. does not have AIDS and is not HIV-positive. She has spoken of her fears about contracting AIDS while caring for her husband. She does not like to feed him or bathe him or touch him in any way. She jokingly said she does "not like to be in the same room with him." The D.'s do not know how Mr. D. contracted AIDS, but Mrs. D. said she thinks her husband "was 'catting' around and is getting his just desserts." She says her husband was never very affectionate with her, but that he must have been affectionate with someone. Mr. D. admits to having had several extramarital affairs, but he says he was always careful because he did not want to expose his wife to any venereal disease. Mrs. D. has expressed her anger verbally toward Mr. D. by screaming obscenities at him. She has refused counseling to address her anger, saying she is too embarrassed to talk with anyone.
> The physician says Mr. D. is getting progressively weaker and will probably die within the next year. He thinks it is too soon to consider a referral to a hospice program. Mrs. D. says her husband will die in this house because "I've got to live here" and that not one cent of her money will ever be used to pay for his care.

When one thinks of increasing services to White middle-class caregivers, certain types of support programs come to mind, such as home health care, medical care delivered by private physician, or adult daycare or day health care (Griffin, 1993). Such may not be the case when one thinks of services in rural Black communities. Kosberg (1983), Jackson (1978), and Johnson (1989) note racial disparities in medical and social services. If, as Jackson (1980) proposed, part of what contributes to elder abuse among African Americans is the lack of community services that can cause caregiver/perpetrators to be overwhelmed with caring for an infirm elder, then as Liu and Yu (1985) note, minority aged are singled out for "differential and inferior treatment" regarding social services. Mrs. D., for example, might be less overwhelmed and angry about caring for her husband with more health and social supports. When one suggests providing services to a population whose needs have been historically underestimated, as in the African American community, one questions where to begin. The community has been systematically underserved. Multiple needs, such as financial, medical, housing, and medication, exist, but services are limited in types and amounts, especially in rural areas. The enormity of the task of providing services should not cause scholars and program planners to avoid making an attempt to address the needs. Such avoidance is a common form of abuse that is cited by professionals who simply do not know where to begin.

Theme 7: Minimalization or Neutralization Behavior Is Identifiable in Both African American Victims and Perpetrators of Elder Maltreatment

In the literature on elderly maltreatment, practitioners are given a range of possibilities concerning why clients may resist involvement with them. When encountered, such resistive behaviors are sometimes viewed as validation of the existence of abuse, such as when the victim, Mrs. B., is loyal to her son and reported abuser, Robert. For her, staying with Robert is preferable to possible alternative placements. Mrs. B. also may be ashamed about what has happened and the reality that her son has taken advantage of her. A similar situation exists for Mrs. J. Likewise, Mr. D. does not acknowledge the neglect and possible psychological abuse he receives from his wife as his physical health deteriorates. Tomita (1990) offers neutralization theory to explain this denial process. She notes the tendency for victims and perpetrators to neutralize, that is, minimize or rationalize, what is happening to them. Tomita warns practitioners to take care not to be triangulated in the denial process with clients.

However, practitioners who expect members of the client system to rationalize or neutralize the discomfort associated with maltreatment risk exhibiting a "reaction" bias that may be just as problematic. Such a "reaction" bias suggests a predisposition on the parts of workers, a preconception that may affect their abilities to view maltreatment complaints impartially. Predisposed workers may be "too sure" about what they see, so sure that they fail to see and hear what their clients are really saying and feeling. In such instances, workers predisposed to the possibility of clients' neutralizing their circumstances can do their clients a great disservice.

Still another perspective is that denial or resistance may be psychological defense mechanisms that both victims and perpetrators use to protect their emotional selves. Or, as with battered women in an unsafe environment, the victim may believe that to feel or behave any differently may increase the potential for harm. So victims employ such defense mechanisms to protect themselves from the abuser. The charge to the practitioner is to be able to distinguish between neutralization or denial and reality.

> Mr. G., a 67-year-old unmarried male, was diagnosed with lung cancer 2 years ago. A veteran of the Korean War, he "caught [tuberculosis] over there and was put in Asheville in the VA hospital for two years in 1953." He recovered and worked for a construction company as a brick layer until he was 60 years old and retired. Between ages 60 and 65, he lived alone in an apartment.
>
> Mr. G. has five adult children, the result of a long-term unmarried relationship. He denied paternity at each child's birth and was not involved in their upbringing; they were cared for by their mother. All of the children know the identity of their father and express anger over his refusal to make them legitimate. None of them are willing to provide ongoing care for him. Mr. G. returns to his aged mother's home when he is "really sick" and in pain. His 83-year-old mother cannot provide adequate medical care for Mr. G.'s deteriorating condition. Otherwise, Mr. G. lives alone in rural Onslow County.
>
> His oldest son, Leon, an alcoholic, sometimes stays with him when the younger man finds himself homeless. But they are verbally abusive to one another. Mr. G. voices much concern about "who will get his money," his Veteran's Administration benefit, upon his death. He expresses much concern about his loneliness and his deteriorating condition. He speaks of not wanting to die alone.

Theme 8: Psychological Demoralization Is Problematic for African American Families

Although she is 41 years old, Irene (Mrs. J.'s daughter) only worked between 1979 and 1980, because she "couldn't get a job." Mrs. W.'s grandson, James, is 45 years old but has "not worked regularly" at any time during his life because he "didn't finish high school" and "has no skills" and because he was "sick." Mrs. P's granddaughter "is needed in the home to care for grandma," but further investigation reveals that she did not finish high school and "never really looked for a job." Mr. G's behavior has isolated him from his children. His only support is from his elderly mother, who allows him to stay with her when he is very ill. Each of these caregivers illustrate what many in society might call a failed or demoralized existence. Cazenave (1981), Hare (1979), and Asbury (1987) note that violence may be a way of reacting to the lack of options or goals available to meet definitions of success generated by society, which are controlled by the majority race. This suggests that whether young or aged African Americans have been able to achieve economic or developmental success, as defined by the majority race, may directly affect how these individuals interact within African American families. Accused by the community of financially abusing his mother, Robert, Mrs. B.'s son, "cannot find a job. I get day labor when I can," but, he explains, "I am needed in the home to look after mother." He acknowledges feeling badly about not having succeeded economically. He characterizes himself as a failure as a son and as a citizen. Yet, he does not look for permanent work; he does "drink too much," a scenario that was repeated again and again during the interviews. Failure to successfully meet the majority race's criteria may promote the potential for socially unacceptable expression.

Staples (1976) suggests that African Americans are not inherently violent and that rates of violence among African Americans in other countries are lower than that of both African Americans and White Americans. He suggests that the explanation for higher rates of violence among African Americans may be due to their social predicament in American society, especially in the southern region of the United States, which has historically reacted violently to African American quests for social equality. If, as has been proposed, the character of African American families has been affected by changes in our society, such as increased poverty and the erosion of traditional natural social-support networks in families and neighborhoods as evidenced by elevated rates of separation and divorce and imprisonment, the results may be increased elder maltreatment (Harper & Alexander, 1990).

Theme 9: African Americans Are Particularly Resistant to Institutional Help

Although the above-mentioned considerations are important, there are other considerations that must be included in the practice mix for those working in the field. The level of resistance or cooperation should not be an implicit signal that maltreatment is occurring.

> Mrs. M. was widowed 23 years ago. At age 91, she has lived in a privately run boarding home in eastern North Carolina since "breaking her hip" 5 years ago. Prior to that, she lived alone in the family home in Pitt County, North Carolina. She was a life-long resident of Pitt County. Mrs. M. worked all of her adult life. She worked as a porter in the railroad station in Rocky Mount until she was 50 years old and later worked as a domestic for several Pitt County families until she retired at age 70.
>
> Mr. and Mrs. M. had one adopted daughter who died at an early age (25 years old). The older couple raised their daughter's two children, ensuring that both completed high school and college. Both of her granddaughters are married with families of their own.
>
> Mrs. M. stubbornly refused to live with either of her two granddaughters, although her doctor repeatedly insisted that she needed supervision and could not live alone. Two nieces tried to live in the home and provide supervision, which did not

prove to be positive experiences for them or Mrs. M. She became argumentative and leveled accusations of theft at them.

Diagnosed with Alzheimer's disease, she now has few lucid moments and does not recognize family or friends. Her finances (Veterans Administration and railroad retirement pensions) are managed by a granddaughter who resides approximately 10 miles away. (Financial exploitation.)

The worker should not be the only "expert" in determining the existence of abuse; aged people's contributions must not be minimized. Little is said about clients' current levels of mistrust of institutions, the history of mistrust of institutions and practitioners employed by them by particular client cultural groups, and fear of inappropriate "handling" by "helper" social-service agencies. If perceived "institutional abuse" is a factor, the "cure" to the client may appear worse than the "disease." Such considerations may influence the level of resistance or cooperation exhibited by Mrs. M. or Mr. N. These notions may seem ridiculous to some practitioners, but that does not make them any less real for clients. Aged adults also may judge situations differently than do practitioners, and the ethnocultural background of the client may influence the practitioner's perception of elderly maltreatment (either in overamplified, stereotypic directions or in more sophisticated constructive ways) as well (Moon & Williams, 1993).

There is a law, but. . . Elder-abuse laws or adult protective service laws, which prohibit abuse or maltreatment of elders, exist in all the states of the Union. The existence of these protective laws substantiate society's value for all individuals and its commitment to protect vulnerable older people. Unfortunately, the laws vary widely. For example, a statewide guardianship office provides guardianship services to impaired, dependent elders in Delaware; county sheriffs serving as "committee" perform the same duties in West Virginia; and area agencies on aging are responsible for such services in Pennsylvania. There is little consistency in terminology, service-delivery models, or levels of protection provided. Differences in interpretations of an individual state's elder-abuse laws may exist among all involved parties: adult protective service workers, physicians and nurses, criminal-justice personnel, suspected abuse victims and suspected perpetrators, and other family members. The potential for different interpretations of existing laws is even greater if any combination of the persons mentioned is from different cultural backgrounds, such as African American and European American. Yet, these people from different cultures must cooperate if abused elders are to be adequately protected. The need for consistent interpretation of existing laws suggests a need for joint education and for information sharing. Information about elderly maltreatment and help for perpetrators is most helpful when it is presented in nonthreatening environments such as community churches, public schools, or neighborhood community centers. Use of such sites allows for maximum dissemination of information without labeling members of the audience.

Theme 10: Definitions of Elder Maltreatment Are Not Sensitive to the Unique Circumstances of African Americans

Available research cites most perpetrators of elder abuse as White, middle-aged daughters or daughters-in-law, who are primary caregivers and with whom elderly victims reside (Steinmetz, 1988). Such studies fail to consider the large number of older African American victims, such as Mrs. B., who provide a home for their adult children, or the large number of older adult victims who may be abused by nonkin adult children and grandchildren—household situations that are common in the African American tradition (Griffin & Williams, 1992). Recognizing that elder maltreatment occurs in all cultural and minority groups, there is little direct evidence and no reason to assume that the existing majority's definition of elderly maltreatment, such as it is, can be validly applied to different ethnic populations (Williams & Griffin, 1991). Indeed, we have learned that in many other areas, such as mental health (Leigh, 1989; Chau, 1989; Sue & Zane, 1987), child abuse, and spouse abuse (Hampton, 1991; Long 1986; Asbury, 1987), such generalizations mask important differences. Applying the characteristics of a condition that exists in one population without reflection to another may inaccurately frame that other population's reality.

The lack of information about the effect of ethnicity on the perception of elderly maltreatment may further obscure populations with less social status, typically minorities. The few studies that focus on elder maltreatment among minorities stress that culture must be included as a factor in the search for more precise definitions and approaches to the problem (Brown, 1989a; Hall, 1986; Cazenave, 1979; Griffin & Williams, 1992; Moon & Williams, 1993; Williams & Griffin, 1991). Brown (1989b), Cazenave (1979), and Griffin and Williams (1992) suggest that characteristics traditionally used to evaluate this phenomenon may produce inaccurate information concerning what exists because researchers frequently exclude variables that define minority life. For example, differences in family patterns, living arrangements, and resource sharing may influence what may be perceived as maltreatment, who is more likely to be the abuser, the form the abuse takes, and how maltreatment is perceived (Griffin & Williams, 1992; Moon & Williams, 1993). In the case of Mrs. B., neither the social worker nor Mrs. B.'s daughters considered that Mrs. B. might be the perpetrator of emotional abuse against Robert, her adult son. The reluctance to think of Robert as a victim may be because neither the majority culture nor minority cultures support such a stance. Similar circumstances exist for Mrs. J. and her female housemates, for Mrs. W. and James, and for Mrs. P. and her granddaughter. Culture provides the context in which the behavior of those involved can be understood.

African Americans tend to define the use and the sharing of resources in a different way than Caucasians, and an ethnically insensitive adult protective service worker might mislabel a situation as financial exploitation, as in Robert's case, with a variety of oppressive consequences for those involved. Researchers and practitioners alike must stress the importance of developing a deeper understanding of diversity to enhance the effectiveness of assessment and intervention.

CONCLUSIONS

This chapter examines the nature of abusive relationships involving African American elders who are located primarily in the southeastern United States, the site of this author's research. Time and again, content analyses of maltreatment situations have revealed that financial abuse and neglect are present, physical abuse and sexual abuse are not. Caregivers repeatedly said, "You just don't hit your momma." Physical abuse does not occur to parents or elders in the African American community. The data reveal the emergence of 10 themes that have been presented in the context of social service delivery concerns and are summarized below.

1 Physically abusing elders is particularly unacceptable among African Americans.

2 There is a relationship between social conditioning and abusive behavior among African Americans.

3 Poverty is pervasive in African American elder maltreatment situations.

4 African American perpetrators of elder abuse may be adults involved in dependent, mutually beneficial relationships with elders. These relationships may involve emotional maltreatment of the adult children in the form of "encouraged" infantilism.

5 Nontraditional "family" constellations are common among African Americans.

6 Elderly maltreatment victims are geographically isolated from services, medical care, family members, and so forth.

7 Minimalization or neutralization behavior is identifiable in both African American victims and perpetrators of elder maltreatment.

8 Psychological demoralization is particularly problematic for African American families.

9 African Americans are particularly resistant to institutional help.

10 Definitions of elder maltreatment are not sensitive to the unique circumstances of African Americans.

RECOMMENDATIONS

Diversity is an essential element in an expanded conceptualization of elder maltreatment. Without allowing for ethnic diversity, any definition is not generalizable, is narrow, and can have negative consequences for all concerned. It is important that the helping professions respond to instances of elder maltreatment in the African American community. But there is a lack of clarity about what maltreatment is and the faces it presents in the African American community. Acquiring empirical information is a necessary first step in improving services to this underserved population. Until such empirical information can be obtained, some helpful measures can be undertaken by the human-services community.

First, community-based education about the existence of elder maltreatment as a problem should be provided to the informal and formal networks within the

African American community. Such efforts would impact kin and nonkin relationships and could be provided through neighborhood groups, churches, senior-citizen centers, mental-health centers, and healthcare centers.

Second, in addition to providing information about the existence of elder maltreatment, attention must be directed toward promoting a nonjudgmental attitude among helpers of both the elderly victims and perpetrators of elder maltreatment. Nonjudgmental attitudes are important if professionals are to cultivate trust in the community, thereby encouraging both victims and abusers to share and to involve themselves in treatment and recovery processes.

A third need is to investigate the symbiotic relationships that can exist between African American victims and perpetrators of maltreatment. Such an investigation may require that professionals examine their inherent biases against suspected perpetrators and honestly look at the behavior of both participants in abusive relationships. The conscious or unconscious behaviors of some older adults to prevent being alone may serve to infantilize adult children.

Fourth, culturally sensitive program staffs and procedures should be required by community agencies. When real sensitivity is exhibited by administrators and workers toward minority issues, they are more likely to successfully diffuse potentially explosive maltreatment situations. Culturally sensitive practitioners and procedures also reduce the likelihood of angry confrontations surrounding investigations and service delivery.

Finally, although education may be one form of primary prevention, other forms of prevention and treatment should be present in the African American community to provide treatment to clients in need of services. Many private and public service agencies are available to the community at large. Research has shown that African Americans do not make adequate use of such agencies. It is necessary then that these agencies' access points be placed within the African American community to encourage use by the minority group.

REFERENCES

American Association of Retired Persons–Andrus Foundation. (1987). *Minority affairs initiative.* Washington, DC: American Association of Retired Persons.

Anetzberger, G. (1987). *The etiology of elder abuse by adult offspring.* Springfield, IL: Charles Thomas.

Asbury, J. (1987). African American women in violent relationships: An exploration of cultural differences. In R. L. Hampton (Ed.), *Violence in the black family: Correlates and consequences* (pp. 89–106). Lexington, MA: Lexington Books.

Barresi, C. M. (1990). Diversity in black family caregiving: Implications for geriatric education. In *Minority aging: Essential curricula content for selected health and allied health professionals.* (DHHS Publication No. HRS-P-DV-90–4). Washington, DC: U.S. Government Printing Office.

Billingsley, A. (1968). *Black families in white America.* Englewood Cliffs, NJ: Prentice-Hall.

Billingsley, A. (1969). Family functioning in the low-income black community. *Casework, 50,* 568–572.

Blanton, P. G. (1989). Zen and the art of adult protective services: In search of a unified view of elder abuse. *Journal of Elder Abuse and Neglect, 1*(1), 27–35.

Breckman, R., & Adelman, R. (1988). *Helping elderly victims of abuse and neglect.* Beverly Hills, CA: Sage Publications.

Brown, A. S. (1989a). A survey on elder abuse at one Native American Tribe. *Journal of Elder Abuse And Neglect, 1*(2), 17–35.

Brown, A. S. (1989b, March). *Increasing the Effectiveness of Informal Support Systems in Rural Areas.* Research brief presented at 31st Annual Meeting of the Western Gerontological Society, Washington, DC.

Carlton-LaNey, I. (1991). Some considerations of the rural elderly Black's underuse of social services. *Journal of Gerontological Social Work, 16*(1/2), 3–17.

Cazenave, N. A. (1979). Family violence and aging African Americans: Theoretical perspectives and research possibilities. *Journal of Minority Aging, 4*, 99–108.

Cazenave, N. A. (1981, October) *Elder abuse and black Americans: Incidence, correlates, treatment and prevention.* Presented at the Annual Meeting of the National Council on Family Relations, Milwaukee, WI.

Chau, K. L. (1989). Sociocultural dissonance among ethnic minority populations. *Social Casework, 70*(4), 224–230.

Crystal, S. (1987). Elder abuse: The latest "crisis." *The Public Interest, 88*(Summer), 56–66.

Godkin, M. A., Wolf, R. S., & Pillemer, K. A. (1989). A case-comparison analysis of elder abuse and neglect. *International Journal on Aging and Human Development, 28*, 207–225.

Greenstein, R., Porter, K., Shapiro, I., Leonard, P., & Barancik, S. (1988). *Still far from the dream: Recent developments in Black income, employment and poverty.* Washington, DC: Center on Budget and Policy Priorities.

Griffin, L. W. (1993). Adult day care and adult protective services. *Journal of Gerontological Social Work, 20*(1/2), 115–133.

Griffin, L. W. (1994). Elder maltreatment among rural African Americans. *Journal of Elder Abuse & Neglect, 6*(1), 1–27.

Griffin, L. W., & Williams, O. J. (1992). Abuse among African American elderly. *Journal of Family Violence, 7*(1), 19–35.

Hall, P. A. (1986). Minority elder maltreatment: Ethnicity, gender, age, and poverty. *Journal of Gerontological Social Work, 9*(4), 53–72.

Hampton, R. L. (1991). *Black family violence: Current research and theory.* Lexington, MA: Lexington Books.

Hare, N. (1979). The relative psychosocial economic suppression of the black male. In W. D. Smith (Ed.), *In reflection of black psychology.* Washington, DC: University Press.

Harper, M. S., & Alexander, C. D. (1990). Profile of the Black elderly. In *Minority aging: Essential curricula content for selected health and allied health professionals.* (DHHS Publication No. HRS-P-DV-90-4). Washington, DC: U.S. Government Printing Office.

Hill, R. B. (1971). *The strengths of Black families.* New York: Emerson Hall.

Hill, R. B. & Shackleford, L. (1975). The black extended family revisited. *The Urban League Review*, Fall, 18–24.

Hudson, M. (1989). Analyses of the concepts of elder mistreatment: Abuse and neglect. *Journal of Elder Abuse and Neglect, 1*(1), 5–27.

Hudson, M. F. (1994). Elder abuse: Its meaning to middle-aged and elder adults. Part II: Pilot results. *Journal of Elder Abuse and Neglect, 6*(1), 55–81.

Hwalek, M. B., & Sengstock, M. C. (1987). Assessing the probability of abuse of the elderly: Toward development of a clinical screening instrument. *Journal of Applied Gerontology, 5*(2), 153–173.

Jackson, J. J. (1978, September–October). Special health problems of aged African Americans. *Aging*, 278–288, 15–20.

Jackson, J. J. (1980).*Minorities and aging.* Belmont, CA: Wadsworth Publishing Co.

Johnson, T. F. (1989). Elder mistreatment identification instruments: Finding common ground. *Journal of Elder Abuse and Neglect, 1*(4), 15–37.

Kosberg, J. I. (1983). *Abuse and maltreatment of the elderly: Causes and interventions.* Boston, MA: John Wright & Sons, Ltd.

Kosberg, J. I. (1988). Preventing elder abuse: Identification of high risk factors prior to placement decisions. *The Gerontologist, 28,* 43–50.

Krischef, C. & Yoelin, M. L. (1981). Differential use of informal and formal helping networks among rural elderly and White Floridians. *Journal of Gerontological Social Work, 3*(Spring), 45–59.

Leigh, J. (1989). *Issues in working with ethnic minorities* (pp. 1–33). Unpublished manuscript, University of Washington School of Social Work.

Liu, W. T., & Yu, E. (1985). Asian/Pacific American elderly: Mortality differentials, health status, and use of health services. *Journal of Applied Gerontology, 4,* 35–64.

Long, K. A. (1986). Cultural considerations in the assessment and treatment of intrafamilial abuse. *American Orthopsychiatric Association, 56*(1), 131–136.

Lucas, E. T. (1989). Elder mistreatment: Is it really abuse? *Free Inquiry in Creative Society, 17,* 95–99.

Moon, A., & Williams, O. J. (1993). Perceptions of elder abuse and help seeking patterns among African American, Caucasian, and Korean-American elderly. *The Gerontologist, 33,* 386–395.

Moore, T., & Thompson, V. (1987) Elder abuse: A review of research, programmes and policy. *The Social Worker, Travailleur Social, 55,* 115–122.

Myers, J. E., & Shelton, B. (1987). Abuse and older persons: Issues and implications for counselors. *Journal of Counseling Development, 65,* 376–380.

Neighbors, H. W., & Jackson, J. S. (1984). The use of informal and formal help: Four patterns of illness behavior in the black community. *American Journal of Community Psychology, 12,* 281–300.

Pillemer, K. (1985). The dangers of dependency: New findings on domestic violence against the elderly. *Social Problems, 33,* 146–158.

Pillemer, K., & Finklehor, D. (1989). Causes of elder abuse: Caregiver stress versus problem relatives. *American Journal of Orthopsychiatry, 59,* 179–187.

Staples, R. (1976). Race and family violence: The internal colonialism perspective. In L. E. Gary & L. P. Brown (Eds.), *Crime and its impact on the Black community.* Washington, DC: Howard University, Institute for Urban Development Center.

Steinmetz, S. K. (1978). Battered parents. *Society, 15,* 54–55.

Steinmetz, S. K. (1988). *Duty bound: Elder abuse and family care.* Newbury Park, CA: Sage Publications.

Straus, M., & Gelles, R. (1986). Societal change and change in family violence from 1975–1985 as revealed by two national studies. *Journal of Marriage and the Family, 48,* 465–479.

Sue, S., & Zane, N. (1987). The role of culture and culture techniques in psychotherapy: A critique and reformulation. *American Psychologist, 42*(1), 37–45.

Taylor, R. J., & Chatters, L. M. (1986). Patterns of informal support to elderly Black adults: Family, friends, and church members. *Social Work,* 432–438.

Thomas, A., & Sillen, S. (1976). *Racism and psychiatry.* Secaucus, NJ: The Citadel Press.

Tomita, S. T. (1990). The denial of elder mistreatment by victims and abusers: The application of neutralization theory. *Violence and Victims, 5*(3), 171–184.

U. S. Congress, Senate Special Committee on Aging. (1977). *Protective services for the elderly: A working paper.* (No. 052–070–04120–0). Washington, DC: U.S. Government Printing Office.

Valentine, D., & Cash, T. (1986). A definitional discussion of elder maltreatment. *Journal of Gerontological Social Work, 9,* 17–28.

Williams, O. J., & Griffin, L. W. (1991). Elder abuse in the Black family. In R. L. Hampton (Ed.), *Black family violence: Current research and theory* (pp. 117–127). Lexington, MA: Lexington Books.

Williams, O. J., & Griffin, L. W. (1996). Elderly maltreatment and cultural diversity: When laws are not enough. *Journal of Multicultural Social Work, 4*(2), 1–13.

Wolf, R., Strugnell, C. P., & Godkin, M. A. (1982). *Preliminary findings from three model projects on elderly abuse.* Worcester, MA: University of Massachusetts Medical Center, Center on Aging.

Chapter 4

African Americans and Elder Mistreatment: Targeting Information for a High-Risk Population

Donna M. Benton

Although the prevalence and incidence of elder mistreatment is still being investigated among minority populations, there is a need to educate these populations about the topic. Education about elder mistreatment is usually presented without reference to specific ethnic or cultural groups. Experience from other health and social-service education, identification, and service-delivery programs strongly suggests that generalized education may not adequately reach the minority elderly. Education programs about elder mistreatment need focused outreach efforts if they are to convey their message to minority elderly. The purpose of this chapter is to determine how information about elder mistreatment is currently being disseminated to African American elderly. This chapter begins with a discussion of risk factors for elder mistreatment among African American elderly. Subsequent sections present data about elder mistreatment among African Americans and discuss concerns about access to information. Concluding sections present the results of a survey of agencies providing information about elder mistreatment, along with recommendations for future education.

INTRODUCTION

As the 21st century nears, demographic trends together with funding constraints have prompted social policy to evolve toward requiring that social services use more "targeted" service delivery. This mandate means that programs must better assess the needs of the elderly population in order to improve service delivery and use. The growing ethnic diversity in the United States is reflected in the elderly population. Minority elderly are the fastest growing subgroup of the elderly population. African Americans constitute the largest ethnic group in the United States and represent the largest subgroup among the minority aged (Urban

League, 1989). The 1990 census data estimate the population of African American elderly (those over the age of 65 years) to be 2.5 million. Of this group, 1.8% were 80 years or older, and this number is expected to rise to 2.7% by the year 2020 (Darnay, 1996). Despite the large numbers, there continues to be little information about this group's strengths and the challenges this population faces. Research about elder mistreatment in the African American family is still very limited (Cazenave, 1979; Griffin, 1994; Griffin & Williams, 1992). Before outreach efforts are looked at, a brief review of risk factors for elder mistreatment is given. Because most studies of elder mistreatment among African Americans have involved small, nonrepresentative samples, it is important not to generalize to the entire population. Differences within the group, such as gender, socioeconomic factors, family configuration, religion, and geographical location, impact on risk factors for elder mistreatment in the African American population (Griffin & Williams, 1992). Therefore, the risk factors presented in this chapter can serve only as a means to highlight the potential need for education; they are not representative of incidence or prevalence of elder mistreatment in the African American community.

Perceptions of Elder Mistreatment and African Americans

A definition of elder mistreatment within the African American community is problematic because there are only a few, small, studies which have addressed cultural interpretations of abuse or mistreatment (Anetzberger, Korbin, & Tomita, 1996; Griffin, 1994; Moon & Williams, 1993; Stein, 1991). What these studies suggest is that there are cultural differences between African Americans and other ethnic groups in how they perceive and define elder mistreatment. The study by Moon and Williams (1993) looked at how 30 African American, Caucasian American, and Korean American (N = 90) elderly persons rated scenarios for presence of abuse, severity of abuse, and what aspect of the situation was abusive. Results suggested that a higher percentage of African American respondents rated scenarios as abusive compared with the other two groups. In a study by Anetzberger, Korbin, and Tomita (1996), four ethnic groups (Native Americans, Japanese, Hispanics, and African Americans) were divided into "baby-boom" generation (1946–1964) and those over 60 years of age. Focus-group discussions were conducted with each group using scenarios and open-ended discussions. Results suggested that both elderly and baby-boom African Americans recognized the most commonly defined forms of abuse (psychological, physical, neglect) and were the only groups to consider financial exploitation a form of elder mistreatment (defined for the purpose of the study in question as the worst thing a family member can do to an elderly person).

Taken together, these studies support the supposition that African Americans do recognize and define some situations as elder mistreatment. This is not to say that there is more elder mistreatment in the African American community, because studies of incidence have found no ethnic-group differences (Pillemer & Finkelhor, 1988) or greater incidence among Whites of European descent (Block & Sinnott, 1979; Chen, Bell, Dolinsky, Doyle, & Dunn, 1981; Giogho & Blakemore, 1983; Giordano & Giordano, 1984; Greenberg, McKibben, & Raymond, 1990). Because elder mistreatment is recognized by this population, it becomes critical that people who need to have help in these situations be aware of where to get services and information. A subsequent section in this chapter argues that targeted outreach may be the most vital link in prevention and detection of abuse among African American elderly.

Risk Factors for Elder Mistreatment in Non-African Americans

Before a "targeted outreach" program is designed, it is necessary to understand who should be "targeted." Risk factors for elder abuse have been primarily defined with reference to the White population. A review of the literature suggests four risk factors for elder mistreatment. Although findings in the research literature on elder mistreatment are often contradictory, owing to differences in methodology, definitions, and populations sampled, nevertheless there is considerable agreement among researchers that external stress, dependency relationships, psychopathology, and social isolation are the four dominant risk factors in elder mistreatment.

It appears that stress levels in society may be increasing. For generations, families have cared for older relatives in the home. However, increased longevity has produced a new family structure in society. This new structure has been termed the "beanpole family." With this type of family structure, there is an increase in the number of living generations within lineages and a decrease in the number of members within each generation. One implication of this changed structure is a lengthening of the duration of family roles for husbands, wives, children, and caregivers. The increased duration of family roles means that families have new challenges to face, one of which is increased long-term care of the older members of the multigenerational family.

Researchers and theorists have hypothesized that caregiver stress is a risk factor for elder mistreatment (Quinn & Tomita, 1986; Steinmetz, 1988). However, empirical studies have been inconsistent in confirming that caregiver stress is related to elder mistreatment (Bookin & Dunkle, 1989; Phillips, 1983; Pillemer & Finklehor, 1989). These inconsistencies often relate to what type of mistreatment is under investigation, how mistreatment is operationally defined, or how caregivers perceive stressful situations. Survey data of professionals who have worked with elder mistreatment cases frequently mention caregiver stress or burden as a factor related to elder mistreatment (Hickey & Douglass, 1981). Moreover, Steinmetz, in a study of 119 dependent elders and their caregivers, found that caregivers who perceived caregiving as being stressful and a burden had significantly higher levels of elder mistreatment (Steinmetz, 1988). In addition, caregivers' problem-solving skills, and their perceived locus of control of events around caregiving, also have been found to be related to elder mistreatment (Bendik, 1992). Therefore, caregiver stress should not be ignored as a possible risk factor for mistreatment.

It has been proposed that elder mistreatment may be the result of an overload of stressful life events (external stress) experienced by the caregiver in areas unconnected to the caregiving situation. Such events may be the death of a friend, loss of a job, moving, low income, pregnancy, marriage, legal problems, or marital difficulties. The overwhelmed caregiver may inappropriately use the dependent elder as a focus for striking out and relieving tension and become abusive. Although this hypothesis is not fully supported by survey research findings (Hickey & Douglass, 1981; Hudson, 1986), it has received some support in empirical research studies (Pillemer & Finkelhor, 1988; Wolf & Pillemer, 1989). Findings suggested that caregivers who were abusive reported a greater number of negative life events than nonabusive caregivers. It is noteworthy that studies have found that the stressful events in caregivers' lives are often related to psychopathological behaviors on the part of the caregiver (Wolf & Pillemer, 1989).

It has been suggested that elder mistreatment is related to the dependency of the older adult on the caregiver for basic activities of daily living (e.g., grooming, feeding, bathing) or instrumental activities of daily living (e.g., housekeeping, financial management, shopping). It has been suggested that as these dependency needs increase, the burden on caregivers increases and so does their stress level. The fastest-growing segment of the population is the group 75 years of age and older, which means that more middle-aged adult children will have "old-old" (75 and over) parents who may need assistance with basic and instrumental activities of daily living. As with caregiver stress, there are conflicting data on whether dependency on the part of the elder is related to elder mistreatment (Hudson, 1986). An interesting finding by Steinmetz (1993) is that caregiver perception of stress is a stronger predictor of abuse than level of dependency in caregiving situations.

What has been found in empirical research is that victims of elder abuse were more likely to be supporting a dependent abuser, and that there is a significant association between dependency of the perpetrator and elder mistreatment (Greenberg et al., 1990; Pillemer, 1985). These data suggest that when addressing elder mistreatment it is important to know about the dependency of family members on older adults, because such dependency increases risk of mistreatment.

Psychopathological risk factors suggest that elder mistreatment appears to be related to the mental and emotional status of the abuser (Anetzberger, 1987; Pillemer, 1993; Pillemer, 1986; Pillemer & Finkelhor, 1989). It has also been suggested that persons who mistreat older adults may have been the victims of abuse at a younger age, but the amount of support for this theory has been inconclusive (Cicirelli, 1986; Suitor & Pillemer, 1988). This hypothesis requires further research, but it has significant indirect support; researchers focusing on age groups other than older adults have found evidence to support the theory of a cycle of family violence (Wolf, 1988). Moreover, it has been found that abusers, and self-neglecting older adults, are more likely to have psychiatric and substance-abuse problems (Galbraith, 1989; Spencer, 1995).

Socially isolated older adults may be more at risk for elder mistreatment than those with good social networks, inasmuch as social isolation makes it harder for the abused older adult to confide in someone about being mistreated. It also makes it harder for others to notice changes in behavior and mental health that may indicate elder mistreatment. Research indicates that mistreated older adults tend to have fewer social contacts and are less satisfied with the quality of these contacts than nonmistreated older adults (Pillemer, 1985). Moreover, this study found that the psychopathological behavior of the abuser often was responsible for the limited contacts of the abused older adult. Social isolation of the abuser has also been related to risk for elder mistreatment (Anetzberger, 1987; Pillemer, 1993).

There are other risk factors suggested by both empirical and incidence research. Among these are theories that link elder mistreatment separately to the abuser being a relative of the victim and to the abuser living with the victim (Hudson, 1986). There does not appear to be a consensus on whether female or male family members are more likely to be perpetrators. A lack of knowledge on the part of caregivers and the older adults themselves of the normal physical and cognitive changes and medical and nutritional needs associated with advancing age may contribute to both active and passive elder mistreatment.

Research into incidence of elder mistreatment among caregivers of dementia patients reports that 11% to 26% of caregivers surveyed admit to having physically abused their relative on at least one occasion (Coyne, Reichman, & Berbig, 1993; Hamel, et al., 1990). In these studies, caregivers who admitted to elder mistreatment provided more care, and had higher depression and burden scores, than caregivers who made no such admission. It also was noted that a third of the caregivers reported that they had been physically assaulted by the dementia patient. Moreover, the experience of services designed to identify elders at risk have recently stressed the importance of considering dementia as a risk factor (Flaherty & Raia, 1994; Haley & Coleton, 1992). High rates of aggression and physical violence have been well documented in patients with dementia (Haller, Binder, & McNeil, 1989; Mansfield-Cohen, Billing, Lipson, Rosenthal, & Pawlson, 1990; Reisberg, Borenstein, & Salob, 1987). Given these data, it is important that dementia be considered a risk factor for elder mistreatment.

The data presented here provide information that service providers can use to formulate outreach strategies to high-risk cases for mistreatment. In doing so, however, service providers cannot ignore the possibility of differences among various ethnic groups with respect to the risk factors themselves as well as their relative importance. Specifically, in the case of the African American ethnic group, risk factors in some areas are more pronounced and other risk factors appear to be less salient. The following sections elucidate these aspects further.

VIOLENCE, CULTURE, AND AFRICAN AMERICANS

The sociocultural contributions of slavery, economic deprivation, and racism have contributed to the anger and hostility within the African American community. This history also has influenced directly how African Americans arrange their lives and family configurations. Consideration of space precludes all but a brief examination of these factors. Ucko (1994) in her examination of the interaction of African and American culture on domestic violence suggests that, in addition to material deprivation, emotional deprivation seems to be related, at least in part, to violence and abuse. Added to this are the conflicting and incompatible cultural expectations of "family-centered" versus "individualistic" approaches to coping with stresses and decisions.

Others suggest that historical violence against African Americans, from both institutions and individuals, is partly responsible for the development of violent behavior in this population, and they use the analogy of victims of abuse, who in turn become abusers themselves (Griffin & Williams, 1992). Although a variety of theories have been advanced to explain data that underscore the rates of violence in the African American community, there is singular unanimity among researchers that theories that postulate a population-wide genetic propensity for such behaviors are not tenable. To the contrary, there have been several studies that point out the influence of socioeconomic and cultural factors (transcending populations that share genetic traits) in the expression of violence (Billingsley, 1968; Staples, 1976).

Looking at demographic data alone, African American elderly exhibit several risk factors for elder mistreatment. Compared with other ethnic sub-groups, they have a higher proportion of people that meet one or more of the following criteria: living alone, being female, being frail, or being poor (Darnay, 1996). Specifically, 33% of African Americans more than 65 years old live alone compared with 31% for Whites and 22% for Hispanics. This percentage represents an increase in the proportion of elderly people living outside of a multigenerational home in the past 30 years (Darnay, 1996).

For the African American elderly, changes in family structure may increase their risk for abuse from people outside the family; multigenerational homes can place elders at risk in their homes (Griffin & Williams, 1992). Overall, African American families of all ages are more likely than Whites to live in an extended family household (Allen & Majidi-ahi, 1979; Angel & Tienda, 1982; Hofferth, 1984). These households consist of both kin and nonkin relatives (Harper & Alexander, 1990). This family structure has been the foundation for support among this population during economic and social hardships. The multigenerational family has allowed many generations to subsist on a minimum income by providing stability, resources, and social support (Jackson, 1980). At the same time, multigenerational homes can be problematic because older African Americans are more likely to have their adult children, grandchildren, and other relatives move into their home. Studies have shown that African American parents over age 50 are most at risk to be victimized by their children, and older African

Americans are more likely to be victimized by a partner (Plass, 1993). This type of living may foster the type of dependency (financial, housing, emotional) cited in cases of elder mistreatment (Anetzberger, 1987; Breckman & Adelman, 1988; Pillemer, 1985). In addition, relatives moving into the home generally do so due to stressful life circumstances, such as divorce, drug problems, or unemployment (Allen & Pifer, 1993; Billingsley, 1968; Harper & Alexander, 1990), which also have been shown to be risk factors for elder mistreatment (Anetzberger, 1987; Pillemer, 1985).

The percentage of low-income African Americans who report fair or poor health (56%) is higher than that of Hispanics (38%) and that of Whites (39%). More disturbing is the expectation that the health of African American elders will decline further in the coming decades. In contrast, the corresponding projections for Whites indicate a decline in reports of fair to poor health (Darnay, 1996). This means that caregivers to the African American elderly population will be caring for very frail elderly. This places additional strain on the potential caregiver and may lead to an increased incidence of neglect or other types of elder mistreatment.

African Americans provide more caregiving assistance than other ethnic groups (Hays & Mindel, 1993; White-Means & Thornton, 1990) for members of their family. Studies of the psychological impact of caring for demented relatives on African American caregivers have shown mixed results. Cox and Monk (1990) examined the caregiving experiences of Black and Latino/Hispanic families of dementia victims. Among the dependent variables analyzed were caregiver health status and mental well-being. Black caregivers were found to be significantly less depressed compared with Latino/Hispanic caregivers and several community samples of older Blacks. On the Center for Epidemiological Studies–Depression (CES–D) scale, the mean score (9.75) for Black caregivers was lower than the CES–D mean of 15 obtained in mostly White samples (Knight, Lutzky, & Olshevski, 1992), indicating that Blacks were less depressed than other people.

Morycz, Malloy, Bozich, and Martz (1987) examined the differential impact of caregiving strain according to race in a sample of 810 patients in a community-based geriatric assessment center in Pittsburgh. The researchers there were interested in ascertaining which set of variables predicted stress for two racial groups of caregivers (Black and White). The data suggested that race, education, and income made little difference in the amount and the experience of stress and strain between the Black and White groups studied. Black families were less burdened caring for a family member with dementia than were Whites and were much less likely than Whites to institutionalize a demented family member. Caregiver burden in Black families was more likely to be correlated with the physical limitations of the relative. Burden was predictive of institutionalization for Whites but not for Blacks.

Similarly, Hinrichsen, and Ramirez (1992) found that African American caregivers, compared with non–African Americans, evidenced less burden and had less desire to institutionalize their relatives with dementia, while expressing more unmet service needs. These unmet needs may stretch the informal networks beyond the caregivers' ability to respond appropriately, thus creating a risk factor for elder mistreatment (Griffin & Williams, 1992).

In a study by Lawton, Rajagopal, Brody, and Kleban (1992), African American caregivers expressed less subjective burden, greater caregiving satisfaction, and less depression even when socioeconomic and personal background differences were accounted for. Mintzer et al. (1992) studied symptoms of depression among African American and White caregivers of demented patients using the CES-D scale and showed that 62% of the White caregivers had significant symptoms of depression, and 30% of the African American sample manifested symptoms of depression over the cut-off value of 16 (CES-D mean values were 19.3 and 12.4, respectively). There were no statistical differences found with respect to such background variables as age, gender, socioeconomic status, educational background, and impairment level of the patient. The researchers also examined if depressive symptoms were correlated with caregiver burden. Burden was measured along two dimensions: objective and perceived burden. Objective burden was measured by counting the number of items of basic and instrumental activities of daily living (out of a total of 15 possible items) with which the patient needed assistance. Perceived burden was the number of items that also added to the caregiver's self-reported level of stress. Only among Whites was perceived burden significantly associated with depressive symptoms.

In general, these studies have found that Blacks self-report lower mean levels of burden, and often of depression, than do Whites. Socioeconomic status does not seem to explain the difference. In fact, in Lawton et al. (1992), Black caregivers who were younger and better educated and had higher incomes experienced higher levels of burden, which was the reverse of the findings for Whites. The lower burden score suggests that African American caregivers appraise the stress of caregiving differently. The appraisal of caregiving as burdensome appears to be at least partly independent of symptoms of emotional distress. In spite of lower subjective appraisal of the burden of caregiving, African American caregivers appear to be caring for more disabled care receivers and to be providing higher levels of assistance, objectively measured (Fredman, Daly, & Lazur, 1995). Because of these studies it would seem caregiver stress, if measured by burden level, may not be a high-risk factor for elder mistreatment in a majority of the African American population. However, as suggested by the work of Lawton et al. (1992), for those African Americans with more income and education, burden may become a risk-factor.

African American elderly are at a high risk for development of dementia of the Alzheimer's type and stroke-related dementia. They are the largest subgroup of the elderly and they are also the fastest growing subpopulation of "old-old." Evidence from community-based epidemiological studies suggests a higher prevalence of dementing illnesses in the African American population than among non-Hispanic Whites (Burnam, Karno, Hough, Escobar, & Forsythe, 1987). However, these figures may be confounded with differences in educational status and selective recruitment practices. The higher prevalence of cardiovascular disease among African Americans implies that the higher rate of dementing illness would be due to multiinfarct dementia. In any case, it seems likely that the prevalence of dementing illness among African Americans at least equals that in White, non-Hispanics. As outlined in the previous section, caring for a relative with dementia may not be perceived of as a burden in the African American population. What may create risk for elder mistreatment in this population are behavioral problems and unmet social service needs, such as respite and appropriate medical care.

Researchers have suggested that one risk for elder abuse in the African American community is the lack of services to offset the overwhelming demand of providing for the needs of relatives who suffer from dementia or who are very frail. (Jackson, 1978). This gap in service must be addressed in the form of outreach programs that provide information about resources. It has even been suggested that program planners who do not attempt to address this need are perpetuating a form of elder mistreatment (i.e., benign neglect) on the African American community (Griffin & Williams, 1992).

The study by Griffin (1994) of 10 African American victims of elder abuse and six of their perpetrators suggests that financial abuse was the most prevalent type of abuse, with physical abuse deemed "particularly unacceptable." The problem of financial abuse in the African American community also was noted in a study by Anetzberger, Korbin, and Tomita (1996). In this focus-group study, the African American population was the only group to list financial exploitation as a type of elder mistreatment. The authors suggested that more research needs to be done to understand factors leading to financial exploitation in multigenerational households. At the same time, it is clear that outreach programs need to address this issue in the African American community.

The characteristics of abusers are different for the African American victim. Whereas for Whites the abuser is usually a male family member, one study reported that in the African American family it is a female relative or daughter 50 years of age or younger (Longres, Raymond, & Kimmel, 1991). This was a small study and not representative, but it has been supported in another study of elder mistreatment (Longres, 1992). This study further found that the perpetrators were less likely to be either living with the older adult or providing care and were more likely to have substance-abuse problems. Substance abuse is clearly a risk factor for elder mistreatment in both the African American and other populations (Galbraith, 1989; Spencer, 1995).

Domestic violence is highest in African American families, the rate being 400% higher than in White families (Strauss, Gelles, & Steinmetz, 1981). This type of abuse has been found to continue as a couple ages (Plass, 1993). Clearly, domestic violence is a high-risk factor in the African American family. In fact, it is disturbing that victimization rates for all types of crimes of violence are highest in the African American population, and the elderly subpopulation is no exception (Ucko, 1994).

It is important that social-service providers be responsive to the real problems of elder abuse in the African American community. As has been discussed here, there are numerous risk factors for elder abuse in the community. Although much remains to be learned from research, measures can be undertaken to educate and assist those at risk for elder mistreatment. Such measures include public education about elder mistreatment.

OUTREACH TO AFRICAN AMERICANS

For African Americans, outreach programs have been shown to be effective in increasing use of services in medical and social service organizations (Hernandez & Schweon, 1989; Milligan, Maryland, Ward, & Ziegler, 1987; Ramashala, 1989). Descriptions of outreach programs on elder mistreatment are scarce (Douglass, 1991; Jurkow, 1991; Weiner, 1991) and even fewer address outreach to African Americans (Njeri & Nerenberg, 1993). Manuals designed as guidelines for development of public-awareness campaigns present six common elements to a successful outreach effort to minority populations (Beach Advertising & University Research Corp., 1996; National Association of State Units on Aging [NASUA], 1995; Nerenberg, 1995):

1 Learn about the community's need.
2 Work with formal and informal local resources.
3 Focus on respect, dignity, and family.
4 Develop outreach materials for the population.
5 Prepare agencies for new inquiries.
6 Provide follow-up and evaluation.

Learning about the community needs means taking the time and effort to understand how ethnic groups define and understand elder mistreatment. This can be done by reviewing research literature and through discussion with the target population. The most frequently used method for eliciting viewpoints is the use of focus groups (Beach, 1996; NASUA, 1995; Nerenberg, 1995; Njeri & Nerenberg, 1993) with representatives from the target population. These groups not only provide information about existing attitudes on a topic but also can be the first step in accessing informal and formal resources in a community.

Dissemination of information about elder mistreatment should be done through local resources. Guidelines consistently encourage linking with "trusted" community leaders (formal and informal), media services, and health and social-service agencies. In addition, outreach coordinators suggest that dissemination of information may be done through nontraditional locations such as beauty shops, cafeterias, or pharmacies (NASUA, 1995). Of course, use of the church is emphasized, but at least a few outreach programs have cautioned against overreliance on church outreach because of competing demands for church participation in other community efforts.

Without exception, guidelines stress that, based on focus-group reports and experience, programs must focus on how knowledge about a topic or service will strengthen families or increase independence. Particularly in minority communities, there is justified distrust and dislike for programs that seem to reinforce negative stereotypes relating to violence, criminal behavior, or poor family relationships (Beach, 1996). For this reason, elder-mistreatment outreach programs must present information in a manner that does not reinforce these stereotypes. For example, the "We are Family" program makes a point of discussing the strengths of the African American family prior to discussing elder mistreatment (Nerenberg, 1995; Njeri & Nerenberg, 1993).

Although every state has brochures or some type of written informational material about elder mistreatment, few have materials that have been designed for ethnic populations. Brochures and materials should be easy to read, use images reflective of the target population, and contain words that convey respect and dignity. Moreover, outreach efforts should not just focus on written forms of communication but also use verbal methods such as music, discussions, and skits (Nerenberg, 1995).

Often forgotten but very important is preparing agencies for calls and inquiries that may be the result of an awareness campaign. Service-agency personnel may need training to help them become more culturally sensitive, aware of referrals, and knowledgeable about elder mistreatment. Moreover, if agencies are not prepared, they may be overwhelmed by new inquiries and may not be able to provide timely responses. The agencies are also a means for evaluating outreach efforts, because they may be enlisted in helping track how people heard about their services, or what prompted a call. This leads into the area of evaluation and follow-up. Programs should attempt to evaluate the impact of an outreach effort. This can be done in several ways, such as prepost counts of calls or inquiries to a service, phone surveys, focus groups, exit polls, or more formal experimental studies tracking outcome. Whatever method is used, evaluation is a critical component of outreach because it is a way to objectively monitor impact. Follow-up refers to discussing with the community or individuals their experience with a program. Often outreach programs believe that their goal is met once "all the brochures are distributed." Without follow-up, it is difficult to state with confidence that an outreach program has met its goal or that the disseminated information reached the intended population.

Using the six guidelines discussed in this section, the author designed a study to identify outreach programs to African Americans on the topic of elder mistreatment in the United States. The study evaluated programs to assess if they used the six guidelines presented in the literature.

A SURVEY STUDY OF OUTREACH TO AFRICAN AMERICANS ABOUT ELDER MISTREATMENT

During a 3-month period in 1996, phone surveys were done with State Departments on Aging and/or Adult Protective Services in 19 states (Alabama, Arizona, California, Florida, Georgia, Illinois, Kentucky, Louisiana, Maryland, Michigan,

Minnesota, Mississippi, Nevada, New Mexico, New York, North Carolina, South Carolina, Texas, and Virginia and the District of Columbia). States were selected based on population size of African American elderly, or referral from members of the National Center for Prevention of Elder Abuse. This purposive sample was surveyed using a semistructured interview of seven open-ended questions (see Appendix A). State Departments on Aging were the first agencies contacted. This contact was chosen because they are generally responsible for oversight of adult-protection departments and planning for elder-mistreatment policies. If a program was in place, then the interviewer asked questions 2 through 6 or skipped to question 7, which asked if the agency felt there was a need for targeted outreach to the African American community. In some cases more than one agency was contacted in a state. Outreach was defined broadly to include written materials, audiovisuals, specialized presentations, and training programs for gatekeepers, professionals, or paraprofessionals.

Data were analyzed using descriptive statistics. For those states that did have some type of targeted outreach, programs were evaluated to see if they met the six guidelines suggested by the literature for effective outreach programs. Of the 19 states surveyed, 65% (13/20) were not aware of targeted outreach programs or materials. States with no targeted outreach were split almost evenly in their opinion as to the need for targeted outreach (60% no, 40% yes). Reasons given for not needing targeted outreach included that all groups need the same information, that there is a lack of resources to handle a potential increase in referrals, and that there is a lack of funding for a program.

In the six states (California, Illinois, New York, Texas, Georgia, and Pennsylvania, plus the District of Columbia) that had some type of targeted outreach, seven programs met three of the six guidelines (learn needs, work with local resources, prepare agencies for referrals). All the programs had enlisted community representatives in their planning and many (71%) were using community volunteers to help disseminate information. Ethnic group–specific material was used by 71% of the agencies, with the most common method being the use of ethnic speakers. Only two programs had a clear respect- and family-focused program as exemplified by written material. Finally, three programs (California, Pennsylvania, and New York) had plans for an evaluation or follow-up of their outreach efforts. An interesting finding was that most outreach programs (5 out of 7) were being organized from public agencies and not within Adult Protective Services or area Agencies on Aging.

Although results of this study are not generalizable because of sampling methodology, some interesting information was obtained and may be valuable for outreach efforts. Clearly, targeted outreach is not seen as a priority by many state agencies empowered to provide education about elder mistreatment. Although funding is a consistent problem for most agencies, it also seems that there may be a lack of awareness of ethnic differences for risk, which underscores the need for such targeting. For those programs in place, it is encouraging that most have followed guidelines suggested by the literature. The findings also suggest that local agencies, and not Adult Protective Services, may be the key agents in providing education about elder mistreatment to African Americans. It is hoped that further research will look at methods to help agencies incorporate ethnic group–specific outreach techniques in elder-mistreatment awareness programs. Such programs will be valuable in the coming decade as the prevalence of risk factors for elder mistreatment increases in the population.

REFERENCES

Allen, I., & Pifer, A. (Eds.). (1993). *Women on the frontlines: Meeting the challenge of an aging America*. Washington, DC: The Urban Institute

Allen, L., & Majidi-ahi, S. (1989). Black American children. In J. T. Gibbs & L. N. Huang (Eds.). *Children of color: psychological intervention in minority youths*. San Francisco, CA: Jossey-bass.

Anetzberger, G. (1987). *The etiology of elder abuse by adult offspring*. Springfield, IL: Charles C. Thomas.

Anetzberger, G. J., Korbin, J. E., & Tomita, S. (1996). Defining elder mistreatment in four ethnic groups across two generations. *Journal of Cross-Cultural Gerontology, 11*, 187–212.

Angel, R., & Tienda, M. (1982). Determinants of extended household structure: Cultural patterns or economic model? *American Journal of Sociology, 87*, 1360–1382.

Beach Advertising & University Research Corp. (1996). *A manual for implementing elder abuse prevention media campaigns for special audiences: African American, Hispanic, rural elderly*. Pennsylvania: Department of Aging Commonwealth of Pennsylvania.

Bendik, M. F. (1992). Reaching the breaking point: Dangers of mistreatment in elder care giving situations. *Journal of Elder Abuse and Neglect, 4*(3), 39–59.

Billingsley, A. (1968). *Black families in white America*. Englewood Cliffs, NJ: Prentice-Hall.

Block, M. R., & Sinnott, J. D. (Eds.). (1979). *The battered elder syndrome: An exploratory study*. College Park, MD: University of Maryland Center on Aging.

Bookin, D., & Dunkle, R. E. (1989). Assessment problems in cases of elder abuse. In R. Filinson & S. R. Ingman (Eds.), *Elder abuse practice and policy* (pp.65–76). New York: Human Sciences Press, Inc.

Breckman, R. S., & Adelman, R. D. (1988). Elder mistreatment defined. In *Strategies for Helping Victims of Elder Mistreatment* (pp. 11–22). Newbury Park, CA: Sage.

Burnam, M. A., Karno, M., Hough, R. L., Escobar, J. I., & Forsythe, A. B. (1983). The Spanish diagnostic interview schedule. *Archives General Psychiatry, 40*, 1189–1196.

Cazenave, N. A. (1979). Family violence and aging blacks: Theoretical perspectives and research possibilities. *Journal of Minority Aging, 4*, 99–108.

Chen, P. N., Bell, S., Dolinsky, D., Doyle, J., & Dunn, M. (1981). Elderly abuse in domestic settings: A pilot study. *Journal of Gerontological Social Work, 4*, 3–17.

Cicirelli, V. (1986). The helping relationship and family neglect in later life. In K. A. Pillemer & R. S. Wolf (Eds.), *Elder abuse: Conflict in the family* (pp. 49–66). Dover, MA: Auburn House.

Cox, C., & Monk, A. (1990). Minority caregivers of dementia victims: A comparison of Black and Hispanic families. *Journal of Applied Gerontology, 9*, 340–354.

Coyne, A. C., Reichman, W. E., & Berbig, L. J. (1993). The relationship between dementia and elder abuse. *American Journal of Psychiatry, 150*, 643–646.

Darnay, A. J. (1996). *Statistical record of older Americans*. Detroit: Gale Research Inc.

Douglass, R. (1991). Reaching 30 million people to prevent abuse and neglect of the elderly: AARP's strategy for public self-education. *Journal of Elder Abuse and Neglect, 3*(4), 73–85.

Flaherty, G., & Raia, P. (1994). Beyond risk: Protection and Alzheimer's Disease. *Journal of Elder Abuse and Neglect, 6*(2), 75–93.

Fredman, L., Daly, M. P., & Lazur, A. M. (1995). Burden among White and Black caregivers to elderly adults. *Journal of Gerontology, 50b*(2), S110–S118.

Galbraith, M. W. (1989). A critical examination of the definitional, methodological and theoretical problems of elder abuse. In R. Filinson, & S. R. Ingman (Eds.), *Elder Abuse Practice and Policy* (pp. 126–166). New York: Human Sciences Press, Inc.

Giogho, G. R., & Blakemore, R. (1983). *Elder abuse in New Jersey: The knowledge and experience of abuse among elder New Jerseyans*. Trenton, NJ: New Jersey Department of Human Resources.

Giordano, N. H., & Giordano, J. A. (1984). Elder abuse: A review of the literature. *Social Work, 29*, 232–236.

Greenberg, J. R., McKibben, M., & Raymond, J. A. (1990). Dependent adult children and elder abuse. *Journal of Elder Abuse and Neglect, 1*(1/2), 73–86.

Griffin, L. W. (1994). Elder maltreatment among rural African-Americans. *Journal of Elder Abuse and Neglect, 6*(1) 1–27.

Griffin, L. W., & Williams, O. J. (1992). Abuse among African-American elderly. *Journal of Family Violence, 7*(1), 19–35.

Haley, W. E., & Coleton, M. I. (1992). Alzheimer's Disease: Special issues in elder abuse and neglect. *Journal of Elder Abuse and Neglect, 4*(4), 71–85.

Haller, E., Binder, R. L., & McNiel, D. E. (1989). Violence in geriatric patients with dementia. *Bulletin of the American Academy of Psychiatry Law, 17*(2), 183–188.

Hamel, M., Gold-Pushkar, D., Andres, D., Reis, M., Dastoor, D., Grauer, H., & Bergman, H. (1990). Predictors and consequences of aggressive behavior by community-based dementia. *The Gerontologist, 30*(2), 206–211.

Harper, M. S., & Alexander, C. D. (1990). *Profile of the black elderly. Minority aging: Essential curricula content for selected health and allied health professions*. Washington, DC: U.S. Dept. of Health and Human Health Services, Public Health Service, Health Resources and Services Administration.

Hays, W. C., & Mindel, C. H. (1993). Extended kinship relations in Black and White families. *Journal of Marriage and the Family, 35*, 51–57.

Hernandez, A. H., & Schweon, C. (1989). Mobile mental health team reaches minorities. *Aging, 359*, 12–13.

Hickey, T., & Douglass, R. L. (1981). Neglect and abuse of older family members: Professionals' perspectives and case experiences. *The Gerontologist, 21*(2), 171–176.

Hinrichsen, G. A., & Ramirez, M. (1992). Black and White dementia caregivers: A comparison of their adaptation, adjustment, and service utilization. *The Gerontologist, 32*(2), 375–381.

Hofferth, S. L. (1984). Kin networks, race and family structure. *Journal of Marriage & the Family, 46*, 791–806.

Hudson, M. F. (1986). Empirical and theoretical perspectives on elder abuse. In K. A. Pillemer & R. S. Wolf (Eds.), *Elder abuse: Conflict in the family* (pp. 126–166). Dover, MA: Auburn House Publishing Co.

Jackson, J. J. (1978). Special health problems of aged blacks. *Aging, 278*(88), 15–20.

Jackson, J. J. (1980). *Minorities and Aging*. Belmont, CA: Wadsworth Publishing Co.

Jurkow, J. (1991). Abuse and neglect of the frail elderly. *Pride Institute Journal of Long Term Home Health Care, 10*(1), 36–39.

Knight, B., Lutzky, S., & Olshevski, J. (1992, June). *Gender differences under chronic stress: A comparison of self-report and psychophysiological measures*. Paper presented at the meeting of the American Psychological Society, San Diego.

Lawton, M. P., Rajagopal, D., Brody, E., & Kleban, M. H. (1992). The dynamics of caring for a demented elder among Black and White families. *Journal of Gerontology, 47*(4), S156–S164.

Longres, J. (1992). Race and type of maltreatment in an elder abuse system. *Journal of Elder Abuse and Neglect, 4*(3), 61–83.

Longres, J. F., Raymond, J. A., & Kimmel, M. S. (1991). Black and White clients in an elder abuse system. In T. Tatara, M. Rittman, & K. J. Flores (Eds.), *Findings of five elder abuse studies* (pp. 53–80). Washington, DC: National Center on Elder Abuse.

Mansfield-Cohen, J., Billing, N., Lipson, S., Rosenthal, A., & Pawlson, L. G. (1990). Medical correlates of agitation in nursing home residents. *Journal of Gerontology, 36,* 150–158.

Milligan, S. E., Maryland, P., Ward, A. L., & Ziegler, H. (1987). Recruitment and training of the natural helper for geriatric health outreach. *Journal of Gerontological Social Work, 11*(3/4), 167–179.

Mintzer, J. E., Rubert, M. P., Loewenstein, D., Gamez, E., Millor, A., Quinteros, R., Flores, L., Miller, M., Rainerman, A., & Eisdorfer, C. (1992). Daughters care giving for Hispanic and Non-Hispanic Alzheimer's patients: Does ethnicity make a difference? *Community Mental Health Journal, 28,* 293–303.

Moon, A., & Williams, O. (1993). Perception of elder abuse and help-seeking patterns among African-American, Caucasian American, and Korean-American elderly women. *The Gerontologist, 33,* 386–395.

Morycz, R. K., Malloy, J., Bozich, M., and Martz, P. (1987). Racial differences in family burden: Clinical implications for social work. *Journal of Gerontological Social Work, 10*(2), 133–154.

National Association of State Units on Aging. (1995). Effective strategies and approaches for outreach to minority elders. Washington, DC: The National Center on Elder Abuse (NCEA).

National Urban League (1989). *The state of Black America.* New York: Author.

Nerenberg, L. (1995). *To reach beyond our grasp: A community outreach guide for professionals in the field of elder abuse.* San Francisco: San Francisco Consortium for Elder Abuse Prevention.

Njeri, M., & Nerenberg, L. (1993). We are family: Outreach to African American Seniors. *Journal of Elder Abuse and Neglect, 5*(4), 5–19.

Phillips, L. R. (1983). Abuse and neglect of the frail elderly at home: An exploration of theoretical relationships. *Journal of Advanced Nursing, 8,* 379–392.

Pillemer, K. (1985). The dangers of dependency: New findings on domestic violence against the elderly. *Social Problems, 33,* 146–158.

Pillemer, K. (1986). Risk factors in elder abuse: results from a case-control study. In K. A. Pillemer & R. S. Wolf (Eds.), *Elder abuse conflict in the family* (pp. 239–263). Dover, MA: Auburn House.

Pillemer, K. (1993). The abused offspring are dependent. Abuse is caused by the deviance and dependence of abusive caregivers. In R. Gelles & D. R. Loseke (Eds.), *Current controversies on family violence* (pp. 237–255). Newbury Park, CA: Sage.

Pillemer, K., & Finkelhor, D. (1988). The prevalence of elder abuse: A random sample survey. *The Gerontologist, 28*(1), 51–57.

Pillemer, K., & Finkelhor, D. (1989). Causes of elder abuse: Caregiver stress versus problem relatives. *American Orthopsychiatric Association, 59*(3), 179–187.

Pillemer, K., & Suitor, J. J. (1992). Violence and violent feelings: What causes them among family caregivers? *Journal of Gerontology: Social Sciences, 47*(4), S165–S172.

Pillemer, K., & Wolf, R. S. (1992). Domestic violence against the elderly: Who depends on whom? What difference does it make? In R. Gelles & D. R. Loseke (Eds.), *Current controversies on family violence* (pp. 202–235). Newbury Park, CA: Sage.

Plass, P. S. (1993). African American family homicide: Patterns in partner, parent, and child victimization, 1985–1987. *Journal of Black Studies, 23*(4), 515–538.

Quinn, M. J., & Tomita, S. K. (1986). *Elder abuse and neglect.* New York: Springer Publishing Company.

Ramashala, M. F. (1989). *Strategies for increasing minority elderly participation in Title III programs in Pennsylvania: Final report.* Lincoln, PA: Lincoln University.

Rathbone, M. E., & Beicker, J. M. (1982). A general framework for elder self-neglect. In M. E. Rathbone & D. R. Fabian (Eds.). *Self-neglecting elders: A clinical dilemma* (pp. 13–26). New York: Auburn House.

Reisberg, B.., Borenstein, J., & Salob, S. P. (1987). Behavioral symptoms in Alzheimer's Disease: Phenomenology and treatment. *Journal of Clinical Psychiatry, 48,* 9–15.

Spencer, C. (1995). New directions for research on interventions with abused older adults. In M. MacLean (Ed.), *Abuse and neglect of older Canadians: Strategies for change* (pp. 143–158). Toronto, Ontario: Thompson.

Staples, R. (1976). Race and family violence: The internal colonialism perspective. In L. E. Gary & L. P. Brown (Eds.), *Crime and its impact on the black community*. Washington, DC: Howard University, Institute for Urban Development Center.

Stein, K. F. (1991). *Working with abused and neglected elders in minority populations: A synthesis of research*. Washington, DC: National Aging Resource Center on Elder Abuse.

Steinmetz, S. (1988). Elder abuse by family caregivers: process and intervention strategies. *Contemporary Family Therapy, 10*(4), 478–201.

Steinmetz, S. (1993). The abused elderly are dependent. Abuse is caused by the perception of stress associated with providing care. In R. Gelles & D. R. Loseke (Eds.), *Current controversies on family violence* (pp. 222–236). Newbury Park, CA: Sage.

Strauss, M. A., Gelles, R. J., & Steinmetz, S. K. (1981). *Behind closed doors: violence in the American family*. Newbury Park, CA: Sage Publications.

Suitor, J., & Pillemer, K. (1988). Intergenerational conflict when adult children and elderly parents live together. *Journal of Marriage and the Family, 50*(4), 1037–1047.

Ucko, L. G. (1994). Culture and Violence: The interaction of Africa and America. *Sex Roles, 31*, 185–204.

Weiner, A. (1991). A community based education model for identification and prevention of elder abuse. *Journal of Gerontological Social Work, 16*(3/4), 107–119.

White-Means, S., & Thornton, M. C. (1990). Ethnic differences in the production of informal home health care. *The Gerontologist, 30*, 738–768.

Wolf, R. S. (1988). Elder abuse: Ten years later. *Journal of American Geriatric Society, 36*(8), 758–762.

Wolf, R. S., & Pillemer, K. A. (1989). *Helping elder victims: The reality of elder abuse*. New York: Columbia University Press.

APPENDIX

1   Do you have a targeted outreach program for African Americans about elder abuse awareness, prevention, or services? What kind of program is it? (Please be as detailed as possible.)

2   In terms of outreach, what have you done indirectly?

3   What type of materials or media did you use? (Please send copies of the materials.)

4   What were your results? Do you have any figures or statistics documented? (Please send copies of anything in writing.)

5   Did you find an increase in referrals as a result of your efforts? If yes, by how much? (Please send any documentation of statistics showing an increase.)

6   Did you work with any communities or organizations? If yes, which ones? If no, why not?

7   Do you feel there is a need to have ethnic-specific materials, particularly for African Americans, on elder abuse? Why or why not?

Part Two

Elder Abuse in
Hispanic Communities

Chapter 5

Elder Mistreatment in Mexican American Communities: The Nevada and Michigan Experiences

Yolanda M. Sanchez

As reports of elder mistreatment increase throughout the country, there also have been notable increases in the number of reports of older individuals in ethnic minority communities across the United States. This is of particular concern for the Latino community, which is now experiencing the greatest rates of growth of any ethnic group, as well as inordinate representation of individuals aged 60 and older, which is discussed in further detail in this chapter.

Due to the limited research on elder mistreatment in communities of color, and in particular the Latino community, this pioneering exploratory study was undertaken to examine elder mistreatment in the Mexican American community. This chapter provides an overview of the changes in demographics and the impact on Latino populations, with specific consideration of the Mexican American. It also addresses the difficulty in and need for dealing with elder mistreatment in communities of color and finally, and it reports on data from this pioneering exploratory study.

DEMOGRAPHICS

In the next 60 years, the United States is set to experience a "gerontological explosion" as the population that is aged more than 65 years increases dramatically. Equally important is the reality that as a result of differential fertility, mortality, and migration rates among minority Americans, the racial and ethnic diversity of the aged also will increase (Angel & Hogan, 1992). It is projected that by the year 2000, Latinos will constitute the largest minority group in the United States (National Council of La Raza, 1992). More significantly, the older segment of the Latino population is growing at an even faster rate than the non-Latino elderly population. The number of elderly Latinos is projected to quadruple in size by

67

the year 2020 (Andrews, 1989), increasing from approximately 4% of America's elderly in 1990 to 9% in 2020, and to 16% by 2050.

Currently, individuals of Mexican origin represent the largest group of Latinos in this country, accounting for 62% of the entire Latino population (Ortiz, 1994). The Mexican population nearly doubled between 1970 and 1980, and again by 1990 (Bureau of the Census, 1993). Moreover, this growth was fueled by a continuous flow of migrants from Mexico to the United States, a trend that will continue to contribute a unique cultural dynamism to the Mexican American population (Baca-Zinn, 1994). Given the changing demographics of the United States, the challenge of providing services to Latino elderly and families has grown and will continue to grow over the course of the next few decades. Moreover, the issue of elder mistreatment in this community will need to be acknowledged and addressed, although this will not be an easy task because of the lack of familiarity with the issue of abuse in communities of color.

MISTREATMENT IN COMMUNITIES OF COLOR

There are many complex factors involved in dealing with the phenomenon of elder mistreatment, ranging from difficulty with definitions to difficulty with etiology (Johnson, 1995). If these problems are considered in relation to ethnic elderly, the issues are further compounded by specific cultural dynamics. It is inappropriate to assume that our present definitions of elder mistreatment explain what occurs among minority groups; so it is essential that diversity be central to the understanding and application of the comprehensive definition (Williams & Griffin, 1996). This will yield a better understanding of the problem and has important implications for all aged people, but it is particularly significant for the aged who are also members of ethnic minority groups (Griffin & Williams, 1992; Moon & Williams, 1993).

The lack of research on elder mistreatment in the Latino community actually may be a result of the tendency of researchers to emphasis family solidarity in Latino families (Anetzberger, Korbin, & Tomita 1996; Farias & Hardy, 1990; Sanchez-Ayendez, 1988). The few studies that are available in communities of color, however, have yielded conflicting findings. Moon and Williams (1993) identified significant group differences among White, African American, and Korean elderly women in relation to their perceptions of elder abuse and help-seeking patterns. Steinmetz (1990) reported higher prevalence rates for Black elderly, while Hwalek and Sengstock (1986) showed no difference in elder abuse patterns of Whites and Blacks. Sanchez (1994) reported that many interactions in Latino families would be perceived as exploitative utilizing majority-culture definitions yet were not identified or perceived as exploitative by Latino respondents. These mixed findings reinforce Williams and Griffin's (1996) position that there is a need to deepen the present conceptualization of elder mistreatment in ethnic communities. Thus, this project focused on comparison of elder mistreatment in two distinct communities with Mexican American representation: Carson City,

Nevada, and Detroit, Michigan. The research design included a quantitative component and qualitative component to allow respondents to elaborate on questions and capture the nuances of cultural expectations and concepts.

METHODOLOGY

Data Collection

Data were drawn from a population of individuals of Mexican origin in both Carson City, Nevada, and Detroit, Michigan. This population was selected because individuals of Mexican origin represent the largest subgroup of Latinos at a national level, as well as in the states of Nevada and Michigan. In Michigan, individuals of Mexican origin account for 62% of the Latino population, and Latinos account for 4% of the population in that state (Michigan State Office of Services to the Aging, 1994). In Nevada, Latinos constitute 12.5% of the population and individuals of Mexican origin account for 74% of the Latino population. Furthermore, projections indicate that by the year 2025, more than 25% of state residents will be Hispanic, ranking the state fifth nationwide in its percentage of Latinos (Hispanic population, 1996).

Data were collected between June and September of 1996 in telephone interviews conducted by this researcher using structured and open-ended questions. The questionnaire was developed and modified from a previous instrument used in the collection of data for the researcher's dissertation. The questionnaire consisted of 18 questions dealing with demographics and 27 questions dealing with elder mistreatment. Prior to pilot testing, the questionnaire was translated into Spanish using "back translation" by a professional Spanish teacher. The Spanish version was reviewed by three independent reviewers of Mexican origin to ensure congruency of terms. Upon completion of translation, the instrument was pilot-tested in both communities and modifications were completed, as necessary.

Respondents were questioned regarding their language preference, and interviews were conducted accordingly, with 26% of the sample requesting that the interview be conducted in Spanish. There were, however, subsample differences, with 48% of the Detroit sample requesting the interview in Spanish and only 5% of the Carson City sample requesting Spanish, although nonparametric testing on language indicated that it was statistically insignificant.

Respondents were questioned regarding their knowledge of elder mistreatment and their perception of elder mistreatment as a problem in the Mexican American community. They were asked to elaborate on what their definitions of mistreatment were and also were asked questions regarding what they would do if (1) a neighbor was being mistreated; (2) the respondent was being mistreated by a family member; and (3) the respondent was being mistreated by someone who is not a family member. The demographic section of the questionnaire requested that the respondents provide information regarding their demographic and socioeconomic backgrounds, including questions regarding U.S. citizenship and the number of years that each had been in the United States.

Population and Sample

Due to the sensitive nature of the topic and the dynamics of working in a cultural community that is generally a closed community, identification of participants for this project presented a challenge. Subsequently, data for this project were drawn from a sample of convenience. The sample was comprised of 62 elderly individuals of Mexican origin (Detroit—32, Carson City—30), 60 years of age or older, who participated in services at community centers in Detroit, Michigan, and Carson City, Nevada. Individuals of Mexican origin were defined as individuals who are Mexican immigrants or self-identify as Mexican American and are currently residing in the United States. Age 60 was used as the onset of old age because, although it is difficult to define age and to conceptualize what it means to be old, Latino individuals maintain a lower life expectancy than their White counterparts (Schaie & Willis, 1995). Community centers were identified as a source that could supply respondents for the study because they provide on-site services to large segments of the older population in their respective cities, and in the Detroit community primarily service the Latino community in the specific area.

Of the total 62 respondents, 66.1% (41) were female and 33.9% were male (Detroit—66% female, 34% male; Carson City—70% female, 30% male). Respondents ranged from 60 to 94 years old, with an average age of 76. With respect to education, the comparative samples had relatively low levels of educational attainment as reflected in Table 5.1.

When education information is combined for this sample, a quarter (25.8%) of respondents had not completed the 8th grade and only 16.1% completed high school. Differences were seen in relation to gender, with females receiving less formal education than males. Only 9.7% had completed some college or four years of college.

Table 5.2 reflects the comparative incomes of the sample. Respondents reported low income, with 21.4% of the Detroit samples and 23.3% of the Carson

Table 5.1 Education Levels of Respondents

Education	Detroit sample, %	Carson City sample, %
Some elementary	14.3	20
Completed 8th grade	21.4	20
Some high school	39.3	36.7
Completed high school	17.9	16.7

Table 5.2 Income of Respondents

Income	Detroit sample, %	Carson City sample, %
Under $5,000	21.4	23.3
$4,500–14,999	67.9	66.7
$15,000–24,999	7.1	6.7
$25,000–34,999	3.6	3.3

Table 5.3 Living Arrangements of Respondents

Arrangement	Detroit sample, %	Carson City sample, %
Live alone	42.9	40
Live with spouse	42.9	40
Live with adult child over age 18 years	14.3	20

City sample averaging under $5,000 per year. Only 7.1% of the Detroit sample and 6.7% of the Carson City sample reported income in excess of $14,999 per year. A significant percentage of the combined sample (90.3%) reported annual incomes below poverty level. Additionally, 69.4% reported being retired; however, only 13.8% reported receiving private retirement benefits.

Table 5.3 reflects living arrangements of the sample. The majority of respondents (53.2%) live alone; 22.4% live with a spouse and 17.7% live with children over the age of 18.

FINDINGS

Perceptions of Abuse

The inferential statistical tests used in this study were descriptive. Due to the small nature of the sample, analysis was limited. Nonparametric testing including reliability coefficients and t-tests were conducted, although no notable statistically significant findings were identified.

Forty respondents (64.5%) indicated that they believe that parents are responsible for helping their children with issues of care for grandchildren and with providing money and other resources as needed and do not consider this exploitative. Conversely, 52 respondents (83.9%) believe that adult children are responsible for helping their parents with care issues and, if necessary, providing financial assistance to their parents, yet they expressed concern that this creates undue stress on their children. Forty-two respondents (67.7%) reported having a general awareness of elder mistreatment. Additionally, 64.3% reported knowing of at least one case of elder mistreatment. Perception of elder mistreatment as a problem in the Mexican American community was much more apparent in the Detroit sample (62%) than in the Carson City sample (2%).

Prevalence of Abuse

A total of 20 respondents (33%) reported awareness of at least one incident of elder abuse in the Mexican American community. Table 5.4 presents descriptions of these forms of abuse, which were categorized into four types.

The information was attained by categorizing 16 behaviors representative of abuse and condensing them into four categories: physical abuse, neglect, financial abuse, and denial of shelter. The latter category was developed because of

Table 5.4   Forms of Abuse

Type	Description
Denial of shelter	Failure to provide clothing and shelter
Neglect	Failure to assist in personal care, medical care, and protection from health and safety hazards
Financial abuse	Use of an older adult's resources for personal use
Physical abuse	Hitting, biting, slapping, shoving, etc.

Table 5.5   Prevalence of Mistreatment

Type	Combined sample, %	Detroit sample, %	Carson City sample, %
Denial of shelter	40.3	53	26.7
Neglect	22.6	31.3	13.3
Financial abuse	12.9	12.5	13.3
Physical abuse	11.3	21.9	—

the significant number of respondents who reported having had shelter or living-arrangement needs denied by family members. This finding supports the work of Chang and Moon (1997), who introduce the concept of culturally specific types of elder maltreatment, in which mistreatment can be best understood in the context of cultural norms for family and parent–child relationships.

Table 5.5 reflects that denial of shelter was cited as the most frequent form of mistreatment (40.3%), followed by neglect (22.6%), financial abuse (12.9%), and physical abuse (11.3%). The most frequently reported type of denial of shelter involved a family member denying an elderly parent a place to live on a long-term basis. If these findings are further considered by subsamples, important differences are noted: Of the Detroit sample, 53% reported being denied shelter, as opposed to Carson City's 26.7%; 31.3% of the Detroit sample reported neglect, compared with 13.3% of the Carson City sample. The most significant difference relates to reports of physical abuse, with 21.9% of the Detroit sample reporting incidents but the Carson City sample reporting physical abuse as nonexistent. The only category in which prevalence rates were higher for the Carson City sample involved reports of financial abuse, with Carson City reporting 13.3% and Detroit 12.5%.

Findings regarding what respondents would do if (1) a neighbor was being mistreated, (2) the respondent was being mistreated by a family member, or (3) the respondent was being mistreated by someone who is not a family member, reflect consistency across subgroup responses as reflected in Table 5.6.

If a neighbor was being abused by his or her family members, 17.9% of the Detroit sample would not say anything; 57.1% would talk to a family member; and 25% reported they would contact authorities. In the Carson City sample, 20% said they would not say anything; 56.7% would talk to a family member; and 23.3% would contact authorities.

Table 5.6   Hypothetical Response to Abuse of a Neighbor

Response	Detroit sample, %	Carson City sample , %
Not say anything	17.9	20
Talk to family member	57.1	56.7
Contact authorities	25	23.3

Table 5.7   Hypothetical Response to Abuse by Family

Response	Detroit sample, %	Carson City sample, %
Not say anything	14.3	13.3
Talk to family member	67.9	76.7
Contact authorities	17.9	10

Table 5.8   Hypothetical Response to Abuse by Nonfamily

Response	Detroit sample, %	Carson City sample, %
Not say anything	14.3	13.3
Talk to family member	25	30
Contact authorities	60.7	56.7

However, as reflected in Table 5.7, if the respondents themselves were being mistreated by family members, a greater number in both samples said they would discuss the problem with family members before contacting authorities (76.7% of the Carson City sample and 67.9% of the Detroit sample). The Detroit sample did indicate that they would contact authorities more frequently (17.9%) than the Carson City sample (10%).

Table 5.8 reflects the actions that respondents would take if they were being mistreated by an individual outside the family. Both subgroup samples indicated that they would contact authorities with greater frequency, which is contrary to responses if family members are implicated in the abuse. Again, if family is implicated in abuse, the tendency is to attempt to deal with it by talking to other family members.

DISCUSSION

This study clearly suggests that elder mistreatment is a concern in the Mexican American community. The most obvious forms of mistreatment reported in this sample revolve around issues of neglect. Careful examination of the data, however, yield interesting findings that cannot be ignored. The most important finding relates to extreme subgroup differences in reports and frequency of reports of elder mistreatment as a problem in the Mexican American community. Additionally, findings regarding what respondents would do if (1) a neighbor was being mistreated, (2) the respondent was being mistreated by a family member, and (3) the respondent was being mistreated by someone who is not a family member, yield important information that is interpreted in greater detail elsewhere in this section.

With respect to reports of mistreatment and perceptions of mistreatment as a problem for the Mexican American community, the issue presents as more of a concern for the Detroit sample. Consideration of this finding in isolation might lead us to believe that mistreatment is of greater concern for individuals of Mexican origin in Detroit. This finding, however, does not necessarily mean that mistreatment is more of a problem for individuals of Mexican origin in Detroit. Rather, it is important to note that respondents from Carson City report difficulty in considering mistreatment in the "greater Mexican American community." They describe that they do "not see themselves as part of the Mexican American community" and do not "actively participate in the Mexican American community." In contrast, Detroit respondents speak of strong identification, participation, and affiliation with the Mexican American community and describe mutual support networks that are fostered and sustained in their community.

The finding that mistreatment is a greater concern in the Detroit sample renders consideration of several factors. First, in any given community one can expect to find three categories of individuals: native-born United States citizens, foreign-born individuals with legal residency, and foreign-born undocumented persons (Valle, 1983). One can assume that the level of acculturation and assimilation is probably greatest for those individuals who are native-born United States citizens. The findings in this study support that a greater number of respondents in the Carson City sample are native-born and have resided in the United States for a longer period of time than the respondents in the Detroit sample. They identify and affiliate with the dominant culture much more than the Detroit sample and do not view themselves as being interconnected with the Mexican American community.

Secondly, participants in the Detroit sample spoke of mutual networks of support that are fostered in the greater community. These were not identified or addressed by the Carson City respondents. In reviewing the responses provided by the Detroit sample, it appears that the networks are rooted in the concept of *familism*, which often has been considered a defining feature of the Latino community.

The nature of familism is comprised of four key components: demographic familism, structural familism, normative familism, and behavioral familism (Baca-Zinn & Eitzen, 1990; Ramirez & Arce, 1980). More specific to this study is the notion of *normative familism*, which taps the value that people of Mexican heritage place on family unity and solidarity. Today, because of internal and external stresses experienced by families that are often a result of changing economic forces, the community is often forced to serve as an extension of *familia*. Communities are now responsible for providing support to family members and meeting important emotional and social needs of the elderly (Sanchez & Villarruel, In press). One could speculate that because the Mexican American community is more concentrated and centralized in Detroit, the "social ills" that confront this community become more visible.

This may help account for the finding that reports of physical abuse were nonexistent in the Carson City sample yet occurred with frequency in the Detroit sample. Perhaps it is not that physical mistreatment of the elderly occurs with greater frequency in Mexican American communities of Detroit but rather, perhaps, that community involvement provides an arena that fosters a greater awareness of the realities that exist with families.

If the reports of physical abuse are considered, all reported incidents implicated victims' immediate families. Additionally, victims often justified the violence, claiming they had instigated the violence and that the problems could be dealt with in *la familia*. This finding is of particular interest and may offer insight into the cultural and familial expectations in Latino families. As previously stated, in many Latino cultures, and particularly the Mexican American culture, key concepts influence actual behavior and provide a basis that helps establish norms and expectations. These ideologies reinforce the view that family is the central and most important institution in life.

For families of Mexican origin, the extended family system and supportive institutions of *la familia* have been a mainstay and may play an important role in tolerance of physical abuse and other forms of mistreatment of the elderly. *La familia,* the family, is perceived as more important than the individual. Selfishness is condemned, and its absence is a virtue (Sanchez, 1997). The notion that one should sacrifice everything for family has its costs, however, and may account for the small number of respondents who would contact authorities if they were being mistreated by a family member. Clearly, if these respondents were being mistreated by a family member, less than a fraction would contact the authorities and the majority would attempt to resolve it with the help of *la familia*.

Another important concept that emerged in this study which may be useful in understanding elder mistreatment in families of Mexican origin is that of *vergüenza*. *Vergüenza* translates as *shame*. It is a powerful concept that extends beyond the standard definition of shame. It is related to *pena* or worry of taking on shame and *losing face*. Admitting that family, and particularly one's children, have mistreated an elderly parent, and in particular physically assaulted the parent, violates important norms regarding *la familia*. Admitting such abuse brings shame to the family, and that is something to be avoided at all costs.Respondents indicated that issues related to mistreatment must first be dealt with in the context of *la familia,* and only on very rare occasions, or when someone's life is in danger, should outside agencies or organizations be involved.

CONCLUSIONS

It is clear that the reliability and generalizability of these findings are hampered by issues related to research methodology. The use of a nonprobability sampling method and the small sample size limit the generalizability of findings. Furthermore, it is important to note that the assumption that all individuals of Mexican origin identify with the greater Latino community may be most detrimental in our work with mistreatment. Caution must be utilized in interpreting the experiences of and perceptions of mistreatment of small groups of individuals and applying these in policy and program development for the greater community.

As an example, if policy and programming were developed to address elder mistreatment in Latino families in Carson City, Nevada, one could assume from reviewing this data that mistreatment is not of concern for individuals of Mexican origin in this area. However, it may be that the individuals in the Carson City area that participated in this study were individuals who were more acculturated and assimilated than individuals in the Detroit sample. The need exists for the researcher to carefully review culturally specific behaviors related and to make efforts to account for acculturation and assimilation.

Given these limitations, however, this study does establish a foundation upon which we can began to consider unique cultural concepts in the Mexican American community and how these may impact on our work with mistreatment. These concepts, although elusive, may be useful in understanding differences in the nature of interactions, exchanges, and expectations, varied and shifting cultural values, and may be useful in helping us understand how elder mistreatment is addressed in the lives of individuals of Mexican origin, the greater Mexican American community, and other Latino communities.

REFERENCES

Andrews, H. (1989). *Poverty and poor health among elderly Hispanic Americans.* Baltimore, MD: Commonwealth Fund Commission on Elderly Living Alone.

Anetzberger, G., Korbin, J., & Tomita, S. (1996). Defining elder mistreatment in four ethnic groups across two generations. *Journal of Cross-Cultural Gerontology, 11*(2), 207–232.

Angel, J., & Hogan, D. (1992). The demography of minority aging popualtions. *Journal of Family History, 17*(1), 95–116.

Baca-Zinn, M. (1994). Mexican heritage families in the United States. In F. Padilla (Ed.), *Handbook of Hispanic Cultures in the United States: Sociology* (pp. 165–166). Houston, TX: Arte Publico Press.

Baca-Zinn, M. & Eitzen, S. D. (1990). *Diversity in families* (2nd ed.). New York: Harper & Row Publishers.

Bureau of the Census (1993). *Statistical abstract of the United States* (113th ed.). Washington, DC: United States Government Printing Office.

Chang, J., & Moon, A. (1997). Korean American elderly's knowledge and perceptions of elder abuse: A qualitative analysis of cultural factors. *Journal of Multicultural Social Work, 6*(1–2), 139–155.

Farias, L., & Hardy, J. (1990). Protective service issues and Hispanic clients: Mexican Americans as an example. In J. Boyajian (Ed.), *Adult Protective Service Practice Guide* (pp. 5–11). St. Paul, MN: Minnesota Department of Human Services.

Griffin, L., & Williams, O. (1992). Abuse among African American elderly. *Journal of Family Violence, 7*(1), 19–35.

Hispanic population surge to outpace Nevada Growth. (1996, November 10) *Reno Gazette Journal,* p. 1.

Hwalek, M. A. & Sengstock, M. (1986). Assessing the probability of abuse of the elderly: Toward development of a clinical screening instrument. *The Journal of Applied Gerontology, 5*(2), 153–173.

Johnson, I. M. (1995). Family members' perceptions and attitudes toward elder abuse. *Families and Society: The Journal of Contemporary Human Services, 76*(4), 220–230.

Michigan Office of Services to the Aging. (1994). *State of Michigan Survey of Hispanic Elders*. Lansing, MI: Author.

Moon, A. & Williams, O. (1993). Perceptions of elder abuse and help seeking patterns among African American, Caucasian American and Korean American elderly women. *The Gerontologist, 33*, 386–395.

National Center on Elder Abuse. (1995). *Understanding the nature and extent of elder abuse in domestic settings*. Washington, DC: National Center on Elder Abuse.

National Council of La Raza. (1992). *Ancianos Network News, 2*(3), 1–4.

Ortiz, V. (1994). Women of color: A demographic overview. In M. Baca-Zinn & B. Thornton-Dill (Eds.), *Women of color in U.S. Society* (p. 15). Philadelphia: Temple University Press.

Ramirez, O., & Arce, C. (1980). The contemporary Chicano family: An empirically based review. In A. Baron, Jr. (Ed.), *Explorations in Chicano psychology* (pp. 8–11). New York: Praeger.

Sanchez, Y. M. (1994). *Perceptions of financial exploitation in Mexican American families*. Unpublished doctoral dissertation, Michigan State University, Lansing.

Sanchez, Y. M. (1997). Families of Mexican Origin. In M. K. DeGenova (Ed.), *Families in cultural context: strengths and challenges in diversity* (pp. 61–79). Mountain View, CA: Mayfield Publishing Company.

Sanchez, Y. M., & Villarruel, F. (In press). Building from within: Meeting the challenges and giving meaning to the lives of Latinos in a Midwest community. In M. Sotomayor (Ed.), *Roles of aging hispanics*. Milwaukee, WI: Family Service America

Sanchez-Ayendez, M. (1988). Puerto Rican elderly women: The cultural dimension of social support networks. *Women and Health, 14*(3/4), 239–253.

Schaie, K. & Willis, S. (1995). *Adult development and aging* (4th ed.). New York: Harper Collins Publishers.

Steinmetz, S. K. (1990). Elder abuse: Myth and reality. In T. H. Brubaker (Ed.), *Family relations in later life* (pp. 193–211). Newbury Park, CA: Sage.

U.S. House Select Committee on Aging. (1990). *Elder abuse: A decade of shame and inaction*. Washington, DC: U.S. Government Printing Office.

Williams, O. & Griffin, L. (1996). Elderly maltreatment & cultural diversity: When laws are not enough. *Journal of Multi-cultural Social Work, 4*(2), 1–13.

Valle, R. (1983). The demography of Mexican American aging. In R. L. McNeely & J. Colen (Eds.), *Aging in minority groups* (pp. 83–85). Beverly Hills, CA: Sage.

Chapter 6

Issues in the Provision of Adult-Protective Services to Mexican American Elders in Texas

Bettye M. Mitchell, Nicolo A. Festa, Adriana C. Franco, Delma Juarez, & Linda L. Lamb[1]

Texas Adult Protective Services (APS) policy requires case workers to recognize the uniqueness of each client and tailor services to address his or her individual needs. Cultural factors, in particular, greatly influence clients as individuals. Although Mexican American elders share characteristics with elders of other ethnic groups, they also may possess distinct cultural characteristics. This chapter addresses some of those attributes and their relationship to maltreatment and service delivery.

This chapter also discusses how Texas APS is ensuring that workers recognize the relationship between cultural characteristics and service delivery. Although all staff are not experts in this area, APS administrators are responsible for providing staff with a basic foundation that supports the provision of culturally competent services.

This chapter is not intended to be an empirical study of Mexican American culture or elder abuse. Rather, it is a compilation of information about Mexican elders from a variety of sources, including anecdotal information provided by APS field staff with extensive experience working with this population. This anecdotal information was obtained through focus groups and field observations.

The chapter specifically focuses on APS issues relating to working with Mexican Americans and Mexican elders. For the purposes of this chapter, we use the term *Mexican American* to include both groups, unless otherwise specified. Al-

[1]The authors gratefully acknowledge the editorial assistance of Paula Mixson, as well as the contributions of other co-workers who helped in various ways to prepare this chapter. The authors especially thank the APS staff whose participation in the survey and the focus groups was essential to this project.

though there is some discussion of basic concepts in the literature concerning Mexican American elders, the intent of the chapter is to describe the current Texas APS experience with clients of Mexican heritage. It reflects work that is still in progress and may be a practical resource for other APS programs seeking to increase their sensitivity to this unique population.

TEXAS PROFILE

To better understand Mexican American elders and the context in which Texas provides APS, a rudimentary knowledge of the geography, history, and demographics of Texas is helpful. Texas is the second-largest state in the United States. Its 267,277-mi^2 area has 254 counties and is geographically diverse, containing woodlands, coastal prairie, hill country, rocky plateaus, desert, rolling plains, mountains, and 624 mi of tidal coastline (Ramos & Plocheck, 1995, pp. 63–67). It shares a border with Mexico and four states. In large areas of Texas, Mexican American culture predominates, and Spanish is the primary language. Coupled with the proximity of Mexico, this factor creates a unique environment for the provision of services.

Texas was originally part of Mexico until declaring its independence in 1836, after which it became a republic. It remained a republic for nine years and in 1845 became part of the United States (ibid., pp. 39–40). Mexican Americans to this day retain their culture, and many maintain strong ties with family in Mexico. For many, culturally speaking, the border is an artificial dividing line.

According to estimates based on the Texas population data prepared by the State Data Center at Texas A&M University and the U.S. Census Profile of Texas, of the 19,307,376 inhabitants of Texas, 29% are Hispanic (primarily Mexican Americans), and they are highly concentrated in the southern half of the state. Of the remaining inhabitants, 56% are white, 11% are African American, and less than 1% are Asian and Native American. The minority population in Texas is depicted in Figure 6.1.

Texas is the fastest growing state in the nation, and much of that growth is in Hispanic population (Drago, 1997). If trends reflected in the state's population growth from 1980 to 1990 continue into the next century, Texas will be less than 50% white by 2008 and 45.9% Hispanic by 2030 (Murdock, Hoque, Michael, White, & Pecotte, 1997, p. 19). This dramatic increase in population will increase the number of Hispanic elders.

APS in Texas

Maltreatment of vulnerable adults crosses all socioeconomic, ethnic, and religious lines. Chapter 48 of the Human Resource Code mandates that the Texas Department of Protective and Regulatory Services (TDPRS) promptly and thoroughly investigate all reports of abuse, neglect, and exploitation of aged persons and persons with disabilities and, when appropriate, provide services to alleviate or prevent further maltreatment. The jurisdiction of the Texas APS program extends to

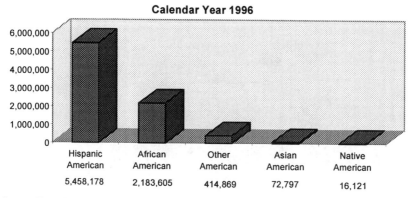

Source: Texas Department of Protective and Regulatory Services, Forecasting Division, V. Chang. Texas population statistics were obtained from Texas A&M University population data center. A&M did not break down the minority population into Asians or Native Americans. The 1990 U.S. Census Profile of Texas breaks down the proportions of the above referenced ethnic groups. TDPRS statistician, Victor Chang, used this data to estimate the population counts of these groups in Texas.

Figure 6.1 Texas Minority Population by Ethnicity

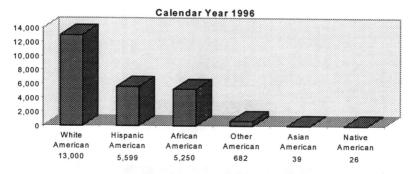

Source: Texas Department of Protective and Regulatory Services Forecasting Division

Figure 6.2 APS Clients 65+ by Ethnicity

persons, regardless of citizenship, who are either aged 65 years or older or under age 65 with a disability, and who are alleged to be abused, neglected, or exploited by a caregiver, family member, or someone with whom the victim has an ongoing relationship. The definition of "neglect" in Texas law includes situations in which individuals have lost the capacity to care for themselves, have no caretaker, and are unable to meet their basic needs (Human Resources Code §48.002). In this type of case, poverty and limitations in or ignorance of available services are often contributing factors. In Texas, APS is practically the only safety net for these vulnerable adults.

In fiscal year 1996, Texas APS workers investigated 49,237 reports of abuse, neglect, and/or exploitation of vulnerable adults who were aged or who were

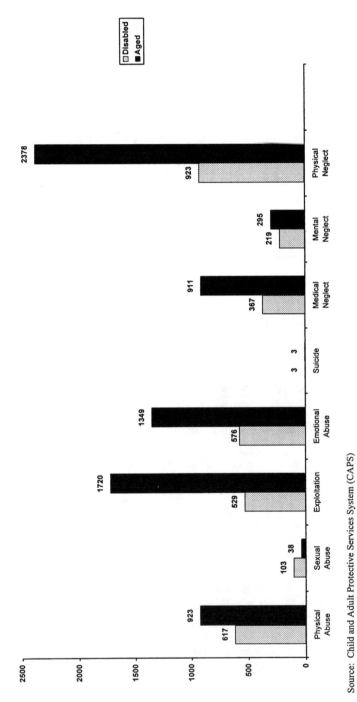

Source: Child and Adult Protective Services System (CAPS)

TDPRS, Fiscal Year 1996

Figure 6.3 Hispanic Aged and Disabled Victims Types of Maltreatment in Texas

younger adults with disabilities. Of the 49,237 investigations, 39,668 cases were validated as abuse, neglect, or exploitation (TDPRS, 1997). Of the 49,237 investigations, 11,187 (22%) concerned clients who are Mexican Americans or Mexican nationals (Chang, 1997a,b,c). The ethnicities of APS clients and the types of maltreatment found among Hispanics in the APS caseload in Texas are depicted in Figures 6.2 and 6.3.

Of the 570 APS staff members employed at TDPRS in fiscal year 1996, 161, or 28%, were bilingual.

Cultural Competence in APS Practice

The demographic shift in Texas is obvious from the data cited in the previous section and drives the need for adapting social programs to current and future realities. Recognizing the relevance of culture to practice, the research forum at the 13th annual Texas APS Conference, cosponsored by the American Public Welfare Association and TDPRS in the Fall of 1996, highlighted issues around providing protective services to minority elders. After the conference, Texas APS state office staff, questioning the sensitivity of the program's service-delivery practices to minority elders, began a process of program evaluation to determine if clients from communities of color have access to services that adequately meet their needs.

The first step in that process was to assess the degree to which staff were culturally competent. This was accomplished by means of surveying staff using a modified version of an instrument called the Cultural Competence Self Assessment Questionnaire. This tool was developed by James Mason of Portland State University in Portland, Oregon, in 1995 and adapted in 1997 by Nicolo Festa for use in the Texas APS program. The survey, to which there was a 93% response rate, produced a great deal of information related to staff's attitudes and beliefs regarding culture and the degree to which they were culturally competent. The findings of the cultural-competency survey indicated that most Texas APS staff demonstrated some degree of cultural sensitivity, but their knowledge and skill levels needed refinement (Festa, 1997).

Focus-Group Discussions

The examination of cultural competence continued after the survey was completed. In the summer of 1997, the APS Director and selected state office APS program specialists facilitated racially balanced focus groups of APS caseworkers, supervisors, and program administrators. The purpose of these groups, held in San Antonio, Lubbock, El Paso, Austin, and Harlingen, was to hear first-hand the perceptions of front-line staff about maltreatment in minority communities and to gather their opinions about strengths and weaknesses of the service-delivery system.

Staff were eager to participate in the focus groups, sharing personal beliefs and values inherent in their respective cultures. The findings of the survey were discussed with each group, which in turn identified issues and best practices based on their professional experiences in working with minority elders. They identified training, procedural, and policy changes needed to improve service delivery.

The following case scenario, developed from an actual case, illustrates some of the issues identified in the focus groups.

> Mr. Juan Ortiz, 87 years old, has allowed his nephew to move into his home 2 years ago. Recently the nephew's girlfriend, a substance abuser, moved in without Mr. Ortiz's consent. The girlfriend bars him from "her" kitchen; eventually, Mr. Ortiz is not allowed out of his bedroom. Mr. Ortiz pays for all household expenses, because neither his nephew nor the girlfriend work. A friend and neighbor who has known the family for 20 years has been bringing Mr. Ortiz a meal every day, but the nephew tells her not to come back; his girlfriend is preparing meals. The nephew also stops the extended family from visiting by intercepting phone calls and telling them that Mr. Ortiz does not feel like having company.
>
> The neighbor calls APS and the family. The family members—two sons, two daughters, and six grandchildren—have a family meeting and decide that the nephew and his girlfriend have to move out. Mr. Ortiz does not want to talk to APS at first, saying that this is a family matter. Neither does he want to evict the nephew. Finally, Mr. Ortiz agrees that the nephew should move. The APS worker gives the nephew and his girlfriend a deadline, but on the day they are supposed to move out, Mr. Ortiz changes his mind. He says he feels guilty about asking his own flesh and blood to leave when he knows that his nephew will be homeless.
>
> Mr. Ortiz continues being exploited and verbally abused by the couple for several months, until the family and APS again intervene. When the nephew and his girlfriend finally move out, they take all of Mr. Ortiz's cash, his automobile (for which they forge a title transfer), and some heirloom jewelry. Mr. Ortiz refuses to talk to law enforcement or press charges against the couple. He dies 6 months later, still expressing guilt about having made his nephew move out.

Themes reflected in the Ortiz case surfaced in each focus group. For example, Mexican Americans traditionally have not trusted "the government" for help. Instead, they rely on families and friends for assistance. During the focus group in Austin, APS worker Letti Guevara affirmed that even she, a Mexican American, is not trusted initially because she is viewed as a part of the system. Ms. Guevara stressed that the element of trust is extremely important in working with elderly Mexican Americans and that extra time is needed to build that trust. This assertion was echoed in other parts of the state. In Lubbock, APS Supervisor Val Joiner noted that workers have to visit with clients two or three times to begin gaining their trust.

Although establishing trust is a cornerstone of effective social work practice, regardless of ethnicity, focus-group members felt that gaining the trust of elderly Mexican Americans is particularly challenging. Focus-group members said that they found elderly Mexican Americans reluctant to admit that they need help, even more reluctant to ask for help from those outside their circle of family and friends, and often embarrassed to discuss personal affairs with a stranger. Staff remarked that these factors often lead some social-service agencies and staff to assume that Mexican American clients typically are noncooperative, do not need or want assistance, and do not want to better themselves.

In all locations, the focus groups identified five common areas in which cultural awareness is needed when working with elders of the Mexican culture. These areas are:

- The extended family,
- Religion,
- Language,
- Change in the family,
- Health care.

The following sections discuss each of these factors in greater detail.

La Familia   The focus groups felt that understanding the roles and dynamics of "*La Familia*" (the family) is vital to providing protective services to the Mexican American client. Participants described the Mexican American family as having strong cultural traditions that have been passed on from generation to generation. Family unity, strong religious beliefs, family traditions, and a constant struggle to maintain high moral values are some of the characteristics that they cited.

The issue of respect and loyalty to the family as a whole was thought to be very important. During the focus-group meeting in San Antonio, APS worker Robert Morales noted that it is vital to respect the roles among the family members when entering a Mexican American household. Robert and the group shared various examples of the need to determine the hierarchy within the family when the APS worker tries to gain access to the client. Robert stated that often, but not always, the male spouse or eldest son is considered the head of the family and should be approached prior to interviewing a female client. Others in the focus groups gave examples of strong matriarchs within families and the need to give recognition to these women.

The family evolves by its social, historical, and cultural experiences (Lockery, 1985). The elders are held with high respect by the younger generations because of past hardships they have endured, including discrimination, racism, poverty, and educational deprivation. The Mexican American family, in times of need, looks for support from the members of the extended family before it considers outside intervention. Often, family members place the needs of their relatives before their own.

Members of the focus groups shared numerous examples that illustrated a credo among Mexican Americans, "*Ahora por él, mañana por mí*" ("Today for him, tomorrow for me"), which reinforces the importance of family unity (Gibson, 1985, p. II-5). When maltreatment occurs, the focus groups were of the opinion that this strong tradition of family loyalty and unity made it especially difficult for the Mexican American elder to accept help, because of the shame that the elder would feel about his or her circumstances. Zuniga (1984), in a discussion of cultural issues in clinical practice with elderly Mexican American women, noted that "[t]he cultural interpretation of shame and the reluctance to allow outsiders to see family skeletons was uniquely Mexican for a relavitely [sic] acculturated family" (p. 6). Admitting abuse, neglect, or exploitation at the hands of a loved one would be acknowledging that *la familia* has broken down. We can certainly surmise that Mr. Ortiz may have shared these feelings. Zuniga, in the same article, also recounts this story:

> A 97-year-old Mexicano told me he was downright angry that when his children needed help both he and his wife were available; now that they need help their children are not around very much. For him it hurt his pride to have an outsider come in to provide services that he felt family could offer. Yet, he would not ask them for help. (p. 13)

Focus-group participants observed that the Mexican American family also includes non-blood members who may be a part of the decision-making process within the family. This tradition, illustrated by the practice of choosing *padrinos* (godparents) when celebrating a wedding, baptism, confirmation, or *quinceañera*, (daughters' 15th birthday), creates a strong bond among the affected parties. If the family is in crisis, these individuals, such as the neighbor in Mr. Ortiz's case, may play a vital role in dealing with the situation and should not be overlooked or ignored by the APS worker.

Religion   The participants were of the opinion that a large proportion of Mexican Americans are Catholic, and that these religious beliefs are as strong as family tradition, serving as a source of comfort in times of need. During the focus group in El Paso, APS worker David Torres said that one question frequently asked by elderly Mexican clients on his initial home visit is, "Are you Catholic?" Mr. Torres noted that these elderly clients seem to feel that the worker can better understand them if the worker and client share religious beliefs.

Focus-groups members said that in their experience, priests are highly trusted among Mexican Americans, being viewed as authority figures—God's representatives here on earth. For example, Mary Jo Garcia, APS worker in San Antonio, described the case of a wife being physically abused by her husband. Despite the availability of protective services, the wife seemed to fear the stigma of divorce more than the abuse. Ms. Garcia said that only after seeking counseling from a priest, who told the woman that she did not deserve to be beaten, did the wife leave the abusive situation.

Language Barriers   The focus groups identified language as one of the greatest barriers for non-Spanish-speaking workers responsible for providing services to Spanish-speaking clients. Graciela Quinteros, APS worker in Lubbock, stated that it has been her experience that the elderly Mexican American prefers to speak to someone who is fluent in Spanish as opposed to someone who can speak only broken Spanish. If a person cannot clearly communicate, the elderly individual may not disclose problems that he or she is experiencing. Focus-group members said that in intervening with clients about issues as sensitive as elder abuse, neglect, and exploitation, communicating in the language in which the elder feels most comfortable enhances the worker's ability to objectively work with the client and family. However, the practitioner's being bilingual or bicultural is no guarantee that interventions will be effective and culturally sensitive. Education and practice insights are still needed (Zuniga, 1984, p. 13).

Changes Within the Mexican American Family   As the younger generation of Mexican Americans is becoming more assimilated, the once-strong support network of the extended family is slowly deteriorating (Lockery, 1985). As a result, the care that the elderly once received from their family members is becoming less common. Jim Sweeney, an APS worker in San Antonio, remarked that after 28 years of casework, he now is seeing the younger generation of Mexican Americans being open to receiving outside agency assistance, such as home health services, for their elders.

Nevertheless, other focus-group members found that many family members still feel that it is their responsibility to care for their elders, and they are hesitant to seek and accept outside assistance. These types of cases often involve neglect, because family members may not be able to provide adequate care for their elderly relatives, primarily for economic reasons. Maria Chavez-Ruiz, an APS supervisor in Victoria, stated it has been her experience that Mexican American clients are hesitant to consider hospital or nursing home care for their elders because they feel death is probable in such settings. The family members may feel that they have failed in their expected roles if they place their elders in any of these environments. Mexican American families will accept a certain level of neglect of their elders in order to keep them at home, feeling that this is their primary duty. The saying, "*Ahora por él, mañana por mí*," clearly reflects this sense of responsibility. One must not ignore, however, that the "lack of time, money, knowledge, or training to adequately provide services" (Arguello & Purdy, 1992, p. 38), which is certainly the case in many poor Mexican American households, can lead to neglectful situations.

Health Care   The accessibility and quality of the health care available to Mexican American elderly individuals is influenced by their income, culture, language, and health status (Council of Scientific Affairs, 1991, p. 249). During statewide focus groups, APS staff noted common health trends among the Mexican American elderly individuals served by APS. These observations are borne out by Texas health data.

In 1994, the Texas Department of Human Services estimated that 40.76% of Hispanics in Texas did not have health insurance (Texas Department of Human Services, 1995, p. 1). The focus groups observed that lack of insurance and limitations in government insurance programs restrict the type of healthcare services that are available to elderly Mexican Americans in Texas. Staff reported finding that elderly Mexican Americans are often uninsured, because they are less likely to have worked in occupations that provided extensive insurance benefits. Historically less educated than other groups of elders, many elderly Mexican Americans worked in low-paying, manual-labor jobs. As a result of being uninsured and having limited financial resources, they may delay or refuse medical treatment, thus increasing the potential for undiagnosed conditions and, ultimately, neglect. Hispanics are uninsured at twice the rate of Whites, and Mexican Americans of all ages have a low rate of physician visits and use of preventative healthcare programs (Trevino, Moyer, Valdez, Stroup-Benham, 1991, pp. 234–237).

Some Mexican Americans prefer to rely on *curanderos* (folk healers) for healthcare and spiritual guidance. APS staff in El Paso, Lubbock, and San Antonio noted that the use of folk medicine in combination with traditional Western medicine is prevalent among Mexican American elderly persons in their caseloads. Staff believe that the use of folk medicine varies among generations and locality and may be more widespread than is commonly known. Members of the focus groups stated that their Mexican American clients are often reluctant to reveal that they use folk medicines and the services of *curanderos*. Only after trust is established between the worker and the client does the recipient of services or members of his or her family admit these practices to APS. The focus-group members said that the Mexican American elder fears ridicule or criticism by agency staff, especially if staff are not sensitive and understanding.

Elderly citizens who live along the border of Texas often seek health care in Mexico, where medical, dental, and pharmaceutical services can be obtained from Spanish-speaking professionals at a much lower cost than in the United States. APS staff members said that they sometimes experience difficulty in locating and consulting with medical professionals in Mexico regarding the health concerns of APS clients. However, even if the Mexican American client has access to health care in Texas, Hispanics are underrepresented among health care professionals here (Ginzberg, 1991, p. 240). Given the general recognition that a person's confidence in medical professionals is strengthened by his or her ability to communicate needs to the physician and develop a trusting relationship with the physician (ibid., p. 238), this culture gap among medical professionals presents another barrier for Mexican American elders needing to obtain mainstream U.S. health care.

There is a high incidence of type II diabetes among Mexican Americans, and the rate of diabetes in the Mexican American population may be two to three times higher than the rate for the non-Hispanic U.S. population (ibid., p. 239). Ginzberg theorizes that the high rate of diabetes among Mexican Americans may be linked to a high rate of obesity, diet, and genetic factors.

APS staff members maintain that it would be very helpful for health professionals recommending restricted diets for diabetic Mexican American elders to suggest healthy alternatives that are culturally appropriate for them, rather than ordering foods that, although healthy, are foreign to the elders. Because it improves their diets, this measure could increase their awareness of the role of proper nutrition in controlling diabetes and heart disease. APS staff members also think that more neglect could be prevented if home health aides and other healthcare professionals would enhance their efforts to provide culturally sensitive training materials in Spanish regarding proper nutrition and health care.

Focus groups in El Paso, San Antonio, Lubbock, and Harlingen stated that there is a lack of available, culturally sensitive mental-health services for Mexican American clients. Their experience has been that Mexican American families routinely minimize or ignore the signs of mental illness. Often, families believe that the mentally ill person has a "nervous condition." Diagnosis and treatment of a mental illness may be delayed until another family member assumes caregiving responsibility for the mentally ill person after the death of a parent or spouse.

APS staff in El Paso and the lower Rio Grande Valley cited environmental factors as adverse influences on the health status of maltreated elderly Mexican Americans residing in the border areas. In 1988, a needs assessment found that there were approximately 140,000 citizens residing in *colonias* (Texas Department of Health, 1985, pp. 1–3). In 1995, the Texas Water Development Board estimated that this number had grown to 340,000 residents (Chapa, 1996). APS workers discussed at great length the substandard living conditions of the *colonias*, which, generally speaking, are rural unincorporated subdivisions characterized by substandard housing; inadequate plumbing, sewage and waste disposal; and inadequate access to clean water. Illegal dumping of waste materials adds to the health risks. Residents often are found in acute states of neglect, in urgent need of better housing, adequate financial resources, improved hygiene, transportation, and medical services.

In working with maltreated elderly Mexican Americans, APS staff noted that clients and family sometimes are reluctant to seek medical assistance. Focus-group members and other staff members recommended various mechanisms by which accessibility to services may be improved, such as the recognition by health professionals of the needs of Mexican American elders and the development of language-sensitive and culturally sensitive diagnostic services. Staff reported that APS interventions that are successful in assisting elderly Mexican American clients to access medical services are most often accomplished with the involvement of family members. Therefore, APS staff thought it important for healthcare professionals to involve family members in all aspects of the elderly person's healthcare when the client so chooses.

Other societal conditions adversely affect elderly Mexican Americans and Mexican nationals. APS staff members are expressing a growing concern about the impact of welfare reform. Although it now appears that services are likely to continue for most elderly legal immigrants who would have lost Supplemental Security Income (SSI), food stamps, and associated medical benefits under the original provisions of the Personal Responsibility and Work Opportunity Reconciliation Act of 1996 (Center for Public Policy Priorities, 1997), the loss of these services is having a very adverse effect on APS clients who are Mexican nationals.

Staff are experiencing great difficulty in providing or arranging for any services to these individuals, who often are found in extreme states of neglect.

ONGOING EFFORTS TO IMPROVE CULTURAL COMPETENCE

In its commitment to ensure the highest quality of services to vulnerable adults in need of protection, Texas APS program leaders continue to evaluate the service-delivery system. For example, a year-long work plan is being implemented to improve services to persons with limited proficiency in English. Efforts involve not only APS but other divisions and outside consultants. The work plan includes policy revisions and additions, training initiatives, procedural changes, and outreach, which will include conducting focus groups in communities of color. The measures being planned reflect a commitment to

- Eliminating cultural and other barriers as they are identified.
- Assuring that staff who are points of entry into the agency are sensitive to the special needs of Mexican American callers.
- Assuring that policies and procedures are written inclusively, rather than exclusively.
- Hiring and retaining bilingual/bicultural professionals who share the culture, language, and values of the groups they serve.
- Developing and delivering a cultural-diversity training curriculum.
- Continuing to obtain and provide resources that eliminate barriers to service delivery.
- Providing bilingual outreach in the electronic and print media.
- Developing and disseminating bilingual publications to senior activity and nutrition centers, Mexican American congregations, healthcare centers, social security offices, grocery stores, and food-stamp offices.

CONCLUSION

Focus groups and the literature confirm that Mexican American elders have unique cultural characteristics that need to be considered when conducting investigations and providing services. If these factors are not considered, investigations and assessments may be inaccurate, clients may refuse assistance, or services may be inappropriate. It is crucial, then, that APS staff working with Mexican American elders understand the family structure, customs, and beliefs of this population.

Ensuring culturally competent staff is partially accomplished by proper training. It is important, however, that staff competence be assessed to ensure that the training is properly designed and applied. For this reason, we recommend the use of a tool like the Cultural Competence Self Assessment Questionnaire prior to beginning training efforts. Training is not the only way, however, to ensure that elders of color have access to culturally sensitive services. Organizational changes in planning policy and procedures are important as well in areas such as gathering community input, recruiting and retaining minority staff, and outreach.

As important as cultural factors are, we must not lose sight of the fact that among Mexican Americans, as in any other ethnic group, there are variances in the culture according to the locale and the generation to which the client belongs. We must be cautious, therefore, about making assumptions and generalizations. As Tello (1985) states:

> We must remember when we work with people of any culture that we are touching persons' lives who have feelings, a spirit, and an identity, all tied to history, tradition, customs, and more importantly, a purpose. The more we respect that purpose, learn from those around us, and utilize our own special gifts, given to us to help others, the more effective we can be (p. III-14).

REFERENCES

Arguello, D., & Purdy, J. K. (1992). Hispanic familism in caretaking of older adults: Is it functional? *Journal of Gerontological Social Work, 19*(2), 29–43.

Center for Public Policy Priorities (1997, July 9). Health and immigration benefit update: Part one. *The Policy Page, 52*(1–2).

Chang, V. (1997a). [APS clients aged 65 by ethnicity, fiscal year 1996]. Unpublished raw data.

Chang, V. (1997b). [Number APS investigations in fiscal year 1996 with clients who were Mexican Americans or Mexican nationals]. Unpublished raw data.

Chang, V. (1997c). [Texas population data base]. Unpublished raw data provided on strip tape.

Chapa, J. (1996). *Colonia housing and infrastructure: Current population and housing characteristics, future growth, and housing, water, and wastewater needs.* A preliminary report by the Policy Research Project on Colonia Housing and Infrastructure, University of Texas at Austin, Lyndon B. Johnson School of Public Affairs.

Council of Scientific Affairs. (1991). Hispanic health in the United States. *Journal of the American Medical Association, 265,* 248–252.

Drago, M. (1997, April 21). Hispanic population outpacing other groups. *Abilene Reporter News,* pp. 1A, 8A.

Festa, N. A. (1997). [Serving elders from communities of color: perceptions of Adult Protective Services workers in Texas]. Unpublished raw data. Austin: Texas Department of Protective and Regulatory Services.

Gibson, G. (1985). The Mexican American family. In M. Guevara (Ed.), *Developing Cultural Competence: A Training Manual for Improving the Efficiency and Effectiveness of Social Services Delivery to the Mexican American Family* (pp. II-1–II-13). Proceedings of a conference of the Texas Migrant Council, Laredo, TX: Texas Migrant Council.

Ginzberg, E. (1991). Access to health care for Hispanics. *Journal of the American Medical Association, 265,* 238–241.

Lockery, S. A. (1985). Care in the minority family. *The Gerontologist, 10*(1), 27–29.

Murdock, S. H., Hoque, M. N., Michael, M., White, S., & Pecotte, B. (1997). *The Texas challenge: Population change and the future of Texas.* College Station, TX: Texas A&M University Press.

Ramos, M. G., & Plocheck, R. (Eds.). (1995). *1996–1997 Texas almanac and state industrial guide.* Dallas: Dallas Morning News, Inc.

Tello, J. (1985). Developing cultural awareness, sensitivity, integration, competence. In M. Guevara (Ed.), *Developing Cultural Competence: A Training Manual for Improving the Efficiency and*

Effectiveness of Social Services Delivery to the Mexican American Family (pp. II-1–II-13). Proceedings of a conference of the Texas Migrant Council, Laredo, TX: Texas Migrant Council.

Texas Department of Health. (1995). *Texas vital statistics*. Austin: Bureau of Vital Statistics.

Texas Department of Human Services. (1995). *General profile of population without insurance in Texas during the calendar year of 1994*. Austin: Budget and Management Department, Forecasting and Demographics.

Texas Department of Protective and Regulatory Services. (1997) *1996 Annual Report*. Austin: Author.

Trevino, F. M., Moyer E., Valdez, B., & Benham-Stroup, C. (1991). Health insurance and utilization of health services by Mexican Americans, mainland Puerto Ricans and Cuban Americans. *Journal of the American Medical Association, 265*, 233–237.

Zuniga, M. E. (1984) Elderly Latina mujeres: Stressors and strengths. In R. Anson (Ed.). *The Hispanic older woman* (pp. 1–14). Washington, DC: National Hispanic Council on Aging.

Chapter 7

Elder Abuse in
the Puerto Rican Context

Carmen D. Sánchez

In Puerto Rico as well as in the United States, the size of the sector of the population 60 years of age and over has been increasing at a more rapid pace than the rest of the population. This increase, reflected in Puerto Rico since the 1950s, has been the result of a reduced birth rate, the emigration of young adults (ages 20–34) to the United States, and the return migration of older Puerto Ricans to the island. The Commonwealth of Puerto Rico (1994a) cites significant shifts of population within age sectors over the past 30 years. The population of those aged 15 years and younger was drastically reduced from 43% of the total population in 1960, to 28% of the total population (3,522,037) in 1990. The population of those aged 60 years and over increased from 6% of the total population in 1960, to 13.2% (465,736) in 1990. Projections for the year 2000 indicate that the percentage of the population 60 years old or older will increase to 14.4% of Puerto Rico's total population. Contributing factors to stated projections may include older Puerto Ricans returning to the island, the "baby-boom" generation continuing to age, continued emigration of young adults, crime rates that tend to impact younger rather than older age groups, a decreasing birth rate, and increased access to more advanced and specialized medical treatment.

The trend toward increased longevity among elderly Puerto Ricans means that more families will extend to four living generations (e.g., middle-aged adults who are already grandparents and have elderly parents). The actual and potential increase in the number and proportion of the aged population, including the multigenerational aspect, presents a challenge for the delivery of health and social services as the number of dependent and frail elderly increases. Clearly, these demographic changes have implications on the tragic phenomena of elder abuse and neglect. More specifically, if Puerto Rico's elderly population is increasing, then there is an increased likelihood that the mistreatment (abuse and neglect) of this population sector may increase also. This correlation necessitates more expansive community resources with which to address elderly mistreatment as a growing social problem. Community care implies providing the health and social services that enable a target population (the elderly sector) to live as independently as possible within their identified communities, despite physical or emotional challenges. Without this intended care, incidents of elderly mistreatment may be expected more frequently. This chapter addresses abuse and neglect of the elderly as it may be observed and experienced in a Puerto Rican context. Significant emphasis on cultural, legislative, and socioeconomic factors is presented, as they are elements essential to the understanding of, as well as accurate assessments of, health and social-service needs for the aged. Furthermore, integration of such elements can assist in successful service delivery and the prevention of what presents a serious threat to the public's health: elderly abuse and neglect.

ELDER ABUSE IN PUERTO RICO

In Puerto Rico, the social epidemiology of elder mistreatment remains unclearly delineated due to underreporting, lack of prevalent data, and a paucity of the research and funding needed to develop a secure foundation for describing the problem, quantifying data, and implementing programmatic remedies. The omitted acknowledgment that elderly mistreatment *does* occur and *is*, indeed, a social problem, is considerably contradictory given this society's notably consistent population increase among the sector 60 years and more of age over the past few decades.

The 1980s marked Puerto Rico's decade of awareness regarding violence against women and children. Subsequently, legislative efforts specified and reiterated both women and children as protected populations. First, the Child Protection Law (Public Law 75, May 28, 1980) defined child abuse and neglect and established the systemic procedures required if such treatment of a child has been found. Similarly, domestic violence is defined, assessed, and penalized according to the Law to Prevent and Intervene with Domestic Violence (Public Law 54, August 15, 1989). The elderly, as a targeted population, have not been a legislative focus in terms of acknowledgment, definition, intervention, or penalization of mistreatment perhaps because, within Puerto Rico, the concepts of elderly abuse and neglect, as separated from familial mistreatment, have not been recognized as social problems in their own right.

Data provided by the Family Department of the Commonwealth of Puerto Rico indicated a total of 342 reports of elder abuse in 1980. By 1990, the Family Department's elderly abuse reports had increased to 2,828. These statistics increased again in 1996 to a total of 5,613 elderly-abuse reports. The Governor's Office for the Aged received 1,226 abuse complaints in 1993 and 1,768 in 1995. These complaints were reported by area Agencies on Aging (Governor's Office for the Aged, 1996). According to police statistics on domestic violence, at the end of 1994 a total of 18,079 cases of domestic violence were reported to that agency, 115 of which concerned women 60 years of age and over (The Commonwealth of Puerto Rico, 1994b; Baba, Colón, & Cruz, 1996). Scarcity of evidence on elder abuse may exist, in part, because the actual mistreatment is often perpetrated within the family setting and goes unreported (Arroyo et al., 1992; Governor's Office for the Aged, 1996; Muñoz, 1985; Baba et al., 1996). In terms of institutional abuse and neglect, the Family Department, which is the agency responsible for supervising and licensing long-term care facilities, in 1989 ordered the closing of 21 establishments in which elders were neglected and emotionally abused (Calero, 1989). The Ombudsman Program, under the Governor's Office for the Aged, detected and received for investigation a total of 2,873 complaints in 1995 and 1996 from long-term care institutions (Governor's Office for the Aged, 1996).

From 1985 to 1996, only four research studies dealing with this topic in Puerto Rico were identified. The research reviewed suggested that many elderly on the island are at risk or have been abused by their caregivers, relatives, or nonrelatives (Muñoz, 1985; Arroyo et al., 1992; Ramos-Tossas, 1991; Baba et al., 1996). The typical victim of abuse is a woman more than 75 years of age who is physically dependent (Muñoz, 1985). The abuser is frequently an adult child of the victim (Arroyo et al., 1992; Muñoz, 1985). The abuse is frequently ongoing and takes various forms, such as neglect or emotional, physical, or financial abuse (Governor's Office for the Aged, 1996; Ramos-Tossas, 1991; Muñoz, 1985). What follows is a brief description of the findings of these research efforts.

The first research in Puerto Rico to assess the prevalence of abuse of elderly people by their caregivers and also the characteristics of both the abused and the abuser was completed by Muñoz in 1985. Muñoz's research analyzed a population of some 86 cases classified under elder abuse or neglect by the Protective Services Unit of the Family Department's Adult Program during the years 1980 through 1984. Variables such as age, sex, level of dependency, education, income source, civil status, living conditions, family composition, abuse incidence and recurrence, and family stress factors were explored. The elderly assessed were 60 years of age and over, living alone or with a relative, friend, or neighbor, and victims of abuse and neglect. Ages ranged from 60 to 104 years. The mean age was 78 years; the majority were between 60 and 74 years old. More than half of the aged were female (54.2%) and widowed (51.8%) and most had low income. Level of dependency was divided into three categories: low (34.6%), high (43.4%), and middle (23.0%).

Definitions of elder abuse and neglect were based on categories used by Block and Sinnott (1979) and Lau and Kosberg (1979). Physical abuse found included malnutrition (38%); lack of personal hygiene (34%); injuries such as bruises or sprains (34%); withholding medical attention (30%); dislocations, abrasions, or lacerations (3%); and sexual assault (2%). Psychological abuse, defined as verbal assaults, isolation, threats, or rejection, was reported in only a small percentage of the cases (5%). Material abuse, defined as misuse of money or properties, was reported in 22% of the situations. Neglect was reported in 50% of the cases in the form of lack of supervision, inconvenient and dirty housing, and inadequate clothing. Neglect constituted the most common form of abuse in the study. Fifty-three percent of the abuse was carried out by a daughter or a son and 10%

by a husband or a wife. In 40% of the situations the victim had been previously abused by another relative.

Muñoz found that 70.8% of the relatives or caregivers were affected by some family stressors. Among the principal stressors identified were mental or physical inability of a family member (70%), alcoholism (31%), inadequate housing conditions (30%), lack of financial resources (18%), unemployment (15%), chronic illness (10%), separation or divorce (10%), drug addiction (10%), and dropping out of school (10%). Almost 50% of the elder's families presented a high number of stress factors. Muñoz's most important conclusions included that abuse was correlated with age and dependency. As age and dependency increased, so did the frequency of abuse. She found no correlation between abuse and sex. The presence or absence of disruptive behaviors among caregivers seemed to be a potential risk factor.

In the research of Arroyo et al. (1992), a total of 134 professionals and practitioners involved in providing supportive services to the elderly in community centers and home healthcare services were interviewed regarding their experience and knowledge of mistreatment of older people in Puerto Rico. Seven different geographical areas of the island were selected as interview sites. These locations represented large metropolitan, suburban, and rural areas. The professionals included nurses, activity coordinators, caseworkers, drivers, social workers, and physical, occupational, and speech therapists. The dimensions of mistreatment in this research included neglect, emotional abuse, physical abuse, exploitation, and sexual abuse. Almost 75% of the subjects of the study identified at least one situation of elder abuse in the past year, representing 5% of the diverse service situations in which they were involved. Home healthcare workers were more likely than the other professionals to identify abuse and neglect situations (69%). The types of mistreatment identified by the respondents were neglect (42%), emotional abuse (36%), physical abuse (11%), exploitation (10%), and sexual abuse (1%). The abuser was a daughter or son in 64% of the instances. The sources of information reported by the professionals were direct observation (51%), the elderly person (34%), a neighbor or friend (16%), another professional (11%), and relatives (2%). This points out the willingness of the elderly to report mistreatment to professionals. In terms of the description of the abused elderly, the study found that the majority of the elderly were between 75 and 84 years of age (50%), female (60%), and widows (60%). One of the explanations for the higher instance of female abuse in Puerto Rico is that life expectancy for women is higher. According to the 1990 census, life expectancy for women was 79 years; for men it was 71 years. For every 100 females, there are only 89 males in the age group 65 years old and older (U.S. Department of Commerce, Census Bureau, 1990). The characteristics of the victims of abuse in this research were similar to earlier research in the United States (Pillemer & Fenkelhor, 1988; Blakely & Dolon, 1989) in terms of the profile of the abused elderly being: female, widows, over 75 years of age, and living with relatives.

Ramos-Tossas's research (1991) focused on elder abuse in long-term care and daycare facilities in the southern part of the island. Two-hundred thirty-five persons 62 years of age and older participated in the study. Each institutionalized participant was administered Brink's Mental Status Scale (Brink, 1979) to determine their capability to participate in the study. Structured and private interviews were conducted with each participant. The categories of abuse included were physical (injuries, bruises, abrasions or lacerations, burns), passive neglect (ignored, left alone, isolated, or forgotten), active neglect (withholding of companionship, medicine, food, exercise, or assistance to a bathroom), verbal or emotional abuse (humiliation, harassment, threats, rejection), sociological abuse (isolation, abandonment, role confusion), and legal abuse (material misuse, theft, or misuse of rights). Variables studied were age, sex, abuse perpetrator, types of abuse, and risk factors. Ramos-Tossas found that more than 50% of the participants had experienced some type of abuse or neglect. Active and passive neglect were the most common types of abuse reported. Men reported being abused more than women. Incidence of abuse was higher in the more dependent elderly, as well as those living in long-term care facilities or with a relative. At the daycare centers, the perpetrators most commonly identified were other participants, administrators, relatives, or nurses. At the long-term care facilities, nurses, social workers, administrators, or other residents were most commonly identified as perpetrators. Data also indicated that daycare centers had fewer incidents of abuse than long-term care facilities. Ramos-Tossas research suggests that Puerto Rican elderly are not well oriented in terms of their legal rights, particularly if these rights have been violated. The elderly Puerto Rican believes that a person should avoid legal confrontations; for example, a dignified elderly man should never be involved in legal battles. According to Rivera-Ramos (1991), Puerto Ricans are sometimes considered docile, nonassertive individuals, which places them in legal disadvantage against the strong and powerful.

Baba, Colón, and Cruz's research (1996) focused on the attitudes toward and knowledge about domestic violence of women 60 years of age and older. Researchers interviewed 100 elderly women residing in urban areas of Puerto Rico. Variables included sociodemographic aspects, views on female roles in society, attitudes towards domestic violence, and knowledge of legal aspects and services on domestic violence. Respondents identified *tolerance* (66%) as one adjective describing women and *aggressiveness* (43%) as describing men. Regarding attitudes towards domestic violence, although the vast majority of the women (99%) repudiated violence in a relationship, 30% considered that men could be violent when women were unfaithful. Fifty percent argued that "a woman should preserve their kid's father no matter what" (Baba et al., 1996, p. 131). Although 80% of the women knew of the existence of a domestic-violence law, only 30% had some knowledge about its content or the rights of a victimized person.

Despite the limited research and data on the topic, there are some risk factors that can be associated with elder abuse on the island. Demographic characteristics of the Puerto Rican older adults indicate that they are members of a familial network system and that most are or have been married and have children. In other words, a large percentage of aged persons are members of a family. The prevalence of family and informal support systems is strong within the Puerto Rican society (Sánchez, 1992). Socioeconomic barriers encountered by the Puerto Rican elderly may make them more dependent on their families. According to the 1990 census data for Puerto Rico, the majority of persons 60 years of age or older were living in family households (371,229 or 79.7%). Nineteen percent, or 88,288, were living alone or sharing a house with nonrelatives, and only 6,219 (1.3%) were in institutional facilities (U.S. Department of Commerce, Census Bureau, 1990). As age increases, the proportion of elderly living in family households decreases and institutionalization increases. In the cohort 60 to 64 years of age, 84.7% were living in family households in 1990, whereas only 74% of the persons aged 85 or more years were living in this type of arrangement. By the same token, institutionalization increased from 0.7% for the cohort 60 to 64 years of age to 5.1% in the cohort 85 years of age or more (U.S. Department of Commerce, Census Bureau, 1990). Nursing homes or long-term care facilities continue to be the last choice for elderly Puerto Ricans or their families.

The rapid socioeconomic changes that Puerto Rican society has undergone in the past 30 years have altered familial and community patterns of interaction. Urbanism and industrialization have affected the structure of the Puerto Rican family. It often is stated that the family pattern has changed from an extended to a nuclear one in which the elderly have no place. However, studies of the Puerto Rican older adults residing in Puerto Rico and in the United States overwhelmingly indicate that the immediate family continues to play a vital function in the delivery of assistance to the aged adult (Sánchez-Ayendez, 1986; Sánchez, 1989; Cruz-López & Pearson, 1985). Despite the changes the Puerto Rican family has undergone in the past decades, it continues to retain many aspects of its ethnic Hispanic identity and cultural values. One such value, known as *familismo*, places a great emphasis on family unity, supports family integrity, and gives shape and direction to the behavior of its members. Being family-centered, members feel an obligation to relatives and a duty to serve in times of crisis. Similarly, the loyalty towards family keeps the elderly from talking about their mistreatment.

In the Puerto Rican community, the family is a source of strength for individuals of all ages. The Puerto Rican cultural heritage is one that underlines family responsibility for care of those in need. This tradition means that the family is a significant primary provider of social services. In accordance with cultural norms and values, and as a practical necessity, the extended family concept is still of great importance. For instance, as previously stated, many Puerto Rican elderly share a household with a child or relative (Sánchez, 1989; U.S. Department of Commerce, Census Bureau, 1990). The fact that Puerto Rican aged are more likely to live in households with other relatives is not only a function of the value system of this community but also a matter of economic necessity. The shared household is one way poorer families meet their housing needs and, in addition, the grandparents often take care of the children in the increasing number of single-parent families, or in families in which both parents work. On the other hand, research on the Puerto Rican elderly on the island consistently demonstrates that most of the elderly are poor and that their meager economic resources do not permit them to use the private healthcare-delivery sector and makes them more dependent on relatives (Sánchez-Ayendez, 1986; Sánchez, 1989). Fifty-six percent of the population 60 years of age and older live below the poverty level, with an annual average income of $5,477 (U.S. Department of Commerce, Census Bureau, 1990).

In addition to the *familismo* value, Puerto Rican culture places a high value on the concept that life is a network of interpersonal relationships. The value of *personalismo* is central for Puerto Ricans. It is described as a "form of individualism that focuses on the inner importance of the person. . . . [it is] rooted in the family, sensing it as an extension of the person and the network of obligations follows" (Fitzpatrick, 1981, p. 211). Thus, Puerto Rican elderly are likely to adhere to traditional and extended family systems. Informal members consist of close friends and special neighbors, who, over a period of years, have proved willing to engage in family matters and events. However, the strong familial and informal support that has sustained and provided the elderly with important roles has begun to weaken.

An important aspect of familial support is what happens when the elder becomes impaired and the family has to provide the needed care. The elderly population in Puerto Rico suffers from ailments encountered among the elderly population of most developed countries in the world. The presence of chronic illness is responsible for more physician visits, more hospitalization and hospital discharges, and longer hospital stays. There is little systematically obtained information concerning mental illness among the Puerto Rican elderly; however, the Puerto Rican Alzheimer Association estimates that approximately 25,000 persons are suffering from this disorder in Puerto Rico. Chronic illnesses frequently imply physical disabilities, mental anguish, and greater reliance on relatives and friends. Ineffective caregiving may very well be the result of a lack of external support to familial networks that could ease the burden. A family history of conflicts, in addition to the combination of feeling compelled to provide care and feeling enraged and frustrated at having to do so, could very well lead to ineffective caregiving and even to abuse in spite of all prevailing cultural values surrounding the family. On the other hand, family values can interfere in the visibility of elder abuse and neglect. Families do not tolerate intromission or interference of strangers in their affairs. Abused members, along with perpetrators, adhere to a silent conspiracy and reject any professional intervention if dysfunction is detected. This value is stronger in older members of the family. Variables such as family ties, loyalty, and interdependent relationships make it hard for victims to go to outside sources for help.

Ageism is mentioned as a precipitant of vulnerability to suffering outside the victim's control (Johnson, 1991). Ageist attitudes can be blamed for the phenomenon of elder abuse not being recognized as a social problem. Ageism suggests that simply being old may be a risk factor in mistreatment. In this regard, mistreatment is based on chronological age and characteristics that are understood to accompany the elderly cohort such as increased frailty, chronic health problems, mental or physical disability, inadequate financial resources, and relational loss, among others. Palmore (1990) mentions three types of ageism that are difficult for the older adult to manage: societal ageism, professional ageism, and community ageism. Societal ageism is manifested in the form of forced retirement, age-discriminatory healthcare policies, and limited Social Security benefits as a function of age, among others. Professional ageism is found if helping professionals who treat or provide care for chronically ill or dysfunctional older adults respond to them as if they were children. Community ageism can be seen in more and better health, recreational, and social services for those other than older adults. Community inattention to the needs of older adults may mean that vulnerable older adults are not protected. No matter how hard the elderly person tries, some of them are unable to prevent possible mistreatment if these forms of elderly discrimination are practiced. For example, in several suburban neighborhoods in Puerto Rico, neighbors have been able to keep nursing homes from opening. In an unprecedented case in Puerto Rico, in 1990, a federal judge ruled that neighbors' complaints against a nursing home were discriminatory against the elderly (United States District Court, 1990). Casa Marie Geriatric Home is a live-in eldercare facility home to approximately 40 elderly, mostly handicapped persons. Some neighbors in the residential area in which the home is located wanted it to cease functioning. The neighbors sought and obtained a state-court judgment ordering the owners to close the home. A group of elderly handicapped residents, precluded by the state court from taking part in those proceedings, joined the owners as plaintiffs alleging that they were being discriminated against for being elderly and handicapped in violation of the Fair Housing Act and the Equal Protection Clause. Plaintiffs alleged that the defendants had violated their civil rights by using the state judicial system to exclude them from Casa Marie. Sufficient facts were alleged for the court to find a continuing violation of the elders' rights. The plaintiffs were not only suffering the effect of some past discriminatory act but continued to suffer from discriminatory conduct each time the defendants went to court with the intention of removing them from Casa Marie. The U.S. District court ruled that the neighbors' complaints were discriminatory and that the victory that they had obtained in local courts violated the nursing home residents' rights under the Fair Housing Act. The judge's opinion had long-term implications for Puerto Rico where, in several places, neighbors have been able to keep nursing homes from opening.

LEGISLATION

Elder abuse and protective-service laws, which prohibit abuse or mistreatment of elders, exist in over 85% of the states in the United States (Johnson, 1991).

Federal and state laws have been enacted to detect, prevent, and remedy mistreatment of the aged. Programs and systems that address abuse include the criminal-justice system, domestic-violence laws; state long-term care ombudsman programs, Adult Protective Service programs, and programs offered through the Older Americans Act. In Puerto Rico, unfortunately, there are no specific laws designed to address the problem of elder abuse, although it is evident that many elderly people suffer from or are vulnerable to certain forms of abuse, often from those who care for them. As adults, elderly persons theoretically have full access to all the legislation or legal services available to other adult members of society following crimes that involve violence. Several pieces of legislation contain a series of separate and quite discrete legal procedures to address issues related to the rights of the elderly.

Puerto Rico Public Law 121 (July 12, 1986) establishes the public policy towards the aged and promulgates the Bill of Rights for the Aged. This piece of legislation constitutes a measure of great importance in terms of social legislation in favor of the aged population. The intended declaration is clear in this respect and summarizes the primary intention of the law: "This government has proposed to do whatever is under its control to improve the living conditions of the aged person, as long as the resources allow it. The Older Adults' Bill of Rights and the Government's Public Policy regarding the aged are a decisive step into guaranteeing the elder's welfare" (Leyes de Puerto Rico, 1986, p. 399). There are specific clauses related to elder abuse in this law. Article 3(a,b,c) establishes the rights of all elderly to live in a dignified environment in which basic housing, food, health, and financial needs are satisfied; to live free of pressure, coercion, or manipulation aimed to lessen their capability or self-determination right, from relatives or particular or State persons; and to receive protection and physical or social security against physical, emotional, or psychological abuses. Article 4(f) addresses specifically the right of an institutionalized elderly person not to be the object of physical or emotional abuse or psychological pressures. Finally, this law decrees the right of every elderly person or his or her tutor, any government official, or any interested person to assist them before the Justice Department Processing of Rights' Violation Unit, to claim any violation of the rights stated in the law. Any noncompliance will result in civil actions.

Public Law 68 of June 11, 1988, created the Governor's Office for Elderly Affairs. This agency is responsible for planning and coordinating the integration of programs and services for the elderly. The Law also designates the Governor's Office for the Aged as the administrative agency responsible for the implementation of the federal programs under the Older Americans Act of 1965. Some of the specific functions of the Office are to collect, analyze, and keep updated statistical data needed for planning, coordination, and use of government resources regarding the elderly; carry out divulgation and orientation activities to develop positive attitudes towards the aged; and provide orientation to the aged regarding services, programs, benefits, and activities offered by private and public agencies.

The Penal Code of Puerto Rico was amended in 1994 (Public Law 33, June 23, 1994) and in 1995 (Public Law 22 and Public Law 23, February 4, 1995) to include specific clauses against elder abuse. Public Law 33 establishes that aggravated assault can be considered if an act is committed against a person aged 60 years or older with the intention of inflicting serious bodily damage. Public Law 22 typifies the act of withholding or denying food to an elderly person as a crime by any husband, wife, or descendant. Public Law 23 typifies abandonment with the intention of desertion as a crime against an elderly person.

Elderly persons who are victims of domestic violence in Puerto Rico have the option to request an injunction to prevent an abusive partner from coming in their vicinity under the Law to Prevent and Intervene with Domestic Violence (Public Law 54, August 15, 1989). This law typifies all violent domestic faults as crimes; establishes the use of psychological violence as criminal behavior; typifies sexual violation in marriage as having same penalties as between strangers; allows for the adoption of restraining orders for victims; and defines the responsibilities and obligations of the Police Department, the Justice Department, and the Correctional Administration regarding the Law.

Protective Service Programs for the elderly are provided by the Division of Adult Services of the Commonwealth of Puerto Rico Family Department. The primary function of this division is to detect and provide protective services for all economically disadvantaged adults. Adult protective service professionals are authorized by the legal political system to enter the private lives of individuals who have been reported by neighbors or relatives as experiencing unnecessary suffering.

The Elder Maintenance Law (Public Law 32, March 28, 1984) has the intention of requesting persons to comply with the legal obligation to feed aged family members; to strengthen family ties between them; and to set the groundwork for eventually establishing a service for protecting aged victims of neglect. Ultimately, the law intends to improve the quality of life of the elderly in their later years. The law authorizes the Family Department to initiate any administrative or judicial action in subrogation of the elderly being served by that agency, localize persons with the legal obligation to maintain the elderly, and initiate any legal action for their support (Equity de Puerto Rico, 1984).

Besides the limited legislation for protection of the abused aged, there is an underuse of legal procedures on the part of the elderly or the professionals. Evidence suggests that some elderly victims of abuse refuse to take legal action against an alleged perpetrator because of family values that move them to protect the abuser against punishment or the liability of fear of retaliation. Other possible reasons may lie in the attitudes or level of experience of the professionals handling the situations.

CONCLUSIONS AND RECOMMENDATIONS

The population growth that some have called the "population revolution" will exert considerable pressure on the delivery system. Great creativity will be needed to adapt the existing services to changes in lifestyles, expectations, and perspectives of our future elderly population. Older adults who are potential or actual victims of elder mistreatment can be better protected from unnecessary suffering if a wide range of human-service agencies and professionals become involved. Because elder mistreatment includes such a broad range of circumstances—physical, psychological, sociological, and legal—the more specialists are involved in the process, the more likely mistreatment will be detected and prevented.

Sound planning must begin with the recognition that the aging experience is heterogeneous. Our health and social services must therefore satisfy the demands of fragile and high-risk elderly persons who suffer serious and disabling chronic health problems, as well as the needs of those family members who are willing to help them. These factors might place the elderly at risk of being abused or neglected. Service providers need to be aware that most families are willing to help their aged members but may need substantial support and specific strategies to provide care. Furthermore, human-service professionals must be alert and knowledgeable about appropriate interventions to be applied in situations in which elderly abuse is suspected. Families whose older members require continuous and special care are likely to experience stress, particularly if they lack outside help. Lack of help could lead to mistreatment, abuse, or negligence in some family settings.

At present, elderly Puerto Ricans who need long-term care rely heavily on their families for assistance, more so than other elderly people. The effect of the economic, physical, and emotional burdens of caregiving borne by these families is unclear. The tendency for the Puerto Rican elderly to live with relatives either in their households or in a relative's home leads to the need for service modalities that incorporate the family into the maintenance and treatment of the aged. This includes putting emphasis on facilitating family caregiving, particularly through in-home assistance and provision of respite care. Preventive measures are one of the best alternatives to elder abuse. There should also be emphasis on the strengthening of community support systems which facilitate a better quality of life.

The existence of protective laws substantiates the value of all individuals to society, and society's commitment to protect vulnerable older people. This should be a concern addressed by Puerto Rican legislation. Furthermore, the weakness of the actual elder-protective legislation should not imply that these persons should be abandoned by service-delivery agencies.

Finally, it is important for all of us, particularly professionals, practitioners, researchers, and policy makers, to understand that the growing ethnic diversity of the United States will require a more systematic appreciation of cultural variables. The lack of information focused on elder abuse among ethnic and racial minorities can lead to misinterpretations that may restrict the abilities of practitioners and researchers to address this issue and make the task of developing services more complex. Adequate information will help to assure that the services for the future elderly population will be more accessible, more sensitive to their needs, and therefore more effective.

REFERENCES

Arroyo, N., Arroyo; E., Aybar, N., Carrión, L., Reyes, F., Rodríguez, Y., & Torres, M. (1992). *El Maltrato a Envejecientes en Puerto Rico (Elder Abuse in Puerto Rico)*. Unpublished Masters Thesis, Graduate School of Social Work, University of Puerto Rico, San Juan.

Baba, J., Colón, M., & Cruz, C. (1996). *Violencia conyugal y la adultez tardía (Domestic violence and late adulthood)*. Unpublished Masters Thesis, Graduate School of Social Work, University of Puerto Rico, San Juan.

Blakely, B., & Dolon, R. (1989). Elder abuse and neglect: A study of adult protective service workers in the United States. *Journal of Elder Abuse & Neglect, 1*(3), 31–49.

Block, M., & Sinnott, J. (1979). *The battered elder syndrome: An exploratory study*. College Park: University of Maryland, Center on Aging.

Brink, T. L. (1979). *Geriatric Psychotherapy*. New York: Human Sciences Press.

Calero, M. S. (1989, June 10). Cierran 21 asilos de ancianos (21 nursing homes ordered closed). *El Mundo*, p. 9.

Commonwealth of Puerto Rico, Junta de Planificación. (1994a). Informe Económico de la población de edad avanzada (Economic report on the aged population). *Boletin Social, 2*(3), 5.

Commonwealth of Puerto Rico, Policía de Puerto Rico. (1994b). *Estadísticas de incidentes de violencia doméstica por edad de víctimas y agresores (Domestic violence statistics by age, victim, and aggression)*. San Juan, PR: División de Estadísticas.

Cruz-López, M., & Pearson, E. (1985). The support needs and resources of Puerto Rican elders. *The Gerontologist, 25*(5), 483–487.

Equity de Puerto Rico. (1984). *Leyes y Resoluciones de Puerto Rico (Laws and Resolutions of Puerto Rico)* (pp. 75–79). 4ta. Sesión Ordinaria, Novena Asamblea Legislativa, San Juan, PR.

Fitzpatrick, J. (1981). *The Puerto Rican family*. In C. Mindel & R. Habenstein (Eds.), *Ethnic Families in America* (pp. 189–215). New York: Elsevier North Holland.

Governor's Office for the Aged. (1996). *Informe Anual del Programa de Ombudsman de cuidado de larga duración (Ombudsman for Long Term Care Annual Report)*. San Juan, PR: Author.

Johnson, T. (1991). *Elder mistreatment: Deciding who is at risk*. New York: Greenwood Press.

Lau, E., & Kosberg, J. (1979). Abuse of the elderly by informal care givers. *Aging, 229*, 10–15.

Leyes de Puerto Rico. (1986). *Leyes Anotadas de Puerto Rico (Annotated Laws of Puerto Rico)*. Ley 121 del 12 de julio, (public Law 121 of July 12), (8)341–347.

Muñoz, M. (1985). *El maltrato a ancianos en la familia (Elder mistreatment in the family)*. Unpublished Masters Thesis, Faculty of Education, University of Puerto Rico, San Juan.

Palmore, E. (1990). *Ageism: Negative and positive*. New York: Springer Publishing Company.

Pillemer, K., & Fenkelhor, D. (1988). The prevalence of elder abuse: A random sample survey. *The Gerontologist, 28*(3), 51–57.

Ramos-Tossas, H. (1991). *Indicadores de Maltrato en una población de hombres y mujeres viejos en los centros de cuidado prolongado y cuidado diurno en la ciudad de Ponce (Indicators of mistreatment in a population of elderly men and women in the city of Ponce)*. Unpublished Doctoral Dissertation, Centro de Estudios Caribeños, San Juan, PR.

Rivera-Ramos, A. N. (1991). *Hacia una psicoterapia para el Puertorriqueño (Toward a psychotherapy for Puerto Ricans)*. Río Piedras: Editorial Edil.

Sánchez-Ayendez, M. (1986). *Puerto Rican Elderly Women: Shared Meaning and Informal Supportive Networks*. In J. B. Cole (Ed.), *All American women: Lines that divide and ties that bind*. New York: The Free Press.

Sánchez, C. (1989). Informal Support Systems of Widows over 60 in Puerto Rico. In Pan American Health Organization and American Association of Retired Persons (Ed.). *Mid-life and older women in Latin America and the Caribbean.* Washington, DC: P.A.H.O. and A.A.R.P.

Sánchez, C. (1992). Mental health issues: The elderly Hispanic. *Journal of Geriatric Psychiatry, 25*(1), 25–30.

U.S. Department of Commerce, Census Bureau. (1990). *Censo de Población y Vivienda de Puerto Rico (Puerto Rico's housing and population census).* Washington, DC: Author.

U.S. District Court. (1990). District of Puerto Rico Civil No. 90-2335 (JAF).

Part Three

Elder Abuse in Asian American Communities

Chapter 8

Elder Abuse and Neglect Among the Korean Elderly in the United States

Ailee Moon

Mrs. Park was 61 years old when she came to the United States with her 27-year-old son Sung in 1979, a year after her husband's death, to join her daughter living in Minneapolis, Minnesota. Her daughter Nancy married a U.S. citizen when he was on duty with the U.S. Army in Korea in the late 1960s. Nancy followed her husband to the United States, became an American citizen, and brought her family to the United States.

Mrs. Park and Nancy hoped that Sung, the only son in the family, who had experienced many problems at school and held various jobs in Korea, would establish a new, productive life in the United States. However, with limited English-speaking ability and job skills, it was difficult for Sung to find a satisfying job. Even when he was employed, it did not last for more than a couple of months. After a period of time, Sung refused to get a job and wanted to start his own business. Mrs. Park gave him all the money she had hoping that he would succeed this time. His restaurant business went bankrupt after only 2 years. Mrs. Park became dependent on Supplemental Security Income (SSI) and moved into a government-subsidized senior-citizen apartment. Reluctant to find a job, Sung began to drink heavily and often asked his mother for money. Meanwhile, Nancy gave up on her brother and refused to see him anymore.

The first day of every month, Sung would take Mrs. Park to the bank to cash her SSI check. He would take most of her money and give her only $50 to live on for the month. Some of Mrs. Park's Korean neighbors living in the same building found out why she always looked sad and hungry. They would occasionally invite Mrs. Park to their apartments for meals.

Her neighbors did not know how else to help Mrs. Park, and nobody wanted to get involved with her family problems. Consequently, no one called for outside help to try to save her from further exploitation and depression. Mrs. Park became weaker and weaker and died in the street on her way to get a free package of dry, canned food in 1989. According to her neighbors, Mrs. Park died from malnutrition and depression.

Mr. Kim and his wife came to the United States in 1982 to help their son Min who had just bought a dry cleaning business. Mr. Kim had retired at the age of 60 as a high-school vice-principal in Korea. Mr. Kim, along with his son and daughter-in-

109

law, worked at the cleaners almost 12 hours a day, 6 days a week. Mrs. Kim, 59 years of age at the time, became responsible for babysitting her two grandchildren, and for cooking, washing, and cleaning the apartment in which they all lived. After 4 years with the help of his parents, Min was able to save enough money to buy his second dry cleaning business. The family moved from a three-bedroom apartment to a five-bedroom house. However, there was little time for social or recreational activities. Even sleep was limited. Mr. and Mrs. Kim were physically tired most of the time. They felt lonely and missed their friends in Korea. Attending a Korean church on Sundays, where they interacted with other Koreans, was the only joy they had in life.

Although Mr. and Mrs. Kim did not mind helping their son, they felt deeply hurt because their son and his family did not seem to care about them. They often felt that Min and his wife only wanted to live with them because they provided free labor at home and at work.

Fourteen years later, Min proposed that Mr. and Mrs. Kim move out of his house and get an apartment for themselves. Their children had grown, and there was no need for a babysitter. Furthermore, Min and his wife complained that living with his parents was uncomfortable for them. Mr. and Mrs. Kim, 74 and 73 years of age, respectively, felt less useful as they became older and weaker. Again, they were hurt by feelings of betrayal, abandonment, and disrespect. They blamed themselves for raising Min improperly.

These true stories, of course, do not portray the lives of most Korean immigrant elderly persons in the United States. Nevertheless, they represent the reality of some devoted and vulnerable Korean immigrant elderly parents. Although most Korean immigrant elders and their adult children grew up in Korea, where the Confucian teaching of filial piety was the social norm governing familial life, filial piety in practice has rapidly become "abandoned and old fashioned" in Korean American families. Mistreatment or exploitation of elderly parents was inconceivable in traditional Korean society. Today, however, elder mistreatment is not a rare phenomenon in Korea nor in the United States among the Korean American community.

Given this background, the purpose of this chapter is to increase the understanding of elder abuse and neglect in families and as a social problem in the Korean American community. The chapter begins with a description of immigration patterns and the demographic profile of Korean American families and the elderly. This is followed by a discussion of research findings on the extent and type of elder abuse in the community, the elder's perceptions and attitudes toward abuse and mistreatment, and their intentions to seek help. Thereafter, implications and conclusions focus on the prevention of elder abuse in the Korean American community.

IMMIGRATION PATTERNS AND DEMOGRAPHIC BACKGROUND

Unlike other Asian American groups, such as the Chinese, Japanese, and Filipinos, who have a relatively long immigration history, it was only after the passage of the Immigration and Naturalization Act of 1965 that Koreans began to immigrate to the United States in large numbers. The immigration pattern of most Korean families begins with adult children establishing residence in the United States. Thereafter, they bring their parents, who initially live with their children (Chang & Moon, 1997). This pattern, combined with a relatively short history of immigration, suggests that many elderly Koreans in the United States were already older when they left Korea, and most of them are monolingual, speaking only Korean.

Due to the massive influx of Korean immigrants in the past three decades, Korean Americans are one of the fastest growing ethnic groups in the United States. The 1990 census counted 798,848 Korean Americans, a 125% increase since 1980 (U.S. Bureau of the Census, 1994). However, the actual number, including those who are undocumented and those who did not participate in the Census, is estimated to exceed 1 million (Kim, 1995; Min & Song, 1998). Census data also revealed that in 1990, 4.4% of the Korean American population, or 35,247 Korean Americans, were 65 years of age or older (U.S. Bureau of the Census, 1994). This number represents a 309% increase since 1980. In 1990, 92% of these elders were foreign born, the majority in Korea. Fifty-eight percent came to the United States in the 1980s, and 63% were women (Young & Gu, 1995).

Although both adult children and their parents initially face similar adjustment problems in the United States, such as language barriers, cultural differences, employment difficulties, and an unfamiliarity with economic and social-service systems, it is generally much harder and takes longer for elderly immigrants to accommodate to the new environment (Kim, Moon, & Shin, 1997). Under these circumstances, most immigrant elders feel insecure and powerless and come to depend on their children for many of the things they did for themselves in Korea, including transportation, making medical appointments, and taking care of other personal business. As a consequence, many of these elders experience a declining status in the family and become vulnerable to mistreatment and exploitation by their children (Chang & Moon, 1997). In addition, due to language and cultural barriers, most of their social activities and contacts tend to be confined to the Korean American community.

THE EXTENT AND TYPE OF ELDER ABUSE AND NEGLECT

A recent study (Chang & Moon, 1997) suggests that a considerable number of Korean immigrant elders have been subjected to elder abuse and neglect, mostly perpetrated by their own family members. When 100 Korean immigrant elderly respondents were asked about elder abuse, 34 respondents (34%) indicated seeing or hearing about at least one incident of Korean American elder abuse that had occurred among their kin, friends, or other social circles during the past 12 months. They also described 46 incidents that they defined as elder abuse, with 8 respondents reporting 2 or more episodes. The study revealed that financial exploitation was the most frequent type of elder abuse. Furthermore, 11 out of 17 elders reported incidents of financial abuse that involved a son taking his elderly parents' SSI benefits.

The finding that most incidents of financial abuse involved adult sons may be explained by the long history of the traditional patriarchal property transfer system in Korean families. Under this system, sons, even after marriage, enjoy almost exclusive inheritance rights; married daughters are no longer considered family members and receive no inheritance from their family of origin (Lee, 1989, cited in Chang & Moon, 1997). The rigidity of traditional inheritance norms in Korea has softened somewhat since the passage of the 1989 Korean Family Law, which in principle grants all children, including married daughters, equal inheritance rights in the absence of the parent's will. However, the long-standing precedent of sons' entitlement to family wealth and property still prevails in both Korean and Korean American families (The Korean Times, 1989). This tradition, when abused, has tended to promote adult sons' financial dependence on and exploitation of their parents (Chang & Moon, 1997).

The common theme of the second-most frequently reported type of elder abuse, psychological abuse, was a lack of respect for and inappropriate treatment of elders by family members. The cases most frequently involved a daughter-in-law disrespecting or treating her mother-in-law improperly. Specific incidents included a daughter-in-law's direct expression of disagreement with the mother-in-law or refusal to eat or talk with her mother-in-law living in the same house, and an adult son and his wife being "too cold" to his elderly parents as indicated by their tone of voice and minimal interaction with the parents (Chang & Moon, 1997). Interestingly, in data from another study's findings (Moon et al., 1998), over 90% of the Korean immigrant elders surveyed indicated that psychological abuse is as hurtful as physical abuse. It is notable that although 7 of 13 identified perpetrators of psychological abuse were daughters-in-law, no sons-in-law or daughters were specifically implicated in any abuse (Chang & Moon, 1997). This partially reflects traditional Korean patriarchal norms, which assign daughters-in-law the lowest family status with the expectation that they perform all household tasks and caregiving responsibilities for elderly parents.

Elderly Korean parents, who are bound by traditions that are particularly harsh on daughters-in-law, might easily view some behaviors that deviate substantially from expectations as abuse. Conversely, sons-in-law are generally considered a "permanent guest" in the traditional Korean family and treated with lavish, yet courteous hospitality by their parents-in-law, with few expectations for them to perform any filial services for their parents-in-law (Lee, 1989).

Chang & Moon (1997) categorized eight separate reported incidents of elder abuse, which involved neglect or psychological abuse, as culturally specific because the respondents' perceptions of these incidents as abuse can be better understood in the context of Korean traditional norms for family and parent–child relationships. Some culturally specific incidents of maltreatment involved an adult son and his wife who did not want to live with his elderly parents, a lack of contact by adult children, placing a frail elderly parent in a nursing home, and adult children delegating caregiving responsibilities for their frail elderly parents to outside helpers.

Whether these incidents specific to Korean culture also would be defined and reported as abuse by White or other ethnic minority elderly populations is unknown. However, in examining the nature of some of the reported psychological and culturally specific elder abuse incidents, the authors pointed out that many elderly Korean respondents tended to apply traditional Korean norms and expectations in their judgment of what constitutes elder abuse (Chang & Moon, 1997).

Traditional filial piety dictates that an adult son, especially the oldest, and his family live with his parents in the same household. It is also expected that the daughter-in-law perform all household tasks and caregiving responsibilities for her parents-in-law with politeness and sincerity (Lee, 1989). Accordingly, some respondents considered an adult son and his wife who were unwilling to provide such living and caretaking arrangements culpable (Chang and Moon, 1997). The expectation of adult children who lived separately from their elderly parents was to fulfill filial responsibilities partially through frequent contacts via visits or telephone calls. Thus, infrequent contact meant denial of basic filial responsibilities. Neglect was not only regarded as disappointing but considered abusive.

Chang and Moon also classified six reported incidents of elder abuse as neglect. Neglect incidents included abandonment of an elderly mother in a motel room, pressuring elderly parents to move out of their children's house, and an adult child's failure to tend to the daily needs of their frail elderly parents (ibid.). Most reported incidents of neglect involved an adult child's denial of their basic caretaking responsibilities and the insecure and vulnerable status of Korean immigrant elders in a new environment. Additionally, there were 2 reported incidents of physical abuse that involved pushing and battering by daughters-in-law. There were no reported incidents of sexual abuse in this study.

All reported incidents of abuse and neglect implicated the victim's immediate family or relatives, particularly sons and their wives. This appears to be a reflection of the lives of most Korean immigrant elderly, who have little or no contact or interaction with people outside the family. This lack of interaction is due mainly to language and cultural barriers. However, it is also possible that Korean immigrant elders tend to perceive and define elder abuse only within the context of family relations, particularly the parent–child relationship. This is based on the traditional Korean norms of filial piety. The study clearly indicates the centrality of "children" in the lives and well-being of Korean immigrant elders, regardless of whether they live with their children or not.

PERCEPTIONS OF AND ATTITUDES TOWARD ELDER ABUSE AND NEGLECT

In a three-group comparison study of perceptions of elder abuse, Moon and Williams (1993) found that Korean immigrant elderly respondents tend to be less sensitive to or more tolerant of potentially abusive situations, compared with Caucasians and African Americans. Respondents were asked for their perceptions about 13 different scenarios that covered various dimensions of elder mistreatment and neglect, including physical, psychological, verbal, sexual, medical, and financial abuse. The overall average percentage of the respondents who perceived each of the 13 scenarios as abusive was lowest among Koreans at 50%, followed by 67% among Caucasians and 73% for African Americans.

One of the most striking group differences was found in respondents' judgments regarding a scenario that involved a daughter (daughter-in-law for Korean respondents) who was frustrated by her mother's (mother-in-law's) embarrassing behavior whenever the daughter invited guests over. In order to control her mother's behavior, the daughter gave the elderly woman tranquilizers but falsely told her that it was prescribed medication. Only 10% of the Korean respondents viewed the scenario as abusive, whereas 36% and 63% of the Caucasian and African American respondents, respectively, regarded the situation as abusive.

Another study by Moon (1996) revealed that although most Korean immigrant elders viewed physical and verbal abuses as unacceptable behavior, many of them were tolerant and accepting of behavior that could be considered financial exploitation by family members. For example, only 12% of the respondents agreed that "it is okay for adult children to yell at their elderly parents," and just 3% agreed that "among elderly couples, occasional battering of a spouse is acceptable behavior." On the other hand, 55% of the Korean sample agreed that "when adult children borrow money from their parents, it is okay not to pay it back, even if the parents want the money back." Thirty-two percent also agreed that "among elderly couples, it is all right if a husband does not allow his wife access to the family's financial resources." The study also uncovered the tendency among some of the Korean immigrant elderly to blame the victim of elder abuse: Fifty-six percent of the respondents agreed that "some elderly people are abused or mistreated because they did something wrong to deserve it."

HELP-SEEKING BEHAVIORS AND ATTITUDES ABOUT REPORTING ELDER ABUSE

According to the findings of the study by Moon and Williams (1993), whether or not an elderly person perceived a situation as abusive or problematic was a strong predictor of their intention to seek help. The data revealed that almost two thirds of the respondents who perceived the scenarios as abusive expressed their intention to seek help had they been the elder in the scenarios, whereas about one third of those who did not perceive the situations as abusive would still seek help.

Given this finding, in conjunction with the discovery that Korean respondents were significantly less likely to perceive the same situations as abusive, it is not surprising that Korean elderly respondents were significantly less likely to seek help compared with the other two groups. Only 36% of the Koreans, as compared with 62% of the Caucasians and 63% of the African Americans, would have sought help had they been the elder in the scenarios.

Moon and Williams (1993) also found that Korean elderly were much more likely to seek help from informal sources (e.g., relatives, friends, and pastors) than elders in the other two groups. Among the respondents who reported that they would seek help, Koreans reported that they would turn to informal rather than formal sources of help (e.g., the police and legal or social-service agencies) 74% of the time. This rate is substantially higher than their African American and Caucasian American counterparts at 36% and 60%, respectively.

There are many factors that seem to contribute to the low use of formal help or services by Korean immigrant elders including Korean values that discourage seeking help from strangers or others outside of the family; norms associated with shame and saving face; language barriers; social alienation; institutional, organizational, and cultural barriers; and the lack of knowledge about available formal services (Chang & Moon, 1997; Koh & Bell, 1987; Moon, Lubben, & Villa, 1998; Moon & Williams, 1993). One recent study found extremely low levels of awareness and utilization of community-based, long-term healthcare and social services among elderly Korean Americans, suggesting from a practical standpoint that most of these services hardly exist for them (Moon, Lubben, & Villa, 1998). With the exception of senior citizen centers and transportation services, an average of only 2.3% of 223 Korean American respondents residing in Los Angeles County, as opposed to 47.1% of 201 non-Hispanic whites, had ever heard of the other 13 elderly services, including homemakers, visiting nurses, adult daycare, legal services, hospices, and meals-on-wheels services.

In addition to their reluctance to seek help for themselves in the event of elder abuse, research findings suggest that Korean immigrant elders are highly unlikely to intervene or seek outside help on behalf of other elders who are being abused (Moon, 1996). Specifically, 74% of 99 Korean elders surveyed indicated that if an elderly person is being abused or mistreated by a family member, individuals outside the family should not intervene. Similarly, only 31% agreed that if one discovers that an elderly neighbor is being abused by his or her children, the abuse should be reported to the authorities, such as the police department and social-service agencies.

IMPLICATIONS AND CONCLUSION

The sad stories of Mrs. Park and Mr. and Mrs. Kim portray the most common types of elder abuse and related issues in the Korean American community: exploitation of labor and finances of elderly parents, neglect of their emotional, social, and functional needs (e.g., transportation, language, and shopping) by adult children, elderly parents' willingness to sacrifice themselves for their children, the elderly's tolerance of potentially abusive situations, and their reluctance to seek help for themselves or other elders who are subject to abuse or mistreatment.

Furthermore, empirical research on elder abuse in the Korean American community, although limited, clearly suggests that elder abuse and neglect is not a rare phenomenon: Rather, it affects a considerable number of Korean elderly. In fact, some abuse incidents identified by Korean elders in previous studies present serious threats to the individual's basic human needs, including the physical and mental health of victimized Korean elders. For example, taking SSI money from poor elderly parents, forcing them out of their own residence, and having them work excessive hours in a family-owned business could endanger their lives.

However, as evident in the tragic story of Mrs. Park and previous research findings, there are many factors that impede their assistance. These factors include Korean elders' tendency to keep family problems to themselves, their reluctance to seek help outside of the family for themselves and for others subject to abuse by family members, language barriers in accessing social services and their unfamiliarity with adult protective services (Chang & Moon, 1997).

The two major reasons given by Korean immigrant elders for not talking to anyone about an abusive situation were their reluctance to reveal their "family shame" to others and fear of creating conflict among their children and relatives (Moon & Williams, 1993). In this regard, Moon and Williams stated:

> It can be argued that their desire to maintain peace in the family at the expense of their suffering must be understood and respected in the context of their culture, which emphasizes family harmony over individual well-being, which denotes some degree of human suffering as a virtue, and which dictates enduring and keeping one's problem to oneself, rather than exposing the problem to others, as a desirable behavior. One can argue, on the other hand, that it goes beyond the reason of culture to ignore the consequent likelihood of the group being at a high risk of elder abuse. (p. 393).

Based on personal observations and conversations with a number of Korean immigrant elderly, this author is inclined to believe that some Korean immigrant elders who are subject to obvious abuse or neglect do not choose to remain in their abusive situations based on an informed decision. Rather, they are unaware of potentially helpful services that provide alternatives to their abusive situations. This is coupled with the misconception that seeking outside help would only result in punishing the perpetrators, who are most likely their own children, without helping the elders or improving their situations.

Therefore, for effective intervention and prevention of elder abuse, social-service agencies, especially Adult Protective Service and Korean American community-based agencies, need to engage in active outreach and public educational efforts to inform Korean Americans, particularly the elderly and their families. This population needs to be educated about the meaning of elder abuse in this country, including its legal implications, reporting requirements, and the types, causes, and consequences of elder abuse.

Most important, this population needs to be informed about the alternatives to suffering silently that are available. Moreover, they need to understand how the available services can help the perpetrator and the victim, as well as how to access the services. Considering that most Korean immigrant elders are monolingual speakers of Korean, the use of Korean American ethnic media and community-based organizations is crucial for effective outreach and public education efforts.

Finally, as evidenced by the psychological and culturally specific abuse incidents discussed previously here, most Korean elders tend to define and identify elder abuse within the context of family relationships, based mostly on the traditional norm for the parent–child relationships. The centrality of "children" in Korean elders' lives and well-being further suggests that the Korean American community, including churches, social clubs, and social-service agencies, can contribute to mitigating and preventing elder mistreatment and neglect by instituting programs that promote interactions and improve relationships between elderly parents and their adult children's families.

In conclusion, for many elderly Koreans in the United States, who have endured hardships and sacrificed for their children, the rejection of the duties of filial piety, justified with excuses of acculturation to American ways of life or "being too busy to take care of parents," seems like a curse. Thus, in the long run, a community-wide movement to revitalize, modernize, and maintain the traditional norm of filial piety will be the most effective means of prevention of elder abuse and neglect, because the practice of filial piety appears to be too valuable a tradition to bury.

REFERENCES

Chang, J., & Moon, A. (1997). Korean American elderly's knowledge and perceptions of elder abuse: A qualitative analysis of cultural factors. *Journal of Multicultural Social Work, 6*(1–2), 139–155.

Kim, J. H., Moon, A., & Shin, H. S. (1997). Elderly Korean American women living in two cultures. In Y. Song & A. Moon (Eds.), *Korean American women living in two cultures* (pp. 191–204). Los Angeles: Academia Koreana, Keimyung-Baylo University.

Kim, N. (1995). Who are the Korean Americans? In S. Gall & I. Natividad (Eds.), *The Asian American almanac: A reference work on Asians in the United States.* Detroit: Gale.

Koh, J. Y., & Bell, W. G. (1987). Korean elders in the United States: Intergenerational relations and living arrangements. *The Gerontologist, 27,* 66–71.

Lee, K. K. (1989). *An analysis of the structure of the Korean family (Han Kuk Ka Jok Eui Ku Jo Pun Suk),* 11th ed. Seoul: Il-Ji Publishing Co.

Min, P. & Song, Y. (1998). The Post-1965 Korean immigrants: Their characteristics and settlement patterns. In Y. Song & A. Moon (Eds.), *Korean American women from tradition to modern feminism* (pp. 45–64). Westport, CT: Greenwood Publishing Co.

Moon, A. (1996). *Attitudes towards elder mistreatment and reporting among Korean American elders.* Unpublished data.

Moon, A., Tomita, S., Talamantes, M., Brown, A., Sanchez, Y., Benton, D., Sanchez, C., & Kim, S. (1998). *A multicultural study of attitudes towards elder mistreatment and reporting.* Research report submitted to the National Center on Elder Abuse.

Moon, A., Lubben, J. E., & Villa, V. (1998). Awareness and utilization of community long-term care services by elderly Korean and non-Hispanic White Americans. *The Gerontologist, 38,* 309–316.

Moon, A., & Williams, O. (1993). Perception of elder abuse and help-seeking patterns among African American, Caucasian American, and Korean-American elderly women. *The Gerontologist, 33,* 386–395. *The Korea Times* (December 30, 1989). Revised family laws' impact on Korean family.

U.S. Bureau of the Census. (1994). *Characteristics of the Asian and Pacific Islander population in the United States*. 1990 Census of Population of Housing. (Subject Summary Tape File SSTF 5).

Young, J. J., & Gu, N. (1995). *Demographic and socio-economic characteristics of elderly Asian and Pacific Island Americans*. Seattle, WA: National Asian Pacific Center on Aging.

Chapter 9

Exploration of Elder Mistreatment Among the Japanese

Susan K. Tomita

Within the context of elder mistreatment, little attention has been paid to ethnicity and cultural norms, that is, standards for behavior that are learned from and shared with others within a subgroup (Straus, 1974b), as independent or causal variables. So far, in the research literature, the majority of the victims have been reported to be Caucasian females, with little being said about cultural and ethnic-group differences (Block & Sinott, 1979; Lau & Kosberg, 1979; Phillips, 1983; Pillemer, 1986; Godkin, Wolf, & Pillemer, 1989).

Caucasians dominate the victim category in the reported data but this may be due to their greater usage of social-service agencies, whose staff are knowledgeable about elder mistreatment, and who make these cases known to investigating agencies and researchers. At this time, it is impossible to conclude that elder mistreatment is not a problem among groups other than Caucasian elderly. Not much is known about how elder mistreatment manifests itself among different groups and if the prevalence of elder mistreatment is higher or lower in these groups. A few studies conducted so far indicate that elder mistreatment is not confined to a few countries or to certain ethnic groups (Anetzberger, Korbin, & Tomita, 1996; Glascock & Feinman, 1981; Kosberg & Garcia, 1995; Reinharz, 1986), and recently it has been reported among African Americans (Griffin, 1994), Native Americans (Brown, 1989; Maxwell & Maxwell, 1992), and the Japanese (Kaneko & Yamada, 1990).

These preliminary studies have contributed a great deal to the idea that the study of elder mistreatment cannot be confined to Western–Caucasian interpretations, that if it were studied in depth among different groups, it would no longer be possible to discuss it in general terms. Elder mistreatment may mean different things to different groups, with age and gender of victims and perpetrators also making a significant difference. This chapter reports on one study that examined the role that cultural patterns may play in the problem of elder mistreatment.

PURPOSE OF STUDY

A primary purpose of this study was to explore the existence of domestic violence, and more specifically elder mistreatment, among Japanese Americans. Questions developed to guide the study were: What are the manifestations of elder mistreatment among Japanese Americans? What cultural variables contribute to elder mistreatment among Japanese Americans? Under what circumstances or conditions does it occur, and what are the consequences of these acts? A decision was made to frame the study within a broad context of domestic violence because it was unclear whether any information would be obtained if the study attempted to have people respond only to the issue of elder mistreatment. Taking an inclusive rather than exclusive approach, a plan was made to approach the topic of conflict in general, then introduce the topic of elder mistreatment. Related to this objective is the exploration of possible links between cultural variables, manifestations of elder mistreatment, and what is done about the mistreatment. Within the context of elder mistreatment, the paucity of information on any group other than Caucasians makes the study of elder mistreatment of the Japanese a potentially fruitful area to pursue. At this point in time, however, it would be premature to conduct quantitative research on the Japanese, utilizing existing definitions of mistreatment and existing measurement tools. Assuming that some elder-mistreatment victims suffer from subtle and often nonphysical forms of mistreatment, Western tools that measure only physical and verbal aggression (Pillemer & Finkelhor, 1988; Straus, 1979), miss other forms of elder mistreatment such as financial or material abuse, abandonment, and covert actions such as silence and avoidance. Not enough is known about domestic violence in general among Japanese Americans, and in order to advance the field, some exploratory research is the first order. It then may be possible to better develop questionnaires and inventories that capture the Japanese American definitions of mistreatment.

Another goal of this study was to conceptualize new theoretical explanations through a grounded theory methodology that may fuel ongoing research. Other explanations, stemming from the catharsis and aggression theories of violence (Berkowitz, 1983; Straus, 1974a) and the negative relationship between intellectualization, an indicator of socioeconomic status of the family, and physical aggression (Straus, 1974a) also may be totally inadequate for contexts or situations in which perpetrators subtly and indefinitely commit acts that keep an elder miserable and passive, and that never culminate in physical or verbal aggression. Although a high level of aggression exists in American society (Gelles & Straus, 1988; Straus, 1974a), the use of physical force among Japanese families may be such a strong violation of norms that it occurs infrequently and is never reported. Subsequently, to conclude that domestic violence in general and elder mistreatment in particular are not problems among the Japanese without exploring alternative manifestations and cultural variables affecting disclosure would be a form of premature closure on the issue.

METHODOLOGY

Grounded Theory

The main method used to explore elder mistreatment in this study is based on grounded theory (Glaser, 1978, 1992; Glaser & Strauss, 1967; Strauss, 1987; Strauss & Corbin, 1990), a qualitative approach that not only studies a phenomenon of interest but also develops a theory or theories that are inductively derived from studying the subject. Glaser and Strauss base their work on inductive qualitative analysis and regard grounded theory as an action- and interaction-oriented method of theory building that tries to capture much of the complexity and movement in the subject of interest. Relevant data are collected and then grouped and given conceptual labels or themes. These concepts are related by means of relationship statements. Codeable data considered appropriate for theory building are secondary sources such as literature, field notes, or transcribed audio tapes of interviews, quotes, and statements. Through a method of constant comparative analysis of data and the categories, and between and within the categories, the data are raised to a conceptual level. The categories are developed in terms of their properties and dimensions, and connections are made between the categories leading to the development of a paradigmatic model and ultimately, through moving between inductive and deductive thinking, to generation of hypotheses and a theory that is grounded in this process (Glaser & Strauss, 1967, pp. 1–18).

Theoretical Sampling Process

The first phase of this study entailed secondary data analysis of transcriptions of two focus groups on elder mistreatment conducted among Japanese Americans, or *Nikkei*, and of interviews of three Japanese American victims of elder mistreatment residing in Hawaii who were reported to Adult Protective Services. These three interviews were part of a research study on elder mistreatment conducted by Pillemer and Wolf. The focus groups were part of a larger project comparing definitions of elder mistreatment among and between old and younger African Americans, Caucasians, Puerto Rican Americans, and Japanese Americans (Anetzberger, Korbin, & Tomita, 1996). The Japanese American group met in Seattle; the other groups met in Cleveland, Ohio.

The second phase and greater part of this study consisted of two 3-hour semistructured interviews of 22 Japanese in Seattle and in Hawaii who were willing to share their recollections and understanding of conflict and elder mistreatment in their families and communities. Theoretical or nonstatistical sampling techniques were applied; that is, the evolving theory determined which samples of populations, incidents, events, and activities were needed to make comparisons between and among these samples. All subjects were guaranteed anonymity and asked to sign an informed consent form that was approved by the University of Washington Human Subjects Committee.

Given the norm of male dominance among the Japanese and assuming that victims of mistreatment most likely would be older women, the initial qualifications for being interviewed were to be elderly (defined as 65 years of age or older), female, and of Japanese ancestry. Theoretical sampling guidelines precluded preselection of the entire sample population. The sampling method consisted of interviewing a few individuals at a time, transcribing and when necessary translating into English the recorded interviews, coding the transcripts, studying the coded transcripts, and writing memos to organize the information conceptually, categorically, and empirically.

The interview process was modified from asking questions in a general manner to asking pointed questions about conflict and mistreatment after those interviewed early on were not forthcoming with information that was felt intuitively to be available. In addition, the sample population was expanded to include both males and females of different ages in order to obtain more depth and variation on the subject. Also, because of the difficulty in getting the participants to discuss conflict coping methods, the focus of this project was expanded to answer questions about why mistreatment is not revealed, adding them to the original questions regarding the existence and manifestations of interpersonal conflict and elder mistreatment. The main questions added were: What cultural and structural factors encourage the Japanese to seek help or keep the Japanese from seeking help for interpersonal conflict? What is distinct about the Japanese culture that makes family conflict and elder mistreatment difficult topics to discuss and resolve? Would younger Japanese who were more acculturated to Western ways be more likely to report family conflict and seek help to resolve it?

The comments made by the focus-group members, the Adult Protective Services cases, and the 22 individual participants comprised the qualitative data from which categories were developed and, in turn, on which the theoretical concepts were built.

Reliability and Validity of the Qualitative Data

Following Swanson-Kauffman's (1986) qualitative research methodology, the content validity of the semistructured interview schedule was addressed by asking each participant at the end of the interview if anything was omitted. No additional questions were suggested at the time of the interviews. Five interviewees were telephoned approximately 1 year later to reflect on the interview and to ask again if they had suggestions for the interview schedule, which had been mailed to them prior to the telephone call. One person said she liked the open-ended questions that allowed her to talk without restriction but did not know if all interviewees were comfortable with the format. Another participant stated that everyone could have been asked, "What will you do when you are older, when you become ill?" She stated that anticipating frailty in the future, she and her friends did not want to enter a nursing home and did not want to be dependent on their children. This question may have revealed more about the elder's and the grown children's expectations of each other. A third stated that he had more to share, especially regarding the sources of conflict. He spoke as if the completed interview had been a warm-up exercise; now he was ready to reveal much more, and he invited this interviewer to interview him again. His perception was that the conflict issues of *Issei* (first-generation Japanese Americans) couples were different from those of the *Issei* and *Nisei* (second-generation Japanese Americans) who lived together, and that many of the conflicts were based on the children and financial issues. The remaining two did not have any suggestions for the interview schedule.

Three persons of Japanese ancestry acted as raters and reviewed the materials containing the data analysis. Two of them were born and raised in Japan and then came to the United States to obtain doctoral degrees. They have remained in the United States for employment purposes, and are familiar with both Japanese and U.S. cultures. The third rater was a participant who was asked to be involved in the review of the data in order to determine if the study adequately captured the experiences and feelings of Japanese people in conflict situations. Each of the raters was compensated with an honorarium; the amount depended on the number of hours that were spent conducting the review.

Reliability   The interviewer's reliability was assessed by the rater who had the most experience in interviewing research subjects. Based on 3 of the 22 transcripts that were chosen randomly, this rater assessed the degree of the interviewer's effectiveness in helping each participant share his or her thoughts. On a scale of 1 to 5, the interviewer was rated as 3, or average, in two of the interviews, and as 4, or somewhat effective, in the third transcript. For the first transcript, the rater felt that the interviewer was perhaps "a little too eager," causing the participant's answers to become shorter. On the other hand, the rater wondered if the short answers came from the participant's assumption that the interviewer should know that "that's the way it was." Had the participant been left to talk in general terms, the rater wondered if conflict issues would have arisen on their own. In the second transcript, the rater felt that in contrast to the second interview, the interviewer could have been more probing and specific with the participant, who the rater felt tended to stay away from his own personal feelings and experiences. For the third transcript, the interviewer was rated higher, as a 4, because the interview flowed better than the other two. For this interview, in which the participant painfully described an abusive marriage, the rater suggested the addition of "placebo" questions to counterbalance the focus on abuse, questions not necessarily germane to the study, but which asked about a positive or happy aspect of the participant's life in order to lighten up or balance the interview.

Interrater reliability was attempted but not achieved by asking two raters to read the two documents containing the data analysis and then rate a participant's transcript for the presence or absence of the reported categories. One rater checked all of the categories as present in the transcript; the other rater's check list was a more accurate measure of the categories that were present in the transcript. For example, the category of *yoshi*, or the husband marrying into the wife's family, was not present in the transcript but was checked by the first rater as present and by the second rater as absent. Budgetary and time constraints prevented the addition of several more raters who probably would have counteracted the first rater's inaccurate results, which were most likely the result of not following directions correctly. Also, during this section of the rating, the second rater had difficulty differentiating between two categories, "Hide the Problems and Wrongdoings of the Japanese" and "A Community Closed to Outsiders." These need to be revisited and their distinctions made clearer, or they could be collapsed into one category.

   Validity   Construct validity, determining whether those things that were observed were adequately described, named, and related conceptually to one another, was maximized by the grounded theory approach, in which the conceptual categories had to fit and be backed up by the data. The categories could not be developed independently either through hypothesis development or by literature review alone. Construct validity also was confirmed by asking the same two raters and one participant to answer four questions: (1) How close did the study come to obtaining the opinions and experiences of the Japanese with regard to conflict? (2) How close did the study come to obtaining the opinions and experiences of the Japanese with regard to elder mistreatment? (3) How well did the categories that were created capture the opinions and experiences of the participants? (4) How well were the categories related conceptually to one another? Each question was answered by a score on a scale of 1 to 5. For the first question, two of the three raters rated the study with a score of 4, and the third with a score of 5, or as coming close and very close to obtaining the opinions and experiences of the Japanese with regard to conflict. With regard to elder mistreatment, the study was rated by two raters as 4, and the third as 5. Regarding the third question on the created categories, two raters scored the categories as 5, and one as 4. For the fourth question, two rated the categories as 4 and one as 5.

   Raters also offered suggestions about other issues that they believed the study should address. One of the raters believed that a category of self-blame was missing from the study. In blaming themselves, the Japanese often say, *watakushi wa waru katta* (I was bad/wrong), thereby taking responsibility for a negative incident even if there was no wrongdoing. A participant who served as one of the three raters believed that readers would appreciate more information on the differences in retaining traditional values between the *kibei* (Japanese Americans who are schooled in Japan) and non-*kibei*. This opinion was based on his own family situation: His siblings were *kibei* but he was not, and the study's analysis of the categorized social structural and social psychological processes helped him understand some of the sources of their differences.

CORE CATEGORY, DIMENSION, AND CONDITIONS

Utilizing the constant-comparison method, the core category of this study and one of its dimensions were identified. The dimension was then divided into subgroups or conditions. In the transcripts, constant comparisons were made between incidents of conflict, and between incidents and categories into which these incidents fell. Taking an inclusive rather than narrow approach, all situations of conflict were used, not only those referring to elder mistreatment, for two main reasons. First, although this interviewer is Japanese, she was not married to a Japanese community member and is considered an outsider. It was speculated that a focus only on elder mistreatment, a relatively foreign and seldom-discussed concept, and by an outsider, would yield minimal information. As a result, a decision was made to maximize the chances of learning about any aspect of elder mistreatment among the Japanese by purposefully taking a nonspecific and nonthreatening approach. The study focused on conflict in general, to make it as comfortable as possible for the interviewees to volunteer information, including about elder mistreatment, to an outsider. The second reason for focusing on conflict in general was to obtain an abundance of rich and varied data with which an inductive analysis could be conducted. By examining elder mistreatment within this broad context of conflict through the constant-comparison method, particular patterns and processes emerged, and concepts on a more abstract level were created for use in hypothesis development in the area of conflict, including elder mistreatment, among the Japanese. As a result of this approach, the developed categories were not confined to elder mistreatment but were conflict-based.

As the transcripts were read and reread, tentative codes were placed on the side of the sentences in the margins. For example, having read a description of the wife leaving the house for a few hours after an argument with the husband, "leaving home" was written in the margins next to the incident described. The sentences with their related codes in the margins of 27 transcripts were assembled. All sentences related to distancing oneself from the perpetrator were placed in one pile. After reading the sentences and their codes in a pile, the pile was given a general code name. For example, all of the incidents describing self-removing events, such as going to live with a relative for a week, leaving the house for three hours, and going to another room after an argument remained in the pile eventually labeled "Self Removal."

In all, approximately 100 cards were used, each with a category listed on it, and piled on each card were the relevant indicators in sentence form from the transcripts. It became very obvious that certain codes and their data would be eliminated from the study. For example, interviewees' accounts of Japanese historical events, coded as "Japanese History," did not tie in with the major portion of the other categories, which had to do with managing and coping with disagreements and uncomfortable situations.

Core Category: Group Above Self

It became clear what would be the core category, containing a pivotal or main theme that meaningfully and easily integrates all the other categories, emerging repeatedly (Glaser, 1978, p. 95). It was chosen because many of the others seemed to be manifestations or aspects of it, and the subjects' actions and their descriptions of why they did what they did and thought what they thought were due to this core category, which was ultimately labeled *Group Above Self*. Other labels considered for this core category were *Family/Group Loyalty, Groupness, Belongingness, Non-Individuality, No-Self-ness*, and *Self-Sacrifice*. This concept can be applied in the context of the family, a group, or a community and helped to make sense of the behaviors chosen in a variety of conflict situations, some of which were elder mistreatment. A core theme or pattern that emerged from the interviews was the lack of importance of the individual, regardless of age. The self was treated as if he or she were discardable (*suterumono*: *suteru* = throw away, *mono* = item), supported by common terms such as *ubasute* (*uba* = old woman/grandmother, *sute(ru)* = throw away) and *jama no mono* (*jama* = in the way, *mono* = item) that objectify human beings. Group survival and group importance seemed paramount, with the individual being sacrificed on behalf of the group.

Part of this family orientation is rooted historically in the Japanese government's expectation that the community and household were collectively responsible for the conduct of its individual members. In some cases, the entire household was punished for one member's wrong doings and banished from the community. One's survival depended on group conformity (Kuwayama, 1992).

Another category under consideration as the core category was *Power*; that is, many of these categories could be labeled as manifestations of individual power*less*ness. Group Above Self seemed more apt, because after a lifetime of acculturation to think first of family and community, power*less*ness is a given condition and is a *result* of Group Above Self. Shaming the family, feeling ashamed when a son misbehaved, not complaining, and accepting one's fate had a stronger and more logical pull toward wanting to belong to a group than toward a power–powerlessness struggle.

Dimension: Conflict Avoidance and Management

Many of the other categories were interrelated through the core category, Group Above Self. For example, for the sake of the group, family, or community, a member exhibits one of these properties or categories: Never Complain, *Gaman*/Endure, *Enryo*/Hold Back Desires, Silence, Don't Retaliate, Accept Fate, and so on. The quantity of categories that supported Group Above Self was striking. In order to show how they supported Group Above Self, one main dimension was created, *Conflict Avoidance and Management*, in which distinct interactive categories explicated the core category. The categories in this dimension were divided into two subgroup conditions, *Conditions for Conflict Management* and *Consequences of Group Above Self*. The rest of this chapter discusses the conditions related to conflict management.[1]

---

[1] This chapter presents a portion of the study results. The other half of the study on the consequences of Group Above Self is not addressed in this chapter.

Conditions For Conflict Management:
Japanese Norms Supporting Nonindividuality

The categories under this first subgroup on conflict management represent long-standing cultural norms that help to explain why the interviewees manifested otherness instead of promoting their own happiness and safety in conflict situations. Before research on elder mistreatment among the Japanese can proceed, it is important to explain and understand the conditions of the broader forms of conflict; only then do some of the behaviors exhibited under duress by the Japanese, including its elderly, make any sense. Two categories, *Operation of Dual and Multiple Selves* and *Hiding of Individual Problems and Wrongdoing of the Japanese*, will help explain the condition termed *Conflict Management*.

The Operation of Dual and Multiple Selves   The Japanese define themselves in relation to the distance or difference from other people and groups, taking into consideration the other's gender, age, and status before acting in that particular context. Fulfillment is through aesthetic efforts that achieve "the final unity of non-self rather than individualism in a sense of essentialism and consistent identity" (Rosenberger, 1992, p. 13). Some describe the Japanese as two-dimensional; others explain the *multiplicity* of the self. What emerges is a shifting, relational self (Johnson, 1993; Rosenberger, 1992).

Seventeen of the individuals and one of the young focus-group members discussed some aspect of this "we–they" or the split of the private and public self, which is elaborated further in the following sections. The seeming hypocrisy and constant switching between dimensions was experienced by individual 7:

> **Individual 7**: It's a two-faced thing that is hypocritical. [I] can understand the concept, but to experience it is different. Grandma would have a really sweet company voice [speaks in falsetto], a really high, when you start talking Japanese . . . sort of automatic . . . it does feel crazy, sort of divorced from reality . . . and without having the Japanese context, it doesn't make any sense. How could you go from being so angry at one moment then showing this face and acting as if nothing happened . . . [I] saw the hypocritical change, where outsiders were treated as if nothing happened.

Interpreting the Japanese self as multiple, outside of the dual-concept context such as *uchi–soto* (inside–outside), Lebra (1992) provides more insight into the complex makeup of the Japanese self and categorizes the self as interactional, inner, and boundless.

Interactional Self   These three dimensions are overlapping layers. The interactional self has a presentational quality, a surface layer, and is visible and exposed to others. The face is the main locus of information, and there is a sense of immediacy and inescapability within the group or audience; this self is an actor in a social theater. Besides being presentational, the interactional self is also empathetic. This is the intimacy-seeking part, wanting love, trust, support, cooperation;

there is an *interdependence* and *interchangeability* of the self and other, a quality often labeled negatively as "codependent" in Western terms. Among Japanese Americans, family members use expressions such as, "On behalf of my rude son, I apologize," or, "As a surrogate of my mother, I want to express my appreciation for the kindness you have shown her and my family," not distinguishing the self from others within the identified group. Within this context, there is no equivalent of "I" in the Western sense, a fixed point of self, or a consistent identity (Rosenberger, 1992, p. 17). Instead, the self is multiple and variable, often relayed as a "no-self" (Lebra, 1992, p. 111). Lebra (1992, p. 118, n. 5) adds that the self and object world are viewed as joined as opposed to dichotomous, as exemplified by the use of phenomena such as the weather to depict one's moods. These explanations help to interpret the transcripts of individuals 20 and 21, whose interviews were conducted in Japanese. Individual 20 never used the equivalent of the Western "I" when discussing her abusive marriage. She spoke of herself in third person, "*bachan ga...*" (Grandma did...), and, most unforgettably, in metaphorical terms, "*ame ga furimashita*" (it rained) to mean "I cried when he beat me." Similarly, individual 21 would refer to her husband as, "*sono kata ga...*" (That person did...)

Inner Self Lebra's second self, the inner self, is described as occupying the Japanese most of the time. Without the demanding social audience, this self is autonomous and morally superior, representing the person's true and pure nature, localized in the chest and, although less so, in the belly. This spirited self is represented by *kokoro*, or heart. Lebra elaborates, "This association of the kokoro (or inner self) with truthfulness gives rise to the paradoxical notion that the "real" truth is inexpressible. Thus words and speech as means of expression are often regarded as potentially deceptive and false, and silence as indicative of the true *kokoro*" (Lebra, 1992, p. 112). Given this, true feelings are hard to come by with words, and for outsiders it is difficult to tap this part of the Japanese self. Individual 1 attempted to explain this nonexpression of true feelings:

> **Interviewer** (discussing indirect behaviors): So, I am thinking, that when the Japanese are unhappy with somebody, they do something very quietly to show anger. I don't know if you remember things like that.
> **Individual 1**: Nobody shows she is angry.
> **Interviewer**: Nobody shows. Just in your head, but outside, you are smiling?
> **Individual 1**: [Nods yes.]
> **Interviewer**: Really?
> **Individual 1**: Outside, inside, always, outside and inside.

Boundless Self Last, the boundless self, derived from the Buddhist concept of transcendentalism, rests in the *hara* or belly and can help the person get beyond the immobile, trapped self, yet at the same time, the boundless self functions only within the confines of *innen* or *en*, or fate and predestination. Perhaps this is why in many of the transcripts, the women in unhappy situations would explain, "that's the way it was," or, "it was my fate," quietly persevering and, as one of them quoted a saying, "bearing the unbearable."

Hide the Individual Problems and Wrongdoings of the Japanese   The cultural message is to protect the community by not revealing or discussing with outsiders anything that would dishonor it. This hiding of problems and wrongdoings of the Japanese is the second subgroup category under the condition of conflict management. At no time did any of the interviewees mention being aided or supported for speaking up about unpleasantries. On the contrary, most of the interviewees were quite vocal about knowing that it was unacceptable to make any utterances about their own or others' problems and that presenting oneself as happy and untroubled was a high priority. Throughout the transcripts, the word *outsider* was used countless times to mean someone other than oneself, anyone outside the nuclear family, such as a cousin or an in-law. Then fanning out, *outsider* referred to people in one's church, club, or community, and ultimately people other than the Japanese, including the *hakujin* (Caucasians). To the interviewees, the culture supported being unpleasant at home but not in public. One interviewee said his father was "good on the outside, but at home, a tyrant." Looking up the term, *uchi benke–soto benke* (inside–outside), one dictionary lists as an example, "A lion at home, a mouse abroad" (Masuda, 1964, p. 1352). Some of the interviewees said the way the Japanese in general fought was "dirty," that the Japanese were, pejoratively speaking, "two-faced," that they were nice on the surface but ugly on the inside. As noted previously, one individual spoke of her grandmother's "sweet company voice," and another used a falsetto voice to show how some hide their upset feelings. One mother said her daughter, with whom she clashes often, was like a cat, "Meow, meow, in front, but you know what is inside, eh." Individual 4 articulated what several mentioned:

Interviewer: Tell me what you don't like about the Japanese culture...
Individual 4: Too phony.
Interviewer: Okay, let's talk about that for a few minutes. What do you mean by phony.
Individual 4: Phony ass [laughs]. Does that explain it? [Laughs more]. Well, what's another word for phony? I think something is so important to them. It's not self-esteem. I don't like the term, lose face, save face, but it's something along those lines. It's so important to them to project an image for others that they... I'm not very good at words. I think it's important that they put on this... image? No... that they're pretty perfect, that they're... not always right. They just wanna project this image of hey, everything's peaches and cream, and I'm peaches and cream myself, and I don't have any problems.
Interviewer: And that's really important.
Individual 4: It is so phony ass important it makes me sick. Why can't you just put things out like they are? So you have a problem, big deal. World gonna come to an end? You know...

Individual 4 [later in interview]: But they're real nicey-nicey to you in person, really nicey-nicey, slurpy over. . . and then once you're you know, they all do that, I just feel that buddha-heads [slang referring to Japanese] are [the] worst people. . .

Long-time residents said that their community was rife with scandals and problems that most other communities had. The difference with the Japanese was that due to the strong cultural sanctions against revealing to outsiders the so-called wrongdoings of its community members, most outsiders, including the media, had a lopsided view of the Japanese, often branding the Japanese as the "model minority." The interviewees said that not every Japanese immigrant was a success story, that there were prostitution and gangster activities during the early years in Seattle's Japantown (cf. Ito, 1973), murder, wife-stealing, shootings, and duplicitous business practices among themselves. "The true picture is much worse. . . most of the *Issei* [first generation Japanese], they never mentioned their shortcoming[s] or shameful things they did. So many people made shameful things," said one individual.

Teishu Kanpaku (Male Dominance)

A central conditional variable that controls and explains the core category of Group Above Self is the culturally ascribed male dominance, brought over from Japan by the *Issei* and still evident today. In her oral history project based on 14 *Issei* who settled in Hood River, Oregon, Tamura (1993), focusing on the women, reports that they were to follow the "three obediences:" to obey their fathers when unmarried, their husbands when they married, and their sons when widowed (p. 97). In addition, these *Issei* were guided by several principles: humility (*hikaeme*), perseverance (*shinbo*), and resignation (*shikata ga nai*), which helped them to withstand horrible conditions that were worse than anyone could imagine (Tamura, 1993, pp. 275–277).

Some of Tamura's subjects, upon arrival, were surprised by how well women were treated in America, how they were cherished. In contrast, the Japanese wife was not cherished; she was subservient during her entire married life. The ideal role of women was to be *ryosai kenbo*, or a dutiful wife and intelligent mother (Tamura, 1993, p. 98). Although Tamura's female interviewees discussed subordination, disappointment in their husbands, and not being cherished, they did not elaborate on the quality of their marital and filial interactions.

As with Tamura's study, most of the male and female interviewees of this study spoke as if it were taken for granted that the Japanese male felt superior, even though among the younger *Nisei*, the *Sansei*, and *Yonsei* this perception was diminishing.

Individual 9: Regarding domestic violence, the Japanese *Issei*, they were born in Japan and grew up. They are a man-predominant country. Therefore, in the deep level they still feel *ibatte* [arrogant]. Some old *Nisei* too because they were influenced by the *Issei*.

This support of male dominance is a prerequisite for supporting the group-focused norms. Males usually made the "big" decisions while the woman carried out the plans on behalf of the family and community. Acting against the community order and male dominance often meant that the woman had to leave the group or resulted in self-removal, a conflict-avoidance and -management strategy. Ten of the women recalled incidents of differential treatment of males in their family, the father, father-in-law, uncle, oldest brother, or only son. They also spoke of their domineering husbands, and being ordered about, as well as domineering males in other families. In addition, eight of the men also recalled their domineering male family members and friends, with two of the men calling the Japanese male "chauvinist" and "male chauvinist pig." One male said, "It's easy for the male to be dominant. My father was that way."

Male Unaccountability Yanagisako (1985) emphasizes that a common theme among the women in her study was their resentment of their husband's interests outside the family. The wife and children suffered when the husband spent precious resources outside the family, sometimes drinking and having sexual affairs. Those married to such husbands felt powerless with no or very little control and needed to play the role of the obedient wife. This feeling was echoed by the interviewees of this study. Emerging from the transcripts was the strong opinion that the Japanese male still does not have to account for his actions and is *entitled* to be silent, with his wife, sister, and daughters not having the right to question him. One male interviewee said, "The woman is the one that's supposed to give in. . . that's the way they were brought up, that's the way. Regardless of where, United States, Japan, or Hawaii, I think it's the same. As long as both folks are Japanese, that's the tradition they followed, I think. Man comes first." This is relayed poignantly by one participant about her parents.

Interviewer: Do you know why your mother wanted to divorce your father?
Individual 21: Ummm, the two could not get along, it was said once. . . my father was drinking, and my father *ranbo shimasu kara ne* [was violent, rough, wild], my mother cannot stand. I was the second child, when I was born, my older sister. . . my neighbors. . . my father sent her there while my mother was working. . . they didn't have children, so they liked my sister a lot, took care of her. . . so they told my father they liked my sister, my father was *hito ga ii hito dakara, sake o nomu keredomo, hito ga ii-n desu, sorede, sono hito ga sonna ni hoshii dattara ne, tsugi ni umarete kuruko ga onna no ko datta ra, agemasu* [my father was very good to people, even if he drank *sake*, so, he said if you like daughter so much, if the next child who is born is a girl, you may have the first daughter. My mother was not consulted, so when I was born, it was done, soon after I was born. [difficult to understand who said what next] It was said [to mother], don't say that this is your child, they want to raise the child as theirs, so that person went away, and I didn't have a sibling. So, my mother, my father drank, she took me and went to Japan. Soon after, my father came to Japan and said he was bad, that he would be more careful with her, and asked her to return to America. But my mother said, she would not return to America. . . and since she wasn't returning to America, she would divorce. So, I was left at my father's hometown home, my mother

divorced, so I was also, removed from my mother, so my father returned to America. I was raised in my [paternal] aunt's home. After my schooling [in Japan], then I went to school in America.

Interviewer: So you never saw your sister?

Individual 21: I never saw her again. They took her back to Japan [explains, then talks about father arranging her first marriage]. The parents planned the marriage. I didn't want to marry, I wanted to remain single, I said, but my father didn't listen. The other side too. . . So that person [future husband] was in [state].

Interviewer: So you went to [state]?

Individual 21: My father arranged it, so. . . then we came to [city], and married here, then returned to [state]. Having gone there, there weren't very many Japanese. He had a [business]. . . I didn't understand words because I had just come from Japan. . . so I was married for three years, but I get along *dekinakatta* [could not get along], *ne*? I was young, so I told the person in Seattle who had taken care of me, she understood, I was taken into their house.

In the same interview, this woman, having reported that her second husband beat her regularly during the early years of their marriage, was asked if her husband ever apologized:

Interviewer: Did he ever say, I'm sorry?

Individual 21: No, he never say sorry.

Individual 19 (serving as interpreter): You know, men never say that, not Japanese. In the past they never say I'm sorry.

Individual 21: Yes, nowadays, I don't know if they do, maybe nowadays, many women and maybe more men say it.

In addition, two wives reported that their husbands apologized only once in their entire marriage, long after many hurtful incidents. As they recalled them, they could recite the dialogue word for word and the circumstances of the apology, as if the apology were one of the most unforgettable incidents in the marriage.

One of these wives, who said the husband was the "big boss" and the woman the "small boss," talked about her husband gambling away the reimbursement checks from her husband's employer for gas and mileage on his own car for business purposes, amounting to approximately $10,000 over several years. Another interviewee said that she would never have married a Japanese male because of the way they treated their wives. She remembered her uncle, with whom she lived for a while, having affairs with his hired help while her aunt did nothing. A third interviewee remembers his uncle staying at his mistress's home when there was conflict in the family home.

Shuran (Male Drunken Violence)   Male dominance is also manifested by drinking and having a violent temper, termed *shuran*. Most of the interviewees who were bilingual understood the term. It was a surprise to discover the extent to which the males known to the study participants drank large amounts of alcohol. With regard to women, only one interviewee reported how a woman known to her family drank alcohol at her job site and was abused by her husband when she would return home late from work. The others freely reported the male family members' and acquaintances' *shuran* behavior. Based on their accounts, the *Issei* men found alcohol consumption to be a favorite pastime and outlet. Thirteen of the interviewees discussed the men's drinking behaviors in two generations. These men were reported to have changed their behavior from hard-working employees to demanding and aggressive men when drinking. Some of the interviewees recollected drinking-related incidents such as one man threatening the family with a butcher knife, one man grabbing a kitchen knife at a party and being kept from stabbing another man, fist fights, husbands arguing with wives, and men demanding sex from their wives or other women. The outstanding impression from these interviewees was the high degree of resignation or acceptance of drunk men and their behavior. These men did not stop drinking when asked by their wives. They were allowed to take advantage of the weaker woman who had less status and power to protest. One interviewee remembers her mother's victimization when she was much younger:

Individual 15: Drinking and violence, yeah, *shuran*. Japanese society in the past was fairly, you know, drinking excessively during festivals. . . fairly accepted, but the problem is some people abuse it tremendously. I have a really bad experience with one of the relatives. . . [we were] living in the only single parent home [father died]. It's not quite owner thing, when I was in the village, once in a while, the village men drank, and coming to our house, because at home, probably they don't have too much sympathy, and coming to my mother. I was [the] person [who would] always say, "Oh, she's not here." I've seen very ugly side of drinking, and I hate it. The other thing is, my mother's life was ruined by one person who drank so much. In the same village, I've seen that elderly person, and once in a while [he] came to my house, and became violent, and unless we serve them more *sake* [rice wine], and just unbelievable. . . if the person is weak, [he] just keep coming, especially the person [I'm] talking about is my mother's father-in-law.

Physical and Verbal Aggression   Some people may stereotype the Japanese as peace-loving, living harmoniously among themselves. On the contrary, the interviewees revealed another side of the Japanese not commonly known to the outside world. The culturally supported male-dominance behaviors as described by the interviewees match those reported in the domestic-violence literature in the United States (Gelles, 1980; Gelles & Conte, 1990; Gondolf, 1987; Ohlin & Tonry, 1989). The general feeling of the interviewees was that male physical aggression was socially accepted and commonplace. Some of them reported incidents of physical arguments among men and spousal abuse; those who had no familiarity with actual cases of physical aggression said that they were sure it existed and that they just had not heard about it. One participant generously revealed her early years of marriage.

Interviewer: When you get into an argument with your children, or your mother, or your husband, sometimes some *Nihonjin* [Japanese] yell at each other, some hit each other, some don't say anything.

Individual 21: Well, this person [referring to husband], at the beginning, in the countryside, especially the husband's home, fisherman's work, he felt he had a little more stature than most, and he also had schooling, so, when we argued, he beat me [laughs]. But I didn't think of leaving. He didn't drink. . . I didn't have to *gaman* [endure] about big issues, all of my life. Big *gaman*, there was not a reason to do big *gaman*, we did argue, about the children and things.
Interviewer: So if I understand you right, he did hit you?
Individual 21: At the beginning [of marriage]. . . When we argued, if he didn't get his way, because he was a male.
Interviewer: So he would hit you one time, when you argued. . .?
Individual 21: It may have been more [laughs], a lot.
Interviewer: Okay. . .
Individual 21: He'd come at me quickly [gestures].
Interviewer: So, by the ear. . .
Individual 21: Head, face, would beat. . . he beat this ear area so much that I can't hear as well from that ear.

Television programs in Japan, videotaped and viewed in the United States, commonly portray the male as aggressive, "needing" to slap the woman because she is "stupid" and needing to be straightened out. One interviewee explained:

Interviewer: So, they hit, Japanese people hit each other?
Individual 9: No, yeah, that. . . uh, officer [in Japan] hit. That's right. Yeah, but you know, we ordinary soldier cannot hit officer, but officer hit. Normal, very normal.
Interviewer: On the face, shoulder, like this [mimics hitting]?
Individual 9: Mmmm, no, face. Well, both ways [slap and punch]. But in the family, sometime, quite often the husband you know, hits his wife you know. If wife is not obedient. . . because the husband's excuse is, uh, when I give order, or order, she did not listen. The only way, use the force. . . discipline. But in America, that's why that uh, seems to me any Japanese man you know, see the Western movie, okay, see the American movie, and sometimes the woman, the wife hit the husband, husband not return, he didn't hit. And they think it's coward [laughs]. One hundred percent opposite. See, American philosophy is if man hit wife, he's coward, but Japanese, gee [laughs], that man is a sissy. So, anyway. . .

Some of the incidents of physical and sexual aggression were associated with drinking alcohol, as described in the preceding section. Other spousal abuse incidents were not alcohol-related; they were attributed to the male having a temper or being "short-tempered," feeling superior, or being a "dictator" and a "tyrant." These behaviors included beating, yelling at, and shoving the wife to the floor. Individual 20 responded in Japanese, with individual 19, who had known her for many years, interpreting.

Individual 19 (to Individual 20): So about. . . were you beaten?
Individual 20: Haaaa. . . if I said anything, [says something not understandable].
Interviewer: What did I miss?

Individual 19: Were you beaten?

Individual 20: [Not understandable.]

Interviewer: Tell me what she said.

Individual 19: She said whenever he's [husband] unhappy, he beat her up. When she object to his working for nothing, he beat her up.

Individual 20: We bought a business, right? So then I had to do all of the "men's" work there. The inspector wondered why I had to do it. I had to do it because my husband did not, I told the inspector. He told me to stop it, but if I didn't do the work, the customers would complain, so I told him I would continue to do the work. My husband bullied and bullied me. It rained a lot [I cried a lot].

Individual 19: Where would he hit you?

Individual 20: He would kick and hit.

Interviewer: Everywhere? Your face?

Individual 20: [Not understandable.]

Interviewer: What did she say?

Individual 19: She said since she married him she could not complain, so he was able to beat her up.

Interviewer: What did you do when he did that? I want to know how you reacted.

Individual 20: He would hit, kick, bully, and I would go to another room. It rained [I cried].

Individual 19: Did you lock the door?

Individual 20: I locked the door all the time... and hid the key. [In response to whether she knew of others who had similar experiences] I have heard, there are others, I haven't seen it, in conversations only, I have heard of it. I met him when I was thirteen–fifteen. He looked good, so I was told to marry him. There are many who had this happen too.

Individual 19: She says lots of them, in [a U.S. city].

Interviewer: When you got beaten, did you tell anybody?

Individual 20: I *gaman*-ed [endured] all the time, it rained [I cried]. I would cook, and if he was unhappy with the food, he would throw it at me. *Gomen nasai, Gomen nasai* [I'm sorry, I'm sorry, was said]. Without playing, I worked hard, cared for the children, worked in the business...

Interviewer: How many years do you remember him beating you?

Individual 20: To speak of this is so *hazukashii* [shameful], he hit me, kick me, he would say he had other women who liked him, so I would say, Well, why didn't you marry them instead of me?... all the time it rained [I cried constantly]. I thought of running away, but, I thought of killing myself and dying early, I thought of it many times.

Individual 19: Did you think of running away?

Individual 20: [Makes gesture representing a coin/money with thumb and first finger] I didn't have [money], I didn't receive any, so I couldn't run away, I would go out... [starts crying, unable to talk].

Individual 19: You know, it's probably the first time these [Japanese] people are able to talk about these things.

Individual 20: He abused me so much that... [cries]. I thought I want to return to Japan, so one time I did return.

Individual 19: You went once, why did you come back?

Individual 20: [Cries]

Individual 19: Because of the children?

Individual 20: Because of the children, they were here [repeats how husband said he could have had other women].

Individual 19: There was a lot of verbal abuse too.

Individual 20: He abused me so much that I went to [street] about midnight. I ran away to [street]. He hit me and kicked me so much.

Interviewer: Did everybody in the community know?

Individual 20: No, no. It was about midnight, so nobody was around. So I returned home because I did not have any money. Could not be helped. I was not given spending money even if I worked.

Individual 19: She didn't have any allowance or anything. That's how [Japanese men] controlled their wives. She isn't the only one. That's what they did. Two things, they didn't have money, and they couldn't talk, and they didn't have any skills. They couldn't make a living.

Individual 20 (later, when asked how long the abuse lasted): *Zutto* [ongoing]. He kept talking about other women even in his old age. He beat me and would throw things. Till he died, he bullied me.

DISCUSSION

For the Japanese, group survival and group importance are paramount, with the individual being sacrificed on behalf of the group. Clearly emerging from the data analysis in this study were categories that had to do with group membership. The transcripts, on which the categories and subsequently the core category are grounded, consistently made references to the self within the context of group membership. The core category was labeled Group Above Self, although some may argue that labels such as this polarize and falsely segregate the individual from his or her own society and do not recognize the strong "we-self" or multiplicity of selves that clearly is not the same self or "I" that has a consistent identity in the Western sense. The choice of Group Above Self over the more integrated labels less connotative of "either–or" was based on what was presented in the transcripts: a struggle of the women who were raised to be obedient; who endured often-unbearable conditions, including physical, emotional and verbal abuse; and who were taught not to reveal the wrongdoings and shameful events beyond their community. The choice of Group Above Self was meant to convey the individual's struggles with imposed norms; most often, the group won over the individual's desires, leaving the individual to suffer quietly.

It becomes clear from this study that in a society whose conditions include group and male primacy and in which wrongdoings are not revealed, the victim of elder mistreatment, especially a female victim, may never be identified. Given the cultural context as reported by the study participants, the elder may not know that she is a victim in the first place if she has been raised from infancy to defer to others and, from a Western viewpoint, if she has suffered a lifetime of abuse. In addition, the strong norm against revealing less-than-perfect situations make the chances of seeking help for elder mistreatment from outside agencies very slim.

Reviewing the raters' comments, suggestions for future studies on sensitive topics such as conflict and elder mistreatment among the Japanese include interviewing all participants at least three times and having a broad repertoire of interview styles to accommodate the participants' varying presentation and degrees of willingness to disclose information. Although this study yielded rich data that enabled the development of the preliminary categories, it is highly likely that additional data would have emerged as the participants became more comfortable with the interviewer and with the topics of conflict and elder mistreatment.

The results of this study provide several practice implications. Because some victims who are bound by strong cultural norms, including silent suffering and quiet endurance, which are syntonic with victimization, do not realize that they are victims, clinical intervention may include gently helping victims realize that others may view their situation differently than they do. In addition, because of the strong sense of we-ness, one proposal is to develop methods to treat the we-self and not the I-self, perhaps involving third parties to support or carry out professionals' interventions. Practitioners also could redefine themselves as the third party with whom the victim can vent before he or she returns to the suffering situation. Based on the transcripts, victims of mistreatment will admit to being mistreated to outsiders only after the perpetrator dies, or when they are certain that the family and the perpetrator will not be affected negatively by revealing the mistreatment. This affirms the need to focus on the family system and to do the greatest good for the entire family system and not just one individual.

On a continuum of reactions to conflict, the Japanese tend to stay on one end. The continuum consists of, on the one end, avoidance, then repression, displacement, management, and on the opposite end, resolution (Lebra, 1984). Given this, it would be presumptuous to ask how the victim feels and what she wants to do to *resolve* the situation. Perhaps interventions should not be considered a resolution process but a process by which respite, safety, and group harmony are promoted through conflict-avoidance and -management techniques.

Centuries of culturally based behaviors manifest themselves differently in conflict situations, elder mistreatment being one of those situations. Ours is a short-term, problem-resolution approach, and this approach may not allow us to detect and treat elder-mistreatment cases among groups such as the Japanese. Perhaps with a greater understanding of the cultural factors that affect our practice, we can modify our approach to be more successful.

REFERENCES

Anetzberger, G., Korbin, J., & Tomita, S. (1996). Defining elder mistreatment in four ethnic groups across two generations. *Journal of Cross-Cultural Gerontology, 11*, 187–212.
Berkowitz, L. (1983). The goals of aggression. In D. Finkelhor, R. J. Gelles, G. T. Hotaling, & M. A. Straus (Eds.), *The dark side of families: Current family violence research* (pp. 166–181). Beverly Hills: Sage.

Block, M., & Sinott, J. (1979). *The Battered Elder Syndrome: An Exploratory Study*. College Park, MD: University of Maryland, Center on Aging.

Brown, A. (1989). A survey on elder abuse at one Native American tribe. *Journal of Elder Abuse and Neglect, 1*(2), 17–37.

Gelles, R. (1980). Violence in the family: A review of research in the seventies. *Journal of Marriage and the Family, 42*, 873–885.

Gelles, R., & Conte, J. (1990). Domestic violence and sexual abuse of children: A review of research in the eighties. *Journal of Marriage and the Family, 52*, 1045–1058.

Gelles, R., & Straus, M. (1988). *Intimate violence*. New York: Simon & Schuster.

Glascock, A., & Feinman, S. (1981). Social assessment of burden: Treatment of the aged in non-industrial societies. In C. Fry (Ed.), *Dimensions: Aging, culture, and health* (pp. 13–31). New York: Praeger Publishers.

Glaser, B. (1978). *Theoretical sensitivity: Advances in the methodology of grounded theory*. Mill Valley, CA: Sociology Press.

Glaser, B. (1992). *Basics of grounded theory analysis: Emergence vs. forcing*. Mill Valley, CA: Sociology Press.

Glaser, B., & Strauss, A. (1967). *The discovery of grounded theory*. Hawthorne, New York: Adline de Guyter.

Godkin, M. A., Wolf, R. S., & Pillemer, K. A. (1989). A case-comparison analysis of elder abuse and neglect. *International Journal of Aging & Human Development, 28*(3), 207–225.

Gondolf, E. W. (1987). Evaluating progress for men who batter: Problems and prospects. *Journal of Family Violence, 2*, 95–108.

Griffin, L. W. (1994). Elder maltreatment among rural African-Americans. *Journal of Elder Abuse and Neglect, 6*(1), 1–27.

Ito, K. (1973). *Issei: A history of Japanese immigrants in North America* (S. Nakamura & J. S. Gerard, Trans). Seattle, WA: Committee for the Publication of *Issei: A History of Japanese Immigrants in North America*.

Johnson, F. A. (1993). *Dependency and Japanese socialization: Psychoanalytic and anthropological investigations into amae*. New York: New York University Press.

Kaneko, Y., & Yamada, Y. (1990). Wives and mothers-in-law: Potential for family conflict in post-war Japan. *Journal of Elder Abuse and Neglect, 2*(1/2), 87–99.

Kosberg, J. I. & Garcia, J. L. (Eds.). (1995). *Elder abuse: International and cross-cultural perspectives*. New York: Haworth Press, Inc.

Kuwayama, T. (1992). The reference other orientation. In N. Rosenberger (Ed.), *Japanese sense of self* (pp. 121–151). Cambridge: Cambridge University Press.

Lau, L., & Kosberg, J. (1979). Abuse of the elderly by informal care providers. *Aging*, September–October: 10–15.

Lebra, T. (1984). Nonconfrontational strategies for management of interpersonal conflicts. In E. Krauss, T. Rohlen, & P. Steinhoff (Eds.), *Conflict in Japan* (pp. 41–59). Honolulu, HI: University of Hawaii Press.

Lebra, T. (1992). Self in Japanese culture. In N. Rosenberger (Ed.), *Japanese sense of self* (pp. 105–120). Cambridge: Cambridge University Press.

Masuda, K. (1964). *Kenkyusha's new pocket Japanese-English dictionary*. Tokyo: Kenkyusha.

Maxwell, E., & Maxwell, R. J. (1992). Insults to the body civil: Mistreatment of elderly in two Plains Indian tribes. *Journal of Cross Cultural Gerontology, 7*(1), 3–23.

Ohlin, L., & Tonry, M. (Eds.). (1989). *Family violence*. Chicago: University of Chicago Press.

Phillips, L. R. (1983). Abuse and neglect of the frail elderly at home: An exploration of theoretical relationships. *Journal of Advanced Nursing, 8*, 379–392.

Pillemer, K. (1986). Risk factors in elder abuse: Results from a case control study. In K. Pillemer & R. Wolf (Eds.), *Elder abuse: Conflict in the family* (pp. 239–263). Dover, MA: Auburn House Publishing Co.

Pillemer, K., & Finkelhor, D. (1988). The prevalence of elder abuse: A random sample survey. *Gerontologist, 28*(1), 51–57.

Reinharz, S. (1986). Loving and hating one's elders: Twin themes in legend and literature. In K. Pillemer & R. Wolf (Eds.), *Elder abuse: Conflict in the family*. (pp. 25–48). Dover, MA: Auburn House Publishing Co.

Rosenberger, N. (1992). Introduction. In N. Rosenberger (Ed.), *Japanese sense of self* (pp. 1–20). Cambridge: Cambridge University Press

Straus, M. (1974a). Leveling, civility, and violence in the family. *Journal of Marriage and the Family, 36*, 13–29.

Straus, M. (1974b). Cultural and social organizational influences on violence between family members. In R. Prince & D. Barrier (Eds.), *Configurations: Biological and cultural factors in sexuality and family life* (pp. 53–69). Lexington, MA: Lexington Books–D.C. Heath.

Straus, M. (1979). Measuring intrafamily conflict and violence: The Conflict Tactics Scale. *Journal of Marriage and the Family, 41*, 75–88.

Strauss, A. (1987). *Qualitative analysis for social scientists*. New York: Cambridge University Press.

Strauss, A., & Corbin, J. (1990). *Basics of qualitative research: Grounded theory procedures and techniques*. Newbury Park, CA: Sage.

Swanson-Kauffman, K. M. (1986). A combined qualitative methodology for nursing research. *Advances in Nursing Science, 8*(3), 58–69.

Tamura, L. (1993). *The Hood River Issei: An oral history of Japanese Settlers in Oregon's Hood River valley*. Urbana and Chicago, IL: University of Illinois Press.

Yanagisako, S. J. (1985). *Transforming the past: Tradition and kinship among Japanese Americans*. Stanford, CA: Stanford University Press.

Part Four

Elder Abuse in American Indian Communities

Chapter 10

Patterns of Abuse Among Native American Elderly

Arnold S. Brown

Although it is commonly acknowledged that most of the attention given to el-der abuse in recent years has been focused on the White majority in this country, Native Americans have been especially ignored among minority populations. As Carson points out, data on elder abuse have been collected from only three Native American tribes (Carson, 1995). Furthermore, the problem has largely been de-fined and studied from the perspective of service providers. Very few of the data have come from elderly people themselves. It is also true that very few corrective programs have been developed and few legal statutes have been passed on behalf of Native American elders.

In recent years critical questions have begun to be raised concerning the prob-lem of elder abuse. Specifically, questions are being asked about how the concept "elder abuse" is defined; how accurate or inaccurate (biased or nonbiased) those definitions are (Moon & Williams, 1993); who is being blamed, and with what amount of justification; and how appropriately or inappropriately the problem is being handled. These are important questions to consider in assessing the problem among people of such diverse cultures as Native Americans. This discussion of the adequacy of the definitions we apply to elder abuse is particularly important in understanding the existence of this phenomenon among Native Americans. For example, if it takes place in the context of the process of younger family mem-bers negotiating the provision of needed long-term care to their elderly family members, as studies have shown, how much more intense the negotiations must be for them than for whites. Traditionally, young family members are expected to provide such care when it is needed, but never before has that obligation been so demanding and never before have their social worlds been changing so drastically.

EVIDENCE OF ELDER ABUSE AMONG NATIVE AMERICANS

Plains Indian Elder-Abuse Study

The most recent study of elder abuse among Native Americans was conducted on two different Plains Indian reservations (Maxwell & Maxwell, 1992). The two reservations (referred to in the report as Lone Mountain Reservation and Abundant Lands Reservation) were compared with regard to patterns of elder abuse. The data in this study were collected on the basis of informal observations on the two reservations and informal interviews mostly with tribal officials, health-care providers, and service providers. The specific categories of elder abuse that were identified by those respondents were physical abuse, or an infliction of personal harm; primary neglect, or purposeful incidences of neglect; and secondary neglect, or neglect that is not deliberate.

From their observations, the investigators learned that the economic and social conditions on one reservation were extremely poor, but they were much better on the other reservation. Lone Mountain Reservation had very little land suitable even for grazing and had almost no opportunities for jobs on the reservation. Thus, young adults either were unemployed and living in poverty or had to leave the reservation to find jobs. Elderly people, in contrast, tended to own what good land there was and had regular monthly income from either Social Security or Supplementary Security Income (SSI). Consequently, all too typically, younger adults were found to be financially dependent upon the older members of their families. Those on the Lone Mountain Reservation were also very isolated from the outside world. In contrast, the Abundant Land Reservation had land that was useful for both grazing and agriculture, and an office-supplies factory provided workers with greater on-reservation job opportunities, making dependency of young people on the elderly less prevalent. In addition, they had greater contact with outsiders.

Maxwell and Maxwell found that there was much less elder abuse on the Abundant Land Reservation than on the Lone Mountain Reservation. Although the Lone Mountain respondents reported many cases of financial exploitation and "primary neglect," the few incidences that were reported by the Abundant Land Reservation workers were almost entirely cases of secondary, or unintentional, abuse. The conclusion that they drew from these data were that elder abuse among the Plains Indians is the result of income deprivation, economic dependency among young adults, and cultural isolation. Having jobs available on the reservation keeps younger people less financially dependent upon the elderly members of their families and tends to alleviate the problem of exploitation. Then, contrary to what might be thought, the Lone Mountain Reservation study found that less contact with outsiders apparently does not necessarily keep the cultural tradition of family interdependency intact and make abuse and neglect less likely.

The data from this research project are somewhat limited in that they are qualitative and tend to be anecdotal and descriptive. Missing are such things as the extent of abuse on either reservation, who the abusers were, circumstantial variables associated with abuse, and the perspective of the elders themselves. The comparative aspect of this study is especially valuable, however. It clearly shows, for example, that the patterns of elder abuse among Native Americans tend to be related to changing economic conditions on reservations.

The Maxwells conclude the analysis of their findings by discussing the policy implications of the data. They note that the solutions attempted on both reservations tended to place blame on individual abusers and treat them "with imprisonment, counseling, or some combination of the two," none of which worked. As they put it, "Policy makers were unaware that one reason individual treatment programs were failing is that they were able to do little if anything to eliminate the structural conditions which lead to incidents of abuse" (Maxwell & Maxwell, 1992, p. 19).

Older Navajo Elder-Abuse Survey

Two studies of elder abuse and neglect have been conducted on the Navajo Indian Reservation in recent years. One was a survey of elderly people themselves and members of their families (Brown, 1989), and the other was a survey of service providers across the reservation (Brown, Fernandez, & Griffith, 1990).

The first of these studies was conducted as a joint effort by the Navajo Office on Aging and the Gerontology Institute at Northern Arizona University. The Navajo Nation is divided into chapters, and one chapter (Oljato) was selected as the target area of the study. A random sample of one third (37) of the 110 elderly people in that chapter (aged 60 years and over), along with one close relative of each elderly person in the sample, were chosen and interviewed.

Data from this study indicated that abuse of various kinds is clearly prevalent among the Navajo aged. Neglect was found to be, by far, the most prevalent form of abuse; cases of verbal and physical abuse were not nearly as prevalent as neglect. In general, abuse among Navajo elderly was particularly related to their dependency on others. It is noteworthy, however, that as elderly Navajos became dependent, their families tended strongly to respond by providing them with care. The greater their dependency the more they and others in the community responded with the care that was needed. Lack of response by families and others was not the primary problem related to abuse. How they responded, however, often did make the elderly vulnerable to abuse.

The most typical pattern found among Navajo families was to share the caregiving responsibilities between a number of family members. If this was the procedure, the chances of abuse, especially in the form of neglect, increased. It is probably a case of "if everyone is responsible no one is responsible." If one person in the family was designated as the primary caregiver, typically that person was a daughter who was widowed or single with children of her own for whom she was solely responsible. This was a situation of burden that easily resulted in either (or both) neglect and psychological abuse.

Three factors related to dependency were found to be related to possible abuse: the suddenness of becoming dependent, the presence of mental problems, and income. If elderly persons suddenly became dependent or developed mental conditions such as confusion, families found themselves in a state of crisis and had difficulty planning for and providing the needed care. Both neglect and even physical abuse were found if families were in a state of crisis. All too often, the family members who became caregivers were the least prepared or capable of providing care for these kinds of elderly people. These were people who tended to be relatively young, be unemployed, have other personal problems, live with the elderly persons for whom they provided care, have poor relationships with the elderly persons for whom they provided care, and have no caregiving help from others in their families.

Income was a "catch-22" phenomenon for the elderly Navajos. Having low income frequently preceded being neglected. Having somewhat better income tended to be associated with either (or both) psychological or physical abuses. Findings in this study showed that having their income used by and for the benefit of other family members was the second-most frequent form of "abuse" that the elderly respondents reported.

Surprisingly, however, financial exploitation was not found to be correlated with the amount of income elderly people had. The problem was obviously not related as much to the amount of income elderly persons received as to the fact that they had any amount of income at all. As also was found at the Lone Mountain Reservation, in some cases elderly Navajos were the only members of their families who received a regular monthly check (Supplemental Security Income, for example). Regardless of the amount, they were apt to have to share it with younger family members. However, we must be cautious about actually defining this as exploitation. All of the elderly people who admitted that this was happening to them explained that it was a matter of their voluntarily sharing what they had with family members who had needs. To them it was clearly a case of living up to an important cultural value.

In general, the picture that these data present is that the greater the dependency of the elderly persons, the more suddenly they become dependent and the more hours of care that are provided by families, the more apt families are to share the caregiver responsibilities. If families shared the caregiver responsibilities, there also is a tendency for some care to be provided by others in the community besides family members. Ironically, the sharing of the caregiver responsibilities often leaves the elderly vulnerable to neglect. In fact, abuses of all kinds often happen if family caregiving is shared. If caregiving is left to individuals who have other family responsibilities and problems of their own, other kinds of abuse may occur. This is particularly the case if the caregiver responsibilities have caused family crises.

Navajo Service-Provider Elder-Abuse Survey

The survey of service providers on the Navajo Reservation was conducted in 1990 with a grant from the Indian Health Service (Brown et al., 1990). All of the reservation service providers who it was possible to reach (152) were interviewed.

They included individuals in social services, healthcare, and law enforcement; tribal officials; and community volunteers. These respondents were asked to indicate their perceptions of, knowledge about, and experiences with elder abuse, as well as the extent of and the circumstances related to four types of abuse: physical abuse, verbal abuse, neglect, and exploitation. They also were questioned about their own personal lives, cultural orientations, and professional backgrounds.

Regarding elder abuse they were asked their opinions about the extent that each of the types of abuse was a problem on the reservation, who the abusers of each type were, whether or not each type of abuse was intentional, the extent to which each type of abuse represented repeat offenses, how they would characterize elderly persons' incomes being spent to benefit other family members, and how older people should spend their incomes.

Neglect and exploitation were seen by service providers as the most common forms of abuse. With regard to who they perceived the abusers to be, they saw elder abuse of all kinds as primarily a family problem, particularly on the part of immediate family members. An indication of how severe the service providers rated abuse among Navajo elders was whether or not they thought the various types of abusive acts were done intentionally. Interestingly, neglect and physical abuse were less often considered to be intentional than were verbal abuse or exploitation. Apparently, even though neglect is seen as the most common form of abuse and physical abuse is seen as very serious when it happens, both of them are viewed as more situational than premeditated and deliberate.

On the question of whether or not acts of elder abuse were repeat offenses, a substantial majority of the service providers on the reservation were convinced that, indeed, acts of all four types of elder abuse were repeat offenses. Determining whether or not these data actually represent forms of pathology or power struggles in a culture with strong family interdependent traditions, however, calls for further and more careful analysis. For one thing, most of the informants in the study not only said that family members were primarily the ones acting abusively, but they also indicated that incidences of abuse happened primarily to elders in particular home situations. For example, respondents described abuse as occurring to women who were very old, were socially isolated in their own homes, had become burdens to their families, lived with their abusers, were in poor physical condition, and were suddenly dependent on others.

Respondents also described the primary characteristics of the abusers as factors that were closely related to their serving as caregivers. Mostly mentioned were being unemployed, feeling burdened by caring for an aged person, being poor and in need of money, and often feeling depressed. The two least mentioned factors were the beliefs that these abusers either had been abused in the past or had a history of abusing others. Abuse as intentional and as repeat offenses seems to be confined to the caregiving situation and does not represent long histories of abuse.

Data from this survey also were analyzed on the basis of respondents' backgrounds and experiences. For that purpose the respondents were classified de-

pending on whether they were Navajos or not, the extent to which they were
oriented toward Navajo values, whether or not they served elderly people directly
in their jobs, and how much actual experience they had had dealing with cases of
elder abuse.

It was found that those who were Navajos, claimed to be the most oriented
toward Navajo values, and provided direct services to elderly people were especially prone to rate the extensiveness of abuse among Navajo elders as high.
Ironically, those with actual experience in dealing with cases of abuse did not rate
extensiveness any higher than those with no such experience. The same can be
said about service providers' judgments of whether or not abuse among Navajo
elderly represented repeat offenses. In this case those who were Navajos, were
most oriented toward Navajo values, and directly served elderly people were less
apt to judge abuse as repeat offenses than were others; experience with cases of
abuse did not influence these judgments. Apparently, perceptions of how extensive elder abuse is and whether it represented repeat offenses are more culturally
than experientially judged.

When it came to whether elder abuse was seen as intentional or not, however,
just the opposite was true. In this case those with actual experience dealing with
cases of abuse were the ones who rated intentionality the highest. This tended to
be more of an experiential than a cultural judgment.

Service providers on the reservation saw exploitation as a somewhat special
form of elder abuse. It was found, for example, that a sizable majority of them defined it as exploitation whenever that happened, regardless of the circumstances.
Ironically, that was especially true of those service providers who were Navajos
and those who claimed to be the most strongly oriented toward Navajo values.
They also were much less apt to say that elderly people ought to be willing to
share their income with their families. Furthermore, they agreed equally with all
of the other respondents that the elderly should spend their money on their own
special needs.

The irony in these data is that the Navajo culture is one that has traditionally
had a strong emphasis on the equal sharing of family resources. Indeed, as noted
previously, that was precisely how the elderly respondents in the survey of elderly
Navajos explained the situation when their money had gone to other members of
their families. How can that discrepancy be explained? One possible explanation
is that the service-provider role itself influenced some people to compromise their
traditional values. Perhaps the training they received and the orientation of the
agencies by which they were employed influenced them to think more in terms of
being strong advocates of individual clients than of interdependent family-support
traditions.

Another possible explanation of the Navajo service providers' definition of
exploitation is that it came out of their experiences with elders. Those service
providers who were Navajos and those who said that they were very much oriented toward traditional Navajo values were more directly involved with elderly
people and tended to spend more time dealing with actual cases of abuse. Thus,

they had more chances than other service providers to observe what was actually happening in the homes of the elderly. Those observations may have told them that the Navajo traditional value of mutual sharing within the family was actually being violated instead of being practiced, with younger family members taking the resources of their elderly parents or grandparents purely for their own individual benefits, with little or no effort to reciprocate. Some data from the study tend to support that kind of explanation. For example, although female family members typically served as the primary caregivers, men were blamed more often for exploitation.

Both of those explanations probably have merit. Certainly, advocacy for individual rights and serving individuals in need are dominant parts of the service-provider perspective. In addition, working with dependent and seemingly vulnerable elderly individuals also seems to contribute to that service-provider perspective.

The service-provider perspective of elder abuse, as well as that of the elderly persons themselves, shows us that it is a serious problem among Navajos and that abuse takes place in the homes of the elderly. Although some abuse of Navajo elderly is seen as being intentional and as repeat offenses in that kind of tension-filled situation, it is not viewed as actions of people with long-standing pathological problems or histories of being abused and abusing in turn. Instead, the personal problems of those accused of elder abuse are seen as situational—resulting from such circumstances as being unemployed, poor, and burdened with caregiving responsibilities within families.

It is clear from the two studies of elder abuse on the Navajo Reservation that the issue of exploitation represents a form of cultural conflict. Although older people themselves insist that benefit derived from their incomes by others in their families is purely a matter of their cultural responsibility to share with their families, Navajo service providers define it entirely as exploitation. Here the culture of the service provider, the culture of the elderly, and the culture of the elder person's family must be examined because all have valid points and each needs to consider the other's views. Particularly, we who deal with elder abuse need to take all three viewpoints into account.

NATIVE AMERICAN ELDER ABUSE AND CULTURAL DIVERSITY

There are hundreds of Native American tribes in the United States and they represent a great deal of cultural diversity. Their environmental conditions vary from the frigid areas of northern Alaska to the mountainous areas of Montana, the plains of the Dakotas, and the deserts of Arizona. Their lifestyles also vary from being spread across the land to being village dwellers. Furthermore, they have had a long history of intertribal conflict and violence. Given those diversities and the very limited amount of empirical data on Native American elder abuse, how is it possible to discuss elder abuse in general terms for all tribes?

Admittedly, no generalization of the existing data on any type of statistical basis is valid. However, there are a number of key cultural and situational similarities between tribes that they do not tend to have in common with White Americans. In addition, most Indian tribes are experiencing similar societal changes as they interact with modern society. These similarities allow us to discuss elder abuse among Native Americans in general with a certain amount of confidence.

Factors Combating Abuse

Native Americans generally share a set of cultural values and norms regarding their social goals and relationships, particularly within their families, that tend to be very different from and even in conflict with those found among White Americans (Weibel-Orlando, 1990). The dominant values of Native Americans in general have the effect of creating and sustaining a sense of community and belonging (Locust, 1988). It begins with a spiritual base, and religious observances are a vital part of their social lives (Dicharry, 1986; Carson, 1995). For many, their basic religious belief is that they come from and continue to be part of the earth. It follows from that, then, that they must live in harmony generally with nature and specifically with their fellow tribesmen. Consequently, they tend to interact with each other primarily on the basis of cooperation and family/clan interdependency (DuBray, 1985). Traditionally, Native Americans have tended to deliberately avoid the kind of intense individual competition that prevails throughout the modern Western world.

Some would contend that these kinds of values are no longer being observed as consistently or devoutly by many today, especially by those who are young (Dicharry, 1986; Williams, 1989). Carson (1995) argues, however, that there is evidence to show that "the extended family is still widespread, and the majority of Indians including the elderly report that their family networks are stable sources of strength and encouragement" (p. 29). DuBray reports evidence that adherence to this way of life still exists even among Indian social workers with Master's degrees (DuBray, 1985). In addition, it was found in the study of the Navajo elderly perspective on elder abuse that families were consistently providing the level of care that the elderly person said he or she needed.

Factors Contributing to Abuse

Although the major values and norms of Native Americans are largely still intact and work to combat abuse of older people, there are also a number of relatively common conditions and experiences on Indian reservations across America that tend to have the opposite effect. These include such factors as changing economics, changing health needs and healthcare resources, new work situations, new and different family arrangements and relationships, and the prevalence of personal and mental problems.

Much has been made of the dire economic conditions that tend to exist on most American Indian reservations. As discussed previously, the differences in economic conditions between the two reservations in the Maxwell study were seen as one of the major factors contributing to the fact that elder abuse was more prevalent on one reservation than the other (Maxwell & Maxwell, 1992).

Being poor is by no means a new phenomenon among American Indian tribes. What is different today than in the past is that the basis for economics on reservations is changing (Hanley, 1991; Sandefur & Sakamoto, 1988). Carson (1995) explains, "Poverty, particularly on the reservation, is manifested by high percentages of unemployment and people on welfare" (p. 19), and that creates a depressive kind of dependency. Being poor in the context of an economy based on family cooperation has nothing to do with "unemployment" or being on "welfare" and does not make individuals dependent upon others. Those are concepts that imply the existence of a modern economic system in which people, as individuals, are paid to independently perform productive roles or are unemployed and dependent on others to survive. Thus, it is changing economics, rather than poverty as such, that results in the kinds of severe relational problems associated with elder abuse. Becoming economically dependent has emerged as a new and problematic issue in how people relate to each other among Native Americans.

Dependency has become a major concern in our attempts to understand elder abuse everywhere. The direction of financial dependency for Native Americans is typically just the opposite of that for modern Americans, among whom the elder is usually dependent upon the family (Boudreau, 1993). Although Native Americans have high rates of unemployment and severe poverty, many of the elderly receive monthly checks from pensions, Social Security, or welfare. Although this money typically does not lift them out of poverty, it is often the only funds available to the elder persons' families (Brown, 1989; Carson, 1995; Williams, 1989). Thus, younger Native American adults are often the ones who are financially dependent, often on their elderly family members with whom they live.

The economic changes taking place on Indian reservations also negatively affect how the Native American kinship systems function. For one thing, the general lack of jobs on reservations or near where people live forces workers to leave home and the reservations to find employment (Carson, 1995; Williams, 1989). This has the effect of leaving elders behind in relative isolation from their families, lacking the care they may need when and where they need it and being in danger of being neglected by their families (Brown, 1989; Carson, 1995; McShane, 1987). It also tends to cause intergenerational conflict over the loss of traditions that have been vital to the elders' way of life (Maxwell & Maxwell, 1992; Dicharry, 1986).

Many young Native Americans also have been assessed as having exceptionally high rates of problems such as drug and alcohol abuse, low self-esteem, and a sense of powerlessness and hopelessness that are thought to be associated with elder abuse (Carson, 1995). McShane (1987) sees these problems as serious enough to warn that relying on the "natural support system" for family care could have negative effects. Interestingly, Carson (1995) does not refer to these kinds of personal problems among Native Americans as serious mental pathologies but rather as "concomitants of reservation poverty" (p. 20). It is noteworthy that these were the very family members found in the survey of older Navajos to typically live with and serve as primary caregivers to their elderly family members (Brown, 1989).

The changes that Native American elders are commonly experiencing with regard to health problems and the need for healthcare constitute still another concern related to elder abuse. Life expectancy among Native Americans has now risen to 73.7 years (Mercer, 1996), and problems of Native American elders, as is true of elderly people in general, have changed from short-term to long-term chronic problems. Over 70% of those over 60 years of age suffer some level of limitation in their capability to take care of their own activities of daily living (Manson, 1989; Manson & Gallaway, 1988).

Part of the problems that Native American elderly are having in meeting their growing long-term care needs is the lack of adequate facilities. The Indian Health Service provides almost no long-term care services (Manson, 1989; Mercer, 1996), and by 1989 only 10 nursing facilities had been built on Indian reservations across the United States, providing services for only 435 residents (Manson). Consequently, at least 4,600 elderly Indians who need skilled nursing-home care reside in far-away, off-reservation nursing homes (Mercer). Manson reports that, when the elderly are discharged from hospitals, they typically go to what he described as "home situations that do not have adequate resources to manage their... health problems" (p. 39). As an illustration of that inadequacy Mercer reports that, of the homes of Navajo elderly, 51% have no piped water or indoor toilets, 46% lack electric lighting, and 80% do not have telephones. A limited amount of in-home nursing care is provided on a number of reservations, but given the distances to travel, the inadequacy of facilities in the homes, and the number of people needing the care it is woefully inadequate to meet the long-term care needs on reservations.

Mercer (1996) recently investigated the admissions processes for elderly Navajos at one of their on-reservation nursing homes. Her findings about the reasons given for requesting admissions are noteworthy. All of them had to do not with the persons' health as such but with conditions in their homes and among their families. The reasons included unsafe homes, lack of needed transportation, having no family to provide care, neglect by children or grandchildren, family members' alcohol problems and physical abuse, verbal abuse by family members, and financial exploitation.

Given that the circumstances discussed here are widespread across many American Indian reservations, it should not be surprising that the patterns of elder abuse found among the Navajo elderly also would be found elsewhere. To be sure, Native Americans, young and old alike, are still very much oriented to providing their elderly members with the care they need. However, providing the very technical kinds of care needed and the amount of time that is required are obviously new and overwhelming phenomena to them. Also, because of the adjustments to changing economic situations that force younger Indian workers to either leave their families behind for job opportunities or face the humiliation of becoming financially dependent upon others, with all of the personal problems related to that experience, elder abuse becomes even more probable. That is especially true if that dependency is upon the very elderly family members for whom they are trying to provide care. This kind of analysis provides us with a clear indication that elder abuse is as apt to exist on any or all Indian reservations as it does among non-Indians. It also helps us to more fully understand how very complex this problem is among Native Americans and, therefore, how complex the solutions will have to be as well.

RECOMMENDED POLICIES AND CORRECTIVE ACTIONS

A number of insightful and meritorious recommendations for actions to prevent elder abuse have been made by analysts both on and off Indian reservations. Included are educational strategies, strategies to improve assessment procedures, and policy and organizational strategies.

Proposed Educational Strategies

It is recognized by many analysts of elder abuse that education is one of the most important ways of attempting to deal with this very serious problem. Even among those who have become aware of the problem, very few understand what kinds of abuse exist, where it takes place, who the abusers are, or what the causal factors are. This basic lack of knowledge is particularly acute among Native Americans on reservations. Thus, education about elder abuse directed toward various parts of reservation populations is seen as effectively dealing with the problem.

Some have called for educational efforts in redefining the problem. In that regard, Callahan calls for educational efforts targeting professional service providers, to show them the inappropriateness of laws on elder abuse. He and others argue that elder abuse should be dealt with in the domain of the social-service system that provides victims with needed care (Callahan, 1988; Hugman, 1995).

Specific kinds of training have been suggested for professional people to enable them to overcome their biases and stereotypes related to abuse and set more realistic expectations about what should and can be done (Callahan, 1988; Hugman, 1995; Kosberg & Garcia, 1995; Lucas, 1991, pp. 10–15). These suggested educational strategies have been made on behalf of the non-Indian elderly population, but there can be little doubt that they are needed on Indian reservations as much if not more than elsewhere. A recommendation for training of professional workers and tribal officials on reservations has come from the participants at a special meeting, "American Indians and Elder Abuse: Exploring the Problem," held in 1989 at Albuquerque, New Mexico. The challenge was that "[t]ribes should arrange for or encourage the delivery of special training for service providers, law enforcement personnel, judges, council members and individual elders" (National Association of State Units on Aging, 1989). According to this proposal, the training should be "designed to raise awareness of the problem of elder abuse and promote the development of coordinated adult protective services efforts" (p. 10).

Recommendations also have been made, specifically targeting Native American families, for educational programs to improve the quality of informal caregiving and thus help to alleviate the elder abuse and neglect taking place in that context (Alley & Brown, 1988). Specifically, it has been recommended that a training package be prepared for families with elderly members to help to anticipate the care that may be needed in the future, plan how the care will be carried out, provide continuous family support to those in the families providing the care, alert them to the dangers of potential abuses, provide caregiver training to equip family members with the needed skills to carry out their duties with confidence, and provide them with an understanding of the physical and mental problems that many elderly people often have. It also has been recommended that seminars or public forums be created in which an intergenerational dialogue can take place about cultural changes, how they take place, and how they affect family interdependency.

Proposed Assessment-Improvement Strategies

Some analysts of elder abuse contend that the assessments of abuse cases done by professional service providers are typically inadequate and inappropriate. All too often cases are neither recognized before they become serious nor appropriately dealt with when they finally are identified. Therefore, assessment must be improved, according to these analysts (Nolan, 1993; Ramsey-Klawsnik, 1995). As Hugman (1995) sees it, the lack of adequate assessments stems from the fact that policies and practices related to elder abuse are based on definitions of abuse that fail to consider the existing evidence about the problem. Specifically, he maintains that the vast majority of cases of elder abuse take place in the context of what he appropriately terms the "obligation of care." Most assessments, therefore, must take that into account so that actions taken deal with the real problems involved.

Kosberg argues that because most elder abuse takes place in the context of the family and in the privacy of the older persons' homes, professional workers often fail to detect and report cases of abuse until they become serious. Thus, they deal with the problem after the fact in ways that fail to overcome the real problems and rarely do anything at all about prevention (Kosberg, 1988; Kosberg & Garcia, 1995). He therefore calls for assessments that have the potential to provide preventative policies and practices (Kosberg, 1988).

Callahan (1988) makes the point that assessments need to be applied to outcomes as well as inputs into the problem. Obviously, some form of intervention is assumed to be necessary whenever we discover cases of elder abuse, but how can we be certain that the specific interventions we adopt really help solve the problem? Callahan's response to this question is that "research should be conducted on the outcomes of social interventions into family problems and family violence. What works, for whom, and under what conditions" (p. 458)?

These analysts have not attempted to apply these ideas about the need for improved assessments to Native Americans, to be sure. They seem clearly to imply, however, that the need for better assessment is universal. Indeed, from what we have learned about elder abuse among Native Americans it seems apparent that even service providers tend to lack adequate definitions, appropriate assessments, and successful interventions (Brown et al., 1990).

Proposed Policy and Organizational Strategies

A number of recommendations have been made by those analyzing elder abuse, with regard to policy decisions and organizational interventions, that address the major factors related to cases of abuse. These suggestions deal specifically with caregiver problems, family relationships, working relationships between the formal and informal caregiver systems, interagency relationships within communities, and economic conditions in communities in which abuse takes place.

It is well established that, both on and off Indian reservations, elder abuse of various kinds is strongly associated with the provision of care by informal caregivers, mostly family members. The stresses and the isolation that those folks experience in the performance of that very demanding role have been identified as especially important contributors to abuse. Therefore, interventions that have the potential to help informal caregivers cope with the stresses and perform their roles more successfully are being proposed. For one thing, the formation of caregiver support groups is seen as an excellent way to help them cope (Alley & Brown, 1988; Steinmetz, 1990).

Intrafamily relationships obviously also constitute part of the problem of elder abuse. It seems clear that the tradition of interdependent cooperation within Native American families is being compromised to some degree today by the social and economic changes that are taking place. One proposal that was made to the Navajos was to form "family/clan interdependent support groups" to cooperatively provide respite and other types of support to each other in their mutual caregiver duties (Alley & Brown, 1988).

In most communities, on as well as off Indian reservations, both formal and informal systems exist that provide care and services for older persons. For the most part those two systems must depend upon each other's resources to be effective. On the one hand, the formal systems lack the resources of time and personnel that the informal system has, to provide the amount of care needed by the elderly in their communities. On the other hand, the informal systems typically lack professional skills and expertise, which the formal systems possess, to accomplish what is needed in providing care to the elderly who need it. This was found to be true among the Navajo elderly who were interviewed about elder abuse. Therefore, it was recommended that "a cooperative caregiver system between professional service providers and family caregivers be created" (Alley & Brown, 1988). Included in that program would be easily accessible information about referral channels and a case-management program in which both professional people and family members would participate in determining how cases ought to be handled. For that type of program to operate the most effectively, to the extent possible, interagency coordination in the form of multidisciplinary teams of professionals would be needed, as recommended by Wolf and Pillemer (1994).

Other practical community organizational recommendations were made by the delegates at the 1989 conference on Native American elder abuse in Albuquerque. Included were recommendations that Adult Protective Services agencies be developed on reservations that do not yet have them, that tribes establish "elder desks" or "offices on senior affairs" to which older people can turn for help, and that abuse advisory committees be formed and include elder representatives. They also proposed that more demonstration and research projects on elder abuse be funded by the federal government (National Association of State Units on Aging, 1989).

Based on the finding from their study of elder abuse on two Indian reservations, the Maxwells pointed to the need for broad-based policy changes. As they explained, "individual treatment programs were failing," and the reason for that was that little if anything was being done "to eliminate the structural conditions which lead to incidents of abuse" (Maxwell & Maxwell, 1992). Specifically, the structural conditions to which they refer are the lack of economic development and the cultural isolation found especially in one of the reservations studied, as noted previously. They recommend that policymakers "focus on structural antecedents to social problems" and "adopt a more holistic perspective" (instead of merely an individual one) about the problem of elder abuse (Maxwell & Maxwell, 1992). In discussing elder abuse in general, Callahan makes a similar point by stating that "policy must recognize the greatest abuse that can beset older persons, that is, failure to provide them with the economic means for a decent life and opportunities to exercise their own choices" (Callahan, 1988).

CONCLUSION

Drawing conclusions about elder abuse among Native Americans is by no means a simple or easy task. The problem has not been adequately or consistently defined. It has been thought of and treated as just another form of family violence with very little consideration given to how it may be a unique form of family abuse. Furthermore, how Native Americans, other minority and racial groups, and the White American majority may understand the problem differently has largely been ignored. Consequently, all-too-often misinformed and ineffective solutions have been tried. In addition, very little attention at all has been given to elder abuse among Native Americans, either in terms of systematic studies of or actions to deal with the problem.

Nevertheless, the available data provide important evidence, not only that elder abuse exists as a real problem among Native Americans, but also of what characterizes that problem. We have learned, for example, that neglect and not physical abuse (as often thought) is the most prevalent and serious form of elder abuse; it is overwhelmingly a family problem (done in the home by family members); it is by-and-large situational rather than pathological; it takes place in the context of an intense negotiation of family roles and relationships; and it is very much related to the economic conditions of families.

Elder abuse among Native Americans could be characterized as a dependency-creating situation. On the one hand, the evidence indicates that most abuse takes place as elderly people lose their capacity to care for themselves and become dependent upon their families to care for them. Becoming dependent within the family constitutes a new and troubling role for elderly persons. Becoming a caregiver, especially when it becomes full time, constitutes a new role for family members. These roles not only are new but must be negotiated often at a time of crisis and with much emotional tension, misunderstanding, and conflict. If neglect, verbal abuse, and occasional physical abuse occur they usually happen in that kind of intense dependency situation.

On the other hand, economic conditions tend to create an opposite type of dependency among Native American elderly. Unemployment among younger family members makes them economically dependent upon others in their families. In some cases they become dependent upon older family members when the older persons are the only ones within the families with regular, although meager, incomes. Using older persons' incomes to benefit younger family members is increasingly labeled as "exploitation" by outside observers. Evidence indicates that most elderly Native Americans reject that label, insisting that they are simply living up to the long tradition of family interdependency. Regardless of how we define it, however, it is an example of younger adults becoming dependent upon older family members.

Obviously, the biggest concern with regard to elder abuse is to find solutions that actually do something to correct the problem or prevent it from happening in the first place. In that regard, much of what has been done thus far could be called "criminalizing" it—passing mandatory reporting laws and prosecuting those found to be the abusers. This process is certainly worthwhile, because at least some cases of abuse constitute criminal behavior in which the perpetrators should be removed from the situations and punished. It does not, however, take into consideration the enormous complexity of the problem or account for the fact that a great deal of what happens is not criminal. Neither does it solve the problematic conditions in which most abuse takes place.

Effective solutions must be based on what the evidence tells us about the situations in which abuse tends to take place; what is culturally sensitive and compatible; what takes all components of the problem into account; and what deals effectively with the issue and respects elderly persons' perspectives of the issues related to abuse. The proposed solutions discussed here represent attempts to meet those criteria. By no means are they offered as the final answers that will overcome elder abuse among Native Americans, however. Three suggestions for further efforts also are made to ensure that the proposed solutions are effective. First, much more research on elder abuse among Native Americans across the nation is needed. Second, a concerted planning effort is needed to implement the solutions that seem to be the most promising. Third, the effectiveness of all solutions that are attempted must be carefully evaluated.

REFERENCES

Alley, J., & Brown, A. S. (1988, March). *Navajo Elder Abuse*. Paper presented at the Annual Meeting of the American Society on Aging, San Diego.

Boudreau, F. A. (1993). Elder abuse. In R. I. Hampton (Ed.), *Family violence: Prevention and treatment* (pp. 142–158). Newbury Park, CA: Sage.

Brown, A. S. (1989). A survey on elder abuse at one Native American tribe. *Journal of Elder Abuse & Neglect, 1*, 17–37.

Brown, A. S., Fernandez, R., & Griffith, T. M. (1990). *Service provider perceptions of elder abuse among the Navajo* (Research Report RR-90-3). Flagstaff, AZ: Northern Arizona University, Social Research Laboratory.

Callahan, J. J. (1988). Elder abuse: Some questions for policymakers. *The Gerontologist, 28*, 453–458.

Carson, D. K. (1995). American Indian elder abuse: Risk and protective factors among the oldest Americans. *Journal of Elder Abuse & Neglect, 7*, 17–39.

Dicharry, E. K. (1986). Delivering home health care to the elderly in Zuni Pueblo. *Journal of Gerontological Nursing, 12*, 25–29.

DuBray, W. H. (1985). American Indian values: Critical factor in casework. *Social Casework: The Journal of Contemporary Social Work*, January, 30–37.

Hanley, C. (1991). Navajo Indians. In J. N. Giger & R. E. Davidhizar (Eds.), *Transcultural nursing: Assessment and Intervention* (pp. 215–237). St. Louis: Mosby-Year Book, Inc.

Hugman, R. (1995). The implications of the term 'elder abuse' for problem definition and response in health and social welfare. *Journal of Social Policy, 24*, 493–507.

Kosberg, J. I. (1988). Preventing elder abuse: Identification of high risk factors prior to placement decisions. *The Gerontologist, 28*, 43–50.

Kosberg, J. I., & Garcia, J. I. (1995). Confronting maltreatment of elders. In S. Tobin, E. A. Robertson-Tchabo, & P. W. Power (Eds.), *Strengthening aging families: Diversity in practice and policy* (pp. 63–79). Thousand Oaks, CA: Sage.

Locust, C. (1988). Wounding the spirit: Discrimination and traditional American Indian belief systems. *Harvard Educational Review, 58*, 315–328.

Lucas, E. T. (1991). *Elder Abuse and its Recognition among Health Service Professionals*. New York: Garland.

Manson, S. M. (1989). Long-term care in American Indian communities: Issues for planning and research. *The Gerontologist, 29*, 38–44.

Manson, S. M., & Gallaway, D. G. (1988). Health and aging among American Indians: Issues and challenges for the Biobehavioral Sciences. In S. M. Manson & N. G. Dinges (Eds.), *Behavioral health issues among American Indians and Alaska natives: Explorations on the frontiers of the biobehavioral sciences* (pp. 160–200). Denver: University of Colorado Health Sciences Center.

Maxwell, E. K., & Maxwell, R. J. (1992). Insults to the body civil: Mistreatment of elderly in two Plains Indian tribes. *Journal of Cross-Cultural Gerontology, 7*, 3–23.

McShane, D. (1987). Mental health and North American Indian/native communities: Cultural transactions, education, and regulation. *American Journal of Community Psychology, 15*, 95–116.

Mercer, S. O. (1996). Navajo elderly people in a reservation nursing home: Admission predictors and culture care practices. *Social Work, 41*, 181–189.

Moon, A., & Williams, O. (1993). Perceptions of elder abuse patterns among African-American, Caucasian American, and Korean-American elderly women. *The Gerontologist, 33*, 386–395.

National Association of State Units on Aging. (1989, November). *American Indians and Elder Abuse: Exploring the Problem* (Report of a meeting in Albuquerque, NM, convened by the National Aging Resource Center on Elder Abuse). Washington, DC: Author.

Nolan, M. (1993). Carer-dependent relationships and the prevention of elder abuse. In P. Decalmer & F. Glendenning (Eds.), *The mistreatment of elderly people* (pp. 148–158). Newbury Park, CA: Sage.

Ramsey-Klawsnik, H. (1995). Investigating suspected elder mistreatment. *Journal of Elder Abuse & Neglect, 7*, 41–67.

Sandefur, G. D., & Sakamoto, A. (1988). American Indian household structure and income. *Demography, 25*, 71–80.

Steinmetz, S. K. (1990). Elder abuse: Myth and reality. In T. H. Brubaker (Ed.), *Family relationships in later life* (pp. 193–211). Newbury Park, CA: Sage.

Weibel-Orlando, J. (1990). Grandparenting styles: Native American perspectives. In J. Sokolovsky (Ed.), *The cultural context of aging: Worldwide perspectives* (pp. 109–125). New York: Bergin & Garvey.

Williams, G. C. (1989). Warriors no more: A Study of the American Indian Elderly. In C. L. Fry (Ed.), *Aging in culture and society* (pp. 101–111). Brooklyn, NY: Bergin Publishing.

Wolf, R. S., & Pillemer, K. (1994). What's new in elder abuse programming? Four bright ideas. *The Gerontologist, 34*, 126–129.

Chapter 11

Dilemmas Surrounding Elder Abuse and Neglect in Native American Communities[1]

David K. Carson[2] & Carol Hand

This chapter reflects the synergy that flows from collaboration between two people from different cultural backgrounds, blending the thoughtful scholarship of a European American professor and researcher with the cultural insight of an Ojibwa practitioner and advocate. One of the most crucial questions that has emerged from this partnership, often neglected in research on "other" groups, is: How can the information discussed in this article benefit the people about whom it is written?

As Goc (1995) points out in a history of the Lac du Flambeau Ojibwa community, American Indian people have been studied more than any other group, by "[m]issionaries, government agents, scholars of various sorts, journalists, and the uncredentialed curious" (p. 76). Yet Indian people, both rural and urban, remain among the most misunderstood and disadvantaged groups within the United States by almost every socioeconomic indicator—income, housing, education, health status, and life expectancy (Manson, 1993; Snipp, 1989). The present generation of Native American elders have faced multidimensional contextual challenges across their life span, resulting in a unique blend of factors that both decrease and increase their risk of experiencing some type of maltreatment during their later years. The purpose of this chapter is to synthesize what is known

[1]The terms *American Indian, Native American*, and *Native American Indian* are sometimes used interchangeably to refer to native people on the North American continent. Such is the case in this chapter. However, technically, *Native American* includes Alaskan Natives (Eskimo and Aleut).

[2]Neither author claims "first authorship" of this chapter, because each contributed equally to its formulation and production. The authors wish to thank Dr. Cecyle Perry at the University of Wyoming for her very helpful comments on an earlier version of this paper. They also wish to thank the Honorable Betty Jo Graveen, Lac du Flambeau Ojiwa Tribal Judge, for her insights and assistance; Jane Raymond, Elder Abuse Policy Coordinator for the Wisconsin Department of Health and Family Services, for sharing information on Tribal initiatives and feminist concerns; and Roseanne Barber, Human Services Facilitator for the Lac Courte Oreailles Ojibwa Tribe, for sharing her ideas regarding the intergenerational nature of family violence and the need for new prevention strategies.

about elder abuse and neglect within Native American communities and to discuss approaches that have proven to be effective in resolving conflict on individual, community-wide, and social-policy levels.

The discussion of elder abuse and neglect within Native American communities that follows addresses a number of questions. To what extent do elder neglect and abuse occur today, and what types of abuse and neglect are present? Are abuse and neglect recent social developments, or have Native elders always been at risk? How can these behaviors be understood within a cultural and historical framework? And more importantly, what implications does this information have for designing and implementing successful, culturally appropriate interventions?

Before we discuss the phenomenon of elder maltreatment within Native American Indian communities today, it is imperative that an historical perspective of aging in these diverse cultures first be provided. Perhaps with no other people on this continent does the past influence and flow into the present more than in Native American tribes, communities, and families.

SOCIOHISTORICAL OVERVIEW

Understanding elder neglect and abuse within Native American communities necessitates an understanding of three significant contextual distinctions. First, Native cultures are often spoken of without acknowledging the tremendous range of cultural diversity that exists today among the more than 500 federally recognized tribes within the United States. Second, these differences have been affected in complex ways by the interplay of culture and the unique sociohistorical experience of each tribal community. Third, unlike other numeric minority groups, American Indian people are members of sovereign nations. The status of tribes as "domestic dependent nations" has been recognized by treaties, the United States Constitution, and a plethora of federal statutes and has been upheld on many occasions by the U.S. Supreme Court (Pevar, 1992).

Sovereign political status is unique to Native American people. Like other racial/ethnic minority groups, American Indians have experienced centuries of discrimination. However, intervention into the lives of American Indians has been reserved primarily as the responsibility of the United States government since the creation of the U.S. Constitution. Until very recent times (the mid 1970s), the aim of federal policies has been to gain control of Native American lands and resources through deliberate assimilationistic practices. It is beyond the scope of the present chapter to discuss this history, which is summarized in Table 11.1.

Shifting federal policies have had profound impacts on the relationships within Native communities and families. Take, for example, the forced use of boarding schools—the practice of removing children from their families and communities, sometimes at gunpoint, and sending them hundreds of miles away to live for years in an institutional setting (O'Brien, 1989). The purpose of boarding schools, operated by both the federal government and religious denominations,

Table 11.1 Major Federal/Tribal Policy Relationships

Dates	Policy	Major legislation	Consequences for American Indian nations
1770s-1820s	International sovereign to international sovereign	1783 Northwest ordinance 1790 Trade and Intercourse Acts Treaties	Guaranteed sovereignty and protection in exchange for land cessions. The Bureau of Indian Affairs was created within the U.S. War Department in 1824 to oversee relationships with tribes.
1830s-1850s	Removal	1830 Indian Removal Act	In violation of original treaty agreements, tribes suffered massive land loss and death as a result of the forced cross-country relocation of Eastern Tribes across the Mississippi River. Relocated tribes were guaranteed that their new homes would remain theirs forever.
1850s-1890s	Reservation	Reservation Treaties	In exchange for large cessions of land, Indian tribes were located on "reserved lands" owned by the tribe as a whole. Small cash settlements and promises of health, education, and other services were to be made in payment.
1870s-1930s	Assimilation	1871 End of treaty making 1885 Major Crimes Act 1887 Allotment Act 1924 Indian Citizenship Act	Congress assumed legislative responsibility for overseeing "Indian issues," assumed criminal jurisdiction over major crimes committed by Indians on reservations, and terminated communal land ownership of Indian lands. Individual Indians were awarded taxable tracts and the surplus lands were opened up for white settlement. Many tribal land owners lost their remaining land to taxes or speculators. Indians were granted U.S. citizenship through the allotment process or special legislation.

(Continued)

Table 11.1 Major Federal/Tribal Policy Relationships (Continued)

Dates	Policy	Major legislation	Consequences for American Indian nations
1930s-1950s	Indian self-government	1934 Indian Reorganization Act 1949 Bureau of Indian Affairs is transferred to new U.S. Department of Interior	In response to the Merriam report of 1928, which documented deplorable health conditions, starvation, and poverty on reservations, Congress recognized tribal rights to organize their own governments with limited sovereignty over tribal lands and members.
1950s-1960s	Termination	1953 Resolution 108 1953 Public Law 280 Urban Relocation Program	The process of disbanding tribal governments was begun with selected tribes, and selected states were granted civil and criminal jurisdiction over tribes that were not terminated. A concerted effort was initiated to relocate reservation Indians to urban areas.
1960s-present	Self-government	1968 Indian Civil Rights Act 1975 Indian Self-Determination Act 1978 Indian Child Welfare Act 1978 Indian Religious Freedom Act	The termination process was stopped and in some cases reversed. Efforts were made to reestablish tribal administrative control over some health, education, and social services. Mechanisms for resuming jurisdiction for child welfare issues were established, and limited religious freedoms were recognized.

Source: Adapted from O'Brien, 1989, p. 258.

was to inculcate dominant values and language by forbidding children to speak their own languages, practice their own religious beliefs, wear their traditional clothing and hair styles, participate in cultural events, or spend time with their families. Infringements were severely punished. Instead of growing up surrounded by loving grandparents and family, generations of children spent their childhood in austere institutions, subjected to discrimination and harsh discipline. Many of those who are now elders were sent to boarding schools, were relocated to urban areas, or are members of tribal communities whose sovereign status was abolished ("terminated") during the Eisenhower years. These policies have left a powerful legacy for individuals, families, and communities.

Despite the harmful effects of such policies, however, many facets of tribal cultures have persisted. During the 1970s, federal–tribal relations entered a new phase: Federal commitment to tribal sovereignty, self-determination, and self-governance was reaffirmed. Self-governance and cultural revitalization have become important foci within many Native communities. The impacts of these new directions have been both positive and negative for tribal elders.

EVIDENCE OF ABUSE AND NEGLECT WITHIN NATIVE AMERICAN COMMUNITIES

Changes in American Indian family life and culture have posed a serious threat to the status, roles, and well-being of older Native people in the latter part of the 20th century. Controls and abuses from outside tribal culture and ongoing turmoil within have put the elderly at greater risk for maltreatment, including various forms of neglect, exploitation, and family violence. Although little is known about elder abuse and neglect among Native American Indians because of the scarcity of national prevalence data in this area among all sociocultural groups, including Native Americans (Wolf, 1989), Resolution 88-14 of the National Indian Health Board designates that elder abuse is a significant health problem that must be investigated and remedied (U.S. Senate Hearing 100–981, 1988). However, cultural and family strengths that have been maintained by Native Americans for generations may continue to serve as protective factors against neglect, abuse, and other forms of domestic abuse. It is likely that the relative strength of risk and protective factors associated with abuse and neglect varies tremendously both within and across tribes.

Reports by tribal members, police, and human-service professionals, as well as findings from two major studies (Brown, 1989; Maxwell & Maxwell, 1992), point to the existence of elder abuse and neglect in some Native American populations. According to Carson (1995, pp. 17–39), common types of abuse and neglect described by Pillemer and Finkelhor (1988) and Wolf and Pillemer (1989) all have been observed among Native people. These include:

1   Physical violence (the infliction of physical pain or injury, physical coercion, sexual molestation, physical restraint).
2   Psychological abuse (the infliction of mental or emotional anguish).
3   Material abuse (the illegal or improper exploitation or use of funds or resources).
4   Active neglect (withholding items necessary for daily living or basic care for the physically dependent person).
5   Passive neglect that leaves the elderly person alone, isolated, or forgotten.

Other expressions of abuse and neglect that may occur in American Indian communities include medical abuse or neglect (Block & Sinnott, 1979), abandonment of the elderly by family members (Eastman, 1984), structural or social–

environmental abuse (Chen, Bell, Dolinsky, Doyle, & Dunn, 1981), and legal abuse (Johnson, 1991). Whether some types of abuse are more common than others (e.g., spousal battering or physical abuse from adult children), and the extent to which there are rural versus urban differences in the manifestations and incidence rates of elder abuse and neglect among Native people, cannot yet be determined from any data source of which we are aware. However, as is shown in this chapter, there is limited evidence that suggests that expressions of neglect and abuse among Americans Indians differ considerably from the "mainstream" and probably across tribal cultures as well. Moreover, because it has been estimated that approximately 50% of elderly Native Americans live in extended family households (Cox, 1996; Hooyman, & Kiyuk, 1996), with so many of them being poor, older Native adults reside in situations that may put them at greater risk for elder abuse and neglect.

SUMMARY OF EMPIRICAL STUDIES OF ELDER MALTREATMENT AMONG NATIVE AMERICANS

We have identified only two empirical investigations of elder abuse and neglect among Native people, one that focused on Navajos (Brown, 1989) and one that studied two unidentified Plains Indian reservations (Maxwell & Maxwell, 1992). Despite the paucity of research, these two studies illustrate many of the risk factors involved in the neglect and abuse of Native American elders. Results indicated that there were both similarities and differences in risk factors and types of elder mistreatment on these reservations. Major findings were that:

    1   Elder abuse and neglect among Navajos (Brown, 1989) and the two Plains Indian tribes (Maxwell & Maxwell, 1992) generally were not common occurrences.
    2   The prevalence of elder abuse appears to be much lower than that found among other groups, including European Americans and African Americans (see, e.g., Wolf & Pillemer, 1989, pp. 32–34).
    3   Neglect and exploitation were the most typical manifestations of elder mistreatment.
    4   There were large differences between these reservations in the frequency of reported abuse and neglect.
    5   Common risk factors on these reservations included economic shortages and a lack of employment opportunities on the reservation (associated in part with the abundance of natural resources and agriculture), dependency and caregiving issues and responsibilities (i.e., between adult children and their elderly parents), mental-health and substance-abuse problems, and the widening cultural gap between Indian youth and the elderly.

    However, risk factors for elder mistreatment within one Plains Indian reservation community appeared to be greater in number and variety than within either the other Plains Indian reservation or the Navajo reservation. Hence, a comparison of these tribes suggests that although the types of risk factors among reservation Indians appear to be similar, the prevalence and severity of these factors varies greatly. In addition, each tribe's unique historical experiences and cultural heritage mediate the ways in which risk (and protective) factors influence or are associated with various sociopsychopathologies such as elder abuse and neglect.

In sum, although there is empirical evidence of elder maltreatment among some Native American tribes, our experience with people on several reservations has been that elder abuse is difficult to substantiate because it typically is kept a secret within the family and rarely reported to the authorities such as the tribal police or judge. Victims may perceive that they do not have the option of leaving their current living situation for many reasons (close, enduring family and cultural ties, or lack of economic, housing, or service options). Additionally, both the victim and the perpetrator might experience tremendous social shame and stigma if the victim were to report his or her abuse or neglect. However, it may be, as Brown (1989) suggests, that most older Native Americans do not view themselves as abused, neglected, or exploited by family members—possibly because of the strong loyalty that exists between the elderly and their families. Our experience is that older Native people are much more likely to report structural or institutional types of abuse or neglect, such as from various health or social-service systems. One example of this type of abuse would be the discriminatory or paternalistic attitudes they confront, the endless "White tape" they have to go through to receive necessary services, and the invasiveness of these information gathering procedures.

THE PROCESS OF GROWING OLD IN TRIBAL CULTURES: AN HISTORICAL OVERVIEW

Although tribal cultures remain diverse, there are some important generalizations that can be made with respect to attitudes toward elders today and in the past. Native American cultures today do share respectful attitudes toward elders. In his 1995 article, Carson noted: "To even raise the issue of whether elder abuse occurs among American Indians may be anathema to many, since for centuries the majority of Indian tribes have emphasized respect for the aged, valued the unique role of grandparents, and held tribal elders in high esteem" (p. 17). For example, the Midewiwin, or Great Medicine Society, Code of the Ojibwa people stresses respect of elders as one of its nine tenets: "Honor the aged: In honoring them you honor life and wisdom."

Yet, there is a tendency among many cultures to equate ideals with behavior and to romanticize the past. Native Americans share this tendency. However, cultural anthropologists have studied the consonance of attitudes and behaviors toward elders within Native communities during the past, both through direct observation and by reviewing archival data recorded by first-contact observers. Using data from a world sample of 41 nonindustrialized societies that included American Indian nations, Glascock and Feinman (1980) and Glascock (1990) catalogued prevailing attitudes toward, and treatment of, elders. They suggest that cultures distinguish between "intact" and "decrepit" elders, according respect primarily to those who are viewed as useful to society (i.e., "intact"). Further, they report three different categories of behavior toward elders: supportive, non-death hastening nonsupportive, and death-hastening.

In 37% of the societies Glascock (1990) studied, both death-hastening and supportive or nonthreatening behavior were present simultaneously, with different types of behavior accorded to different categories of elders within that society. Glascock notes: "The killing of the elderly *does* occur in other societies, and when killing, forsaking, and abandoning are combined into the broad category of death hastening, the elderly are dispatched in 50% of the societies with data in the... [sample]. The sex of the individual does not appear to make a difference, since both males and females have their deaths hastened... Death hastening is directed toward individuals who have passed from being active and productive to being inactive and nonproductive members of the social group" (p. 51). Glascock notes a relationship between attitudes, behaviors, and the nature of the physical environment in which communities are located. Those societies that were located in harsh environments (particularly desert or tundra areas) were less able to care for frail individuals and were more likely to practice some type of death-hastening treatment of elders. The Ojibwa people, whose behavioral code has been cited here, were among those societies in which elders were killed, usually after a decision was made jointly by an elder and his or her family (Glascock). From a perspective of cultural relativity, nonsupportive and death-hastening practices served to maximize the chances of survival for communities facing harsh environments, even though attitudes and behaviors were generally the social norm.

These findings are significant. They demonstrate that balanced, healthy relationships are an ideal toward which all societies strive, albeit imperfectly. Elder neglect and abuse are not necessarily a new phenomenon among Native Americans, although the reasons behind their occurrence may be different than in the past.

It is important to point out that, because life expectancy of Native Americans is approximately 8 years less than that of the general population, and because American Indian people at age 45 years experience the same health and functional limitations as their white counterparts do at age 65 years (see National Indian Council on Aging, 1988), the concept of *old* or *elderly* means something very different to Native people, even compared with other ethnic and cultural groups in the United States. Hence, it may be appropriate to consider Native Americans as "older" at a younger chronological age than members of the majority population (John, 1988; Saravanabhavan & Marshall, 1994), with "elderly" referring to individuals between 50 and 60 years of age and older (see also Gelfand, 1987). There are also no exact figures regarding the number of elderly Native Americans living in urban areas as compared with those on or near reservations, although the distributions in each domain may be fairly equal, with probably somewhat greater numbers residing on reservations (U.S. Bureau of the Census, 1992).

CONCEPTUAL FRAMEWORKS FOR UNDERSTANDING ELDER ABUSE AND NEGLECT AMONG NATIVE AMERICANS

No single theory, as Filinson and Ingman (1989) rightly assert, can adequately explain elder abuse and neglect among any group of people. Moreover, clear and inclusive definitions of elder neglect and abuse that apply to Indian people are difficult if not impossible to formulate, given their great cultural diversity, the lack of data on elder abuse and neglect among Native Americans, and the variety of forms it may take. As Biggs, Phillipson, and Kingston (1995) have recently argued, theoretical approaches to elder abuse and neglect tend to be either pragmatic or conceptual. Pragmatic approaches tend to be drawn from practice settings (e.g., health- or human service–related), whereas conceptual approaches have arisen from sociological or psychological theories and then been applied to various forms of family violence, including that directed toward elders. Central to pragmatic theories is a risk- and protective-factors approach to understanding elder abuse and neglect. From a conceptual point of view, some of the numerous theories that have been offered to explain or predict elder abuse and neglect within the majority culture have included psychopathological, structural–functional, learning, social exchange, interactionist, situational, symbolic interactionist, conflict, systems-ecological (or ecosystemic), and environmental press (stressors or demands) theory.[3] Each of these perspectives, in our opinion, sheds some light on these complex phenomena and is somewhat useful when applied to Indian people.

For example, exchange theories and conflict theories might focus on power and control dynamics in Native American families, in which older adults are perceived as weak, vulnerable, and incapable (and perhaps easily exploited); a continual source of burden given their limited health or financial status; and taking more than they give back to relationships (unequal cost–benefit ratio). Maltreatment thus would be more likely to occur. Systems-ecological and environmental-press approaches to explaining elder abuse and neglect would emphasize the difficulties that families experience in their current sociocultural milieus, the pile-up of these stresses and strains over time that can tear at the fabric of family life, and the resources (both material and human) that family members have available to them to cope with these difficulties. Environmental presses in the lives of many Native Americans may outweigh the competencies or adaptive abilities of certain individuals in the family on a consistent basis. With regard to older Indians, this might include both individual limitations (e.g., physical or mental disabilities)

---

[3]Environmental press is explained in N. Hooyman & H. A. Kiyak (1996). This text defines environment as "the larger society, the community, the neighborhood, or the home. Environmental press refers to the demands that social and physical environments make on the individual to adapt, respond, or change" (p. 6). The text also defines the concept of "individual competence... as the theoretical upper limit of an individual's abilities to function in the areas of health, social behavior, and cognition. Some of the abilities needed to adapt to environmental press include good health, effective problem solving and learning, skills, job performance and the ability to manage the basic activities of daily living such as dressing, grooming, and cooking" (p. 7). It was first referenced and defined in M. P. Lawton and L. Nahemow (1973).

and circumstances (e.g., crowded living arrangements and geographical isolation) that prevent them from utilizing their full range of biological, sensorimotor, cognitive, social, and emotional capacities to meet the demands of their everyday lives. The "presses" of caring for an aging parent or relative also may exceed the adult caregiver's ability to cope with ongoing demands, thus contributing to abusive or neglectful behavior.

Despite the positive contributions of the theoretical approach, our emphasis in this chapter is the pragmatic approach—particularly an examination of protective and risk factors that may be associated with elder maltreatment among Native Americans.

A RISK- AND PROTECTIVE-FACTORS APPROACH TO UNDERSTANDING ELDER ABUSE AND NEGLECT IN NATIVE AMERICAN COMMUNITIES

Protective Factors Involved in Elder Abuse and Neglect

The tribal and cultural strengths of Native people have for centuries contributed to individual and family survival and resiliency under the most adverse of conditions (Hodge, 1981; Snipp, 1989). Although not an exhaustive list, these strengths have included an emphasis on family and tribal interdependence and support; community conscience and responsibility; group participation and success; cooperation and noncompetition except in playful, ceremonial (e.g., pow wow), or athletic activities; values rooted deeply in tribal culture (e.g., cooperation, reciprocity, generosity); optimism and contentment that come from a cosmic identity; a deep sense of spirituality; ritualistic or religious practices; and a priority of living in harmony with all creation (Lewis, 1981; Olson and Wilson, 1984). Some tribal groups have been able to maintain these values and practices much more than others in the 20th century.

Furthermore, although the extended family is changing, according to some reports it is not necessarily breaking down (Lewis, 1981; Medicine, 1981; Stauss, 1988). The majority of Native people (including the elderly) indicates that their family networks and fictive kin relationships continue to be stable sources of strength and encouragement (Miller, 1981; Red Horse, 1980; Snipp, 1989). Sandefur and Sakamoto (1988) report that the presence of traditional couple-headed households is actually higher among Native American families than in European American and African American families. Other investigators have observed that older family members are frequently involved in childrearing and supervision, and the transgenerational transmission of teachings and customs (John, 1988; Robbins, 1984; Stauss, 1986).

Respect for elders, both tribal and familial, is instilled in children from a young age. Historically in most tribes, the majority of older adults have not been deserted or isolated from the family or tribe, and tribal elders today still perform many important spiritual, political, and tribal functions (Burgess, 1980; John,

1988). They serve as role models and sources of historical and cultural information (oral tradition), for example regarding legends, songs, dances, prayers, and spiritual practices. They are also teachers of tribal language, traditional arts and crafts, and methods of hunting, and they fulfill roles of ritual specialists and masters of ceremonies at tribal programs and events (Edwards, 1983; Schweitzer, 1983). In many Indian households older adults perform significant roles and functions, such as story-telling and caring for children. Older adults also provide an important link between family, clan, and tribe. The emphasis on community responsibility for the welfare of children and the elderly in most tribes also may serve as a buffer against various types of family violence (Benokraitis, 1996; Staples & Mirande, 1980; Yates, 1987).

In some tribes elders have been able to hold on to their unique status, responsibilities, and power. For example, Arapaho elders in Wyoming maintain their prestige by controlling religious rituals and functions (Fowler, 1990). Older Navajo women are responsible for ensuring reciprocity in the family and tribe, and are central figures in kin relationships and tribal dealings. In fact, the renewed interest in preserving the Indian race, culture, and history in many Native American communities has focused on the crucial role of elders (Curley, 1987). Further, during the current era of cultural revitalization among many American Indian communities, both rural and urban, the importance of elders who have retained cultural knowledge and language facility has been heightened.

Grandparents have held a unique position of respect in most Native American cultures. Grandparents transmit cultural values and beliefs and educate children about the physical, social, and spiritual worlds by communicating to their grandchildren tribal history, traditions, philosophies, myths, and stories or special events (Weibel-Orlando, 1990). Grandparents are often viewed as being at the center of family life, and grandmothers, especially, often serve as kin-keepers and parental surrogates to grandchildren (Shomaker, 1990; Weibel-Orlando, 1990). It also has been our observation that grandparents and other older relatives serve as foster parents, either formally or informally.

Finally, many American Indian cultures have retained paradigms for viewing and resolving intra- and interfamily disputes that differ from European American views in fundamental ways. We suggest, as Hand (1996) has argued, that tribes represent "communities of relatedness"—communities characterized by relationships that have endured from one generation to the next for centuries. Although the nature of these relationships has been profoundly affected by such federal interventions as boarding schools and relocation, they have nonetheless withstood the test of time and remain powerful connections among people. Yet, federal interventions can be characterized as policies developed to maintain order and address problems experienced by "collectivities of strangers" (Hand, 1996). Historian Linda Gordon (1989, 1994) provides some support for this view in her careful scholarly review of the attitudes of those who were instrumental in designing income maintenance and child welfare programs in the United States. According to Gordon, the architects of these programs came from economically advantaged

European American backgrounds, while the intended targets of these programs were poor and largely immigrant "others."

Policies designed for "collectivities of strangers" are often punitive, paternalistic, or, as Gordon (1994) asserts, maternalistic models of intervention. Such approaches fit very poorly in communities of relatedness. Yet, such approaches have constituted the very fabric of interventions imposed on tribal communities. Dominant-culture policies that guide interventions are narrowly targeted by age, income status, or individual deviance (Dolgoff, Feldstein, & Skolnik, 1993). They fail to accommodate the needs of individuals who are integral members of multi-generational families and communities, individuals whose ties to others within their social network are close and enduring. Furthermore, the preoccupation of judging an individual on the basis of one behavior and focusing solely on punishment is predominate in the field of elder abuse and neglect within the United States, as it does with many behaviors that are categorized as deviant or criminal.

Many American Indian communities still adhere, at least partially, to a broader dispute-resolution paradigm that emerged from communities of relatedness (O'Brien, 1993). Each individual is an integral part of the community as a whole; each person's actions reflect a distinctive life path that cannot be judged by others; and the goodness or harm one shows to others will return to the life of the sender. Each has a role to play in community survival. Traditional approaches for resolving conflict and disputes recognize these connections, focusing more on healing relationships, and teaching and reinforcing appropriate behavior among community members. The aim is not individual punishment, but rather the maintaining of interpersonal relationships and the functional integrity of the entire community. This is a significant cultural difference and an enduring community strength. Some of the emerging theoretical paradigms within the field of social work offer the promise of improved models for intervention (see, e.g., Miley, O'Melia, & DuBois, 1995).

Risk Factors Involved in Elder Abuse and Neglect

Risk factors involved in elder abuse and neglect in the mainstream culture have been discussed at length by a number of investigators. For instance, Johnson (1991) categorizes her lengthy discussion of risk factors in elder maltreatment under two major rubrics—the primary risk factor of the precipitator and/or victim being overwhelmed with their lives, and secondary risk factors that include a lack of knowledge among adult children and other caregivers with regard to providing care for older adults, a lack of resources to care for elders adequately, social isolation of those living on reservations, and inappropriate expectations about what older adults can and should do for themselves and others. Other excellent reviews have been presented, for example, by Biggs et al. (1995) and Decalmer and Glendenning (1993). However, the integrative perspectives of Pillemer (1986) and Wolf & Pillemer (1989) provide some of the most useful frameworks for understanding elder maltreatment in various populations, including (in our view) Native Americans. Their approach encompasses a discussion of external stress (e.g., unemployment or economic conditions), dependency and exchange relations between abuser and abused (including caregiver stress and abuser dependency and sense of powerlessness), intergenerational transmission of family patterns (i.e., the cycle of violence), and intraindividual dynamics (i.e., the psychopathology of the abuser, including substance abuse or mental or emotional problems). Factors in each of these domains, in addition to possible social isolation (sometimes due to geographic isolation), appear to play a role in elder abuse and neglect among American Indians.

External Stress Given the long-standing and intrusive nature of federal policies governing American Indians and the quasicolonial status of tribal communities, many of the factors that increase the risk of elder maltreatment and other forms of interpersonal violence are associated with external, or sociostructural, stressors. Continued imposition of government rules and regulations from outside the tribe (e.g., termination, relocation, lack of federal recognition of tribal entities, increased governmental restrictions, or exploitation of reservation land by non-Indians) have eroded political sovereignty, jeopardized economic survival, disrupted family and community relationships, and left a legacy of competing, often dissonant, cultural ideologies (Deloria & Lytle, 1984; Olson & Wilson, 1984; Snipp, 1989).

Among specific factors that place older Native people at risk for abuse and neglect, the first that must be discussed is poverty and its concomitants. Poverty rates among Native Americans are among the highest of any ethnic group in the United States (Antonucci & Cantor, 1994; Bureau of Indian Affairs, 1987; Sandefur & Sakamoto, 1988; Snipp, 1989), and it is believed that elderly Native Americans constitute the most underserved group of individuals in the United States (Cook, 1990; Kramer, 1991; National Indian Council on Aging, 1984). Poverty among Native people is manifested in numerous ways, including inadequate healthcare, low-quality housing and a lack of home ownership (Benokraitis, 1996; Carson, Dail, Greeley, & Kenote, 1990; Duvall & Miller, 1985), high percentages of unemployment and people on welfare (Sandefur & Sakamoto, 1988; Staples & Mirande, 1980), overrepresentation at the lower end of the socioeconomic scale (Bureau of Indian Affairs, 1987; Stauss, 1988), significantly lower levels of education than non-Indians (Duvall & Miller, 1985; Morgan & O'Connell, 1987), and an exceptionally high dependency ratio (i.e., the percentage of dependents in each family, which includes people too young or too old to work) (Antonucci & Cantor, 1994; John, 1994).

The lack of employment, especially on reservations, has forced many elderly Native Americans and their families to rely on Social Security and Supplemental Security Income benefits received by older family members for financial survival (Williams, 1980). This breakdown in community economic life sets the stage for financial exploitation of the elderly by adult family members and increases the likelihood of other forms of maltreatment. Moreover, because thousands of elderly individuals are without a secure economic base (John, 1994), family and tribal members are finding it increasingly difficult to care for them (e.g., because of migration of children or grandchildren to urban areas, or inaccessibility of and lack of transportation to health care facilities) (John, 1986, 1988; Markides & Mindel, 1987).

Dependency and Exchange Relations   The dependency or interdependency between elderly Indians and their adult children may increase conflict across generations, and thus the probability of elder maltreatment (Carson, 1995; John, 1988). Older Native Americans tend to report having multiple diseases (e.g., hypertension, cataracts, arthritis, pneumonia, obesity, diabetes, and dental problems), mental-health problems that include depression and substance-abuse disorders, and physical disabilities that limit such functions as sight, mobility, and physical agility (Meketon, 1983; Novak, 1997; Stuart & Rathbone-McCuan, 1988). Data collected from older Native people in Los Angeles (Kramer, 1992) and Denver (Saravanabhavan & Marshall, 1994) support the notion that these handicapping conditions make self-care difficult and may increase the probability of caregiver burden.

Older Native Americans may risk victimization as they continue to lose some of the status once ascribed to them, and as extended family ties loosen at a slow but steady pace (Yellowbird & Snipp, 1994). The tendency for families today is toward greater nuclearity, bilaterality, and self-reliance among both reservation and nonreservation Indians (Medicine, 1981; Miller, 1981; Red Horse, 1978, 1980, 1981; Stauss, 1986). This trend may result in less assistance and support provided by extended family members (John, 1988; Ryan, 1981). Divorce rates and percentages of homes in which fathers are absent among many tribal groups are also unusually high (Miller & Moore, 1979; Stauss, 1986; Yellowbird & Snipp, 1994). Moreover, pressure to assimilate into the mainstream culture has contributed to greater anomie because traditional norms, values, beliefs, roles, and ritualistic practices in the family and tribe are becoming more ambiguous, obsolete, or difficult to maintain (Hodge, 1981; Stauss, 1988). Other influences on extended-family relationships, as well as cultural traditions and practices in general, include increasing intermarriage outside the tribe, continued opposition to tribal sovereignty and self-determination, and threats to family unity and individual safety (e.g., as represented by high homicide and suicide rates among many Native American groups) (Carson et al., 1990; Edwards, 1983; Yellowbird & Snipp, 1994). Because changes in extended-family relationships and support have been linked to child abuse and neglect on some reservations (see, e.g., Fischler, 1985; or Oakland and Kane's 1973 study of the Navajo), these changes also may contribute to elder maltreatment.

Intergenerational Transmission of Family Patterns   Patterns of violence may be transmitted from one generation to the next but reflect in large measure a legacy of the treatment of Indian children in boarding schools. However, generational relations may be a factor in another way. A number of investigators have indicated that intergenerational stress and conflict have steadily increased among Native people (Burgess, 1980; John, 1994; McLemore, 1991; Price, 1976; Williams, 1980). Sources of conflict include modern lifestyles of the younger generation; the loss of traditional American Indian beliefs, values, and practices; contradictory values concerning time orientation (i.e., past and present versus future); group versus individual involvement, achievement, or productivity; and living in harmony with rather than dominating nature, or "being" versus "doing" (Goodman, 1985; Miller & Moore, 1979; Red Horse, Lewis, Feit, & Decker, 1978). Adult caregivers of the elderly who espouse Anglo ways may have values and lifestyle conflicts with their older family members. On the other hand, if caregivers maintain a traditional way of life, they may find themselves at odds with the dominant culture and thus experience significant degrees of pressure to integrate and acculturate. Intergenerational conflict may occur if members of the younger generation adopt values and lifestyles that are contrary to those of the older generation (e.g., greater independence and emphasis on individual achievement and competition, egocentricity, materialism, and so forth). These sources of intergenerational conflict may put elderly persons at greater risk for abuse and neglect.

Acculturation stress presents one of the greatest challenges to Native American beliefs and practices today. Reservation Indians appear to be more opposed to assimilation into the dominant society than any other sizable ethnic population (Deloria & Lytle, 1984). According to Price (1976), acculturation stress tends to be greater in Native people because they least resemble the majority culture, have less contact with the majority culture, and have been uprooted and dominated at the expense of their traditional practices and social-support systems. Because as many as half of all Native Americans at any given time may be in transition between the majority culture and their own, often struggling with a marginal status in each (Byler, 1977; Miller & Moore, 1979), large numbers of Native people may be experiencing a compromise or perhaps complete elimination of their Indian culture, language, and values. In contrast, Indian people who are able to maintain strong family ties and cultural identity while attempting to become bicultural or transcultural tend to have fewer personal difficulties than those who fail to do so (Stanford & Du Bois, 1992; Stuart & Rathbone-McCuan, 1988).

Intraindividual Dynamics   Other factors that have been correlated with elder abuse in non-Indian populations (e.g., low incomes, higher rates of alcoholism and mental-health problems than most other ethnic or cultural groups) (see, e.g., Anetzberger, 1987; Pillemer, 1986; Quinn & Tomita, 1986; Steinmetz, 1988; Wolf & Pillemer, 1989) may also be involved in Native American Elder Abuse and Neglect (EAN).

Extrapolating from Williams' (1980) discussion of Native American elderly, the factors that may put older American Indians at greater risk for abuse and neglect today include all of those discussed previously as well as additional concerns: financial dependency of large numbers of adult children on their parents (and mutual or reverse dependency); the generally poor health status and high disability rates of older Native people that make them difficult to care for; the potential negative effects of technology and "progress" (e.g., survival and adaptational skills being totally different today for most older Indians); a change in values from the wisdom of the elders to the abilities and ambition of the youth (and an emphasis on productivity and material contributions to the tribe in some cases); a general lack of interest that some of the young have in the old; and the fact that in most tribes today it is the young or middle-aged Indians who are conducting the affairs of the tribe and not the elderly (see also Carson, 1995; Kramer, 1992). Further, the decreasing participation of most older adults in the economic, political, and legal activities of the tribe may breed animosity between generations (John, 1986; Yellowbird & Snipp, 1994).

Finally, that elderly people both on and off the reservation have the lowest formal level of service utilization of any Native American age group (partly because of distance, transportation problems, and distrust of those associated with health and social-service systems) makes it more difficult to determine if abuse or neglect has occurred (John, 1985). Because family members are often the facilitators of service use by older Indian people in both urban and reservation settings, there is heavy reliance on adult children for information about and transportation to various services (e.g., medical, social services, shopping). This dependence on family members places an additional burden on caregivers, increasing the risk of abuse or neglect.

SUMMARY AND CONCLUSIONS REGARDING RESEARCH INTO ELDER ABUSE AND NEGLECT IN NATIVE AMERICAN COMMUNITIES

The connection between elder abuse and neglect and risk and protective factors in Native American populations is admittedly complex, and assertions about cause–effect relationships should always be made with caution. Studies concentrating on risk and protective factors involved in the etiology and expression of elder mistreatment among diverse groups of Indian people are long overdue. Other research needs and policy agendas have been discussed elsewhere (e.g., Carson, 1995). However, research into sensitive areas of Native American family life (including elder neglect and abuse) is not met without resistance. Potential barriers include the vast cultural and linguistic differences that exist among tribes; the ongoing debate within many tribal groups (and within the federal government) as to who is Indian; the tremendous geographical scatter of Indian people on this continent and the rural isolation of many families and individuals; the controversy over federal recognition or nonrecognition of Indian tribes; the great variations in family structures and definitions of family within and between tribes, and the interconnectedness of family and tribe; the differences between urban, rural (nonreservation), and reservation Indians; low population size (less than 1% of the U.S. population); a lack of culturally sensitive and appropriate measures and methods of data collection; the general suspicion of Indians toward non-Indian investigators and social-science research (not without cause), and the tendency for non-Indian researchers to focus on risk factors, deviance, and pathology rather than protective factors, strengths, and adaptive behavior—a practice strongly disliked by many Native Americans today; expense, time, effort, and the distance of researchers from reservations; and the unwillingness or inability of investigators to conduct applied or policy-relevant research among Native people (Carson et al., 1990; John, 1990). Although elder abuse and neglect may be held at bay in tribes in which adaptation to the modern world and majority culture has been balanced with the maintenance of traditional beliefs, values, and practices, rapid changes within and pressures from outside these cultural groups are making life increasingly stressful and difficult and, hence, abuse more probable. Theory-driven basic and applied research is sorely needed that will heighten our understanding of factors that facilitate or impede elder maltreatment among both rural and urban Native Americans.

Needed Programs, Services, and Changes in Legislation and Social Policy with Regard to Elder Abuse and Neglect in Native American Communities

The following recommendations are drawn not only from our understanding of the research literature, but also from our own experiences as caregivers for elderly parents. Through the challenge of assuring good quality care, particularly within the context of a reservation community, as caregivers we have had an invaluable opportunity to understand the difficulties elders, families, and communities confront.

Policy Level Federal legislation must explicitly recognize and reaffirm tribal sovereignty over all health and human services for members who reside within reservation communities, allowing tribes to choose the degree to which they wish to exercise jurisdiction and assume control. States and counties are not the best level of government in which to lodge control and jurisdiction. Further, it is the responsibility of legislators and executive-branch staff to become far more knowledgeable about the Native American communities that they have been elected or employed to serve. Uninformed beliefs about "free" healthcare and education, monthly checks from the federal government, or the wealth-generating capacity of casinos have resulted for too long in the continuation of structural discrimination and inadequately funded programs.

Currently, Native Americans who live on reservations rely on Indian Health Service, under the Public Health Service, Department of Health and Human Services, to meet their healthcare needs. As Manson (1993) points out, Indian Health Service targets its limited funding to provide acute care in the areas of maternal and child health. Long-term care options are extremely rare (Manson, 1993).

The best way to help elders and their caregivers is to assure access to in-home assistance, assisted-living housing options, and health-maintenance services.

Finally, it is crucial that income maintenance policies reflect the intergenerational structure of American Indian families, both on and off the reservation. Studies have shown the devastating rates of poverty and unemployment, and the importance of elders' Social Security and Supplemental Security Income as family income. In these times of "welfare reform," we may well be placing elders at greater risk. *Of course* elders will spend their income to care for children and grandchildren during hard times. It is precisely this unquestioned reciprocity and connectedness that has enabled Native American communities to survive. It may be politically unrealistic to suggest that welfare reform reflect what we have learned from recipients: Dependence is lessened only through education, jobs that pay adequate salaries, continuing access to healthcare, and affordable, high-quality child daycare and elder-care services. Merely cutting already miserly income awards places not only elders and children at risk, but also entire families and communities. Further, by assuring adequate income, improved education, and meaningful employment, future generations of American Indian elders will in all likelihood be healthier and more economically secure.

These policy-level suggestions may appear unrealistic, or not directly related to the topic of elder abuse. However, as Minkler (1996) argues: "We, as gerontologists, must share what we have learned, in as personal a form as possible, and call out for policies and programmes [sic] that address poverty in old age, combat racism, sexism and ageism, and facilitate the empowerment of elderly people, not by calling upon them and their families to 'do more for themselves,' but by reclaiming the sense of community that would have us recognise [sic] that we are indeed all in this together" (p. 483). As researchers, practitioners, gerontologists, educators, and advocates, we must confront the structural inequalities that place many elders at greater risk within an affluent society.

Community Level   As sovereign governments and close-knit communities, tribes are in the best position to direct their own members: to envision and create community relationships that reflect their values and beliefs. Traditions of respect for elders and alternative modes of dispute resolution are powerful strengths on which to build successful prevention and intervention. Community-education efforts can be undertaken more easily within smaller, close-knit contexts. Informal communication ("the moccasin telegraph") has continued to serve as an effective way for identifying problems of abuse and neglect. Many educational efforts thus far, however, have focused only on abuse and neglect without including opportunities to explore culturally appropriate prevention and intervention approaches. Further, the lack of acceptable options for resolving problems and the inability to assure improved conditions for elders and families in ways that do not shame or blame prevent those who know about problems from reporting them to authorities.

Tribal leadership must set an example of balanced, caring relationships and draw on traditions to help set standards of personal and family responsibility. As Rolling Thunder notes (Boyd, 1974): "The most basic principle of all is that of not harming others, and that includes all people and all life and all things. It means not controlling or manipulating others, not trying to manage their affairs" (p. 199). Change cannot be forced or hurried. The situations that have led to neglect and abuse have evolved over the course of centuries. If resolutions are to be acceptable, traditions of building community consensus must be followed. Community members must "own" respectful treatment of elders as a priority and must be an integral part of envisioning and building the types of relationships that they wish to be the norm within their community.

Further, tribal leaders need to look at the policies and practices guiding tribal-health, social-service, educational, and judicial agencies. The policies that usually guide these agencies reflect dominant cultural values and practice modalities for dealing with "collectivities of strangers." Services are fragmented, narrowly targeted, and administered and staffed primarily by non-Indians, or by Indian people who do not feel that they can question "the way things are done." Tribes not only *can* question policies and practices, they have a *responsibility* to do so and to assure that their members are not harmed.

For example, in one tribal community, the lack of coordination among agencies serving elders, and a general lack of accountability to the community, resulted in difficulties for elders and unnecessary risks to their well-being. Elder housing, in which many seriously ill residents reside, is unstaffed and rarely visited by public-housing employees. Transportation is generally unavailable. Overworked community health staff are unable to visit frail elders regularly, and lunches are delivered at 10:30 AM because the number of elders who need this service within the community is so large. Some elders have no furniture, no curtains on their windows to give them privacy, no dishes or utensils. There are no activities to bring elders together, and no help for those who spend their monthly incomes on drinking or gambling. Despite the lack of action on the part of tribal leadership, community members do volunteer their time to provide assistance, and to reduce the loneliness and isolation of elders. However, many needs go unmet. In all fairness, these problems may result not only from lack of leadership but also in part from a lack of the financial resources needed to build the types of systems that are necessary.

Often, the easiest intervention available to tribal communities is the enactment of elder-neglect and -abuse ordinances. Tribal codes, such as the model code that was developed by the American Indian Law Center (Grossman, 1990) do help establish clear behavioral norms. However, as the authors note: "Elder protective laws are not a solution to what, is, essentially, a human relationship problem. . . In many, if not most instances of elder abuse, services, resources, and support systems could have abated or even prevented the abuse, making the necessity for codes less compelling" (p. iv). The author also adds that their model code "is not a criminal code whose purpose is to punish abusers. Rather, it provides a framework to assist tribes in dealing with abuse and neglect, where possible, as a civil matter, so as to be non-threatening to families and to their elders. Studies of child abuse and neglect indicate that outcomes for abused children are better if the family can be maintained as a unit. The same can be said for elders and their families" (p. v). Criminal proceedings are reserved for those situations in which this is the only way to ensure an elder's physical safety. Tribal codes and elder-abuse reporting hotlines, without the services necessary to help elders and their families, often punish families and further harm and isolate elder victims.

Summary

Clearly, the most effective way of responding to existing elder neglect and abuse within Native American communities, as well as preventing future harm, lies in our willingness as a society to provide real long-term support for elders and their families. Just as Minkler (1996) advises us that we should not expect families to do more without help, we cannot expect tribal communities to respond without the necessary political control or financial resources. It is within our power to begin working toward the vision of caring communities, recognizing the wealth to be found in preserving the diversity of wisdom that all of our elders have to share.

REFERENCES

Anetzberger, G. J. (1987). *The etiology of elder abuse by adult offspring.* Springfield, IL: Charles C. Thomas.

Antonucci, T. C., & Cantor, M. H. (1994). Strengthing the support system for older minority persons. In *Minority elders: Five goals toward building a public policy base* (2nd ed.) (pp. 40–45). Washington, DC: Gerontological Society of America.

Benokraitis, N. V. (1996). *Marriages and families: Changes, choices, and constraints.* Upper Saddle River, NJ: Prentice-Hall.

Biggs, S., Phillipson, C., & Kingston, P. (1995). *Elder abuse in perspective.* Philadelphia: Open University Press.

Block, M. R., & Sinnott, J. D. (1979). *The battered elder syndrome: An exploratory study.* College Park, MD: University of Maryland, Center on Aging.

Boyd, D. (1974). *Rolling Thunder.* New York: Random House.

Brown, A. S. (1989). A survey on elder abuse at one Native American tribe. *Journal of Elder Abuse and Neglect, 1*(2), 17–37.

Bureau of Indian Affairs, Department of the Interior (1987). *Indian service population and labor force estimates.* Washington, DC: Author.

Burgess, B. J. (1980). Parenting in the Native American community. In M. D. Fantini & R. Cardinas (Eds.), *Parenting in a multicultural society* (pp. 63–73). New York: Longman Press.

Byler, W. (1977). The destruction of American Indian families. In S. Unger (Ed.), *The destruction of American Indian families* (pp. 1–11). New York: New York Association on American Indian Affairs.

Carson, D. K. (1995). American Indian elder abuse: Risk and protective factors among the oldest Americans. *Journal of Elder Abuse and Neglect, 7*(1), 17–39.

Carson, D. K., Dail, P., Greeley, S., & Kenote, T. (1990). Stresses and strengths of Native American reservation families in poverty. *Family Perspective, 24*(4), 383–400.

Chen, P. N., Bell, S., Dolinsky, D., Doyle, J., & Dunn, M. (1981). Elder abuse in domestic settings: A pilot study. *Journal of Gerontological Social Work, 4*, 3–17.

Cook, C. D. (1990). American Indian elderly and public policy issues. In M. S. Harper (Ed.), *Minority aging: Essential curricula content for selected health and allied health professions* (pp. 137–143). DHHS Publication No. HRS P-DV-90–4. Washington, DC: U.S. Government Printing Office.

Cox, H. G. (1996). *Later life: The realities of aging* (4th ed.). Upper Saddle River, NJ: Prentice-Hall.

Curley, L. (1987). Native American aged. In G. L. Maddox (Ed.), *The encyclopedia of aging* (pp. 469–470). New York: Springer.

Decalmer, P., & Glendenning, F. (Eds.). (1993). *The mistreatment of elderly people.* Newbury Park, CA: Sage.

Deloria, V. Jr., & Lytle, C. M. (1984). *The nations within: The past and future of American Indian sovereignty.* New York: Pantheon Books.

Dolgoff, R., Feldstein, D., & Skolnik, L. (1993). *Understanding social welfare* (3rd ed.). New York: Longman.

Duvall, E., & Miller, B. C. (1985). *Marriage and the family* (6th ed.). New York: Harper and Row.

Eastman, M. (1984). *Old age abuse.* Mitcham, England: Age Concern England.

Edwards, E. D. (1983). Native American elders: Current issues and social policy implications. In R. L. McNeely & J. L. Colen (Eds.), *Aging in minority groups* (pp. 74–82). Beverly Hills, CA: Sage.

Filinson, R., & Ingman, S. R. (Eds.). (1989). *Elder abuse: Practice and policy.* New York: Human Sciences Press.

Fischler, R. S. (1985). Child abuse and neglect in American Indian communities. *Child Abuse and Neglect, 9*(1), 95–106.

Fowler, L. (1990). Colonial context and age group relations among Plains Indians. *Journal of Cross-Cultural Gerontology, 5,* 149–168.

Gelfand, D. (1987). Older American Act. In G. L. Maddox (Ed.), *The encyclopedia of aging* (pp. 499–502). New York: Springer.

Glascock, A. P. (1990). In any other name, it is still killing: A comparison of the treatment of the elderly in America and other societies. In J. Sokolvsky (Ed.), *The cultural context of aging: Worldwide perspectives* (pp. 43–56). New York: Bergin & Garvey Publishers.

Glascock, A., & Feinman, S. L. (1980). Toward a comparative framework: Propositions concerning the treatment of the aged in non-industrial societies. In C. L. Fry & J. Keith (Eds.), *New methods for old age research: Anthropological alternatives* (pp. 204–222). Chicago: Loyola University Press of Chicago.

Goc, M. J. (1995). *Reflections of Lac du Flambeau: An illustrated history of Lac du Flambeau, Wisconsin 1745–1995.* Friendship, WI: New Past Press, Inc.

Goodman, J. M. (1985). The Native American. In J. O. McKee (Ed.), *Ethnicity in contemporary America: A geographical appraisal* (pp. 31–53). Dubuque, IA: Kendall/Hunt.

Gordon, L. (1989). *Heroes of their own lives: The politics and history of family violence: Boston 1880–1960.* New York: Penguin Books.

Gordon, L. (1994). *Pitied but not entitled: Single mothers and the history of welfare: 1890–1935.* New York: The Free Press.

Grossman, T. F. (1990). *The Model Tribal Elder Protection Code.* Washington, DC: American Indian Law Center, Inc.

Hand, C. (1996, November). *Dilemmas surrounding elder abuse and neglect in Native American communities.* Paper presented at the 13th annual Adult Protective Services Conference of the Texas Department of Protective and Regulatory Services and the American Public Welfare Association, San Antonio, TX.

Hodge, W. H. (1981). *The first Americans: Then and now.* New York: Holt, Rinehart and Winston.

Hooyman, N., & Kiyuk, H. A. (1996). *Social Gerontology: A multidisciplinary perspective* (4th ed.). Boston: Allyn and Bacon.

John, R. (1985). Service needs and support networks of elderly Native Americans: Family, friends, and social service agencies. In W. A. Peterson & J. Quadagno (Eds.), *Social bonds in later life: Aging and interdependence* (pp. 229–247). Beverly Hills, CA: Sage.

John, R. (1986). Social policy and planning for aging Americans: Provision of services by formal and informal support networks. In J. R. Joe (Ed.), *American Indian policy and cultural values: Conflict and accommodation* (pp. 111–133). Los Angeles: American Indian Studies Center, University of California.

John, R. (1988). The Native American family. In C. H. Mindel, R. W. Habenstein, & W. Rooselvelt Jr. (Eds.), *Ethnic families in America: Patterns and variations* (pp. 325–363). New York: Elsevier Science Pub. Co., Inc.

John, R. (1990). *Setting a research agenda on American Indian aging.* Unpublished manuscript.

John, R. (1994). The state of research on American Indian elders' health, income security, and social supports. In *Minority elders: Five goals toward building a public policy base* (2nd ed.) (pp. 45–58). Washington, DC: Gerontological Society of America.

Johnson, T. F. (1991). *Elder mistreatment: Deciding who is at risk.* Westport, CT: Greenwood Press.

Kramer, J. B. (1991). Urban American Indian aging. *Journal of Cross-Cultural Gerontology, 6,* 205–217.

Kramer, J. B. (1992). Serving American Indian elderly in cities: An invisible minority. *Aging Magazine,* pp. 48–51, 363–364.

Lawton, M. P., & Nahemow, L. (1973). Ecology and aging process. In C. Eisdorfer & M. P. Lawton (Eds.), *The psychology of adult development and aging* (pp. 619–674). Washington, DC: American Psychological Association.

Lewis, R. (1981). Patterns of strengths of American Indian families. The American Indian family: Stresses and strengths. In J. R. Red Horse, A. Shattuck, & F. Hoffman (Eds.), *Proceedings of the Conference on Research Issues, Phoenix, Arizona, April, 1980* (pp. 101–106). Isleta, NM: American Indian Social Research and Development Associates.

Manson, S. M. (1993). Long-term care of older American Indians: Challenges in the development of institutional services. In C. M. Barresi & D. E. Stull (Eds.), *Ethnic elderly and long-term care* (pp. 130–143). New York: Springer Publishing Company.

Markides, K. S., & Mindel, C. H. (1987). *Aging and ethnicity.* Newbury Park, CA: Sage.

Maxwell, E. K., & Maxwell, R. J. (1992). Insults to the body civil: Mistreatment of elderly in two Plains Indian tribes. *Journal of Cross-Cultural Gerontology, 7,* 3–23.

McLemore, S. D. (1991). *Racial and ethnic relations in America* (3rd ed.). Boston: Allyn & Bacon.

Medicine, B. (1981). American Indian family: Cultural change and adaptive strategies. *The Journal of Ethnic Studies, 8*(4), 12–13.

Meketon, M. J. (1983). Indian mental health: An orientation. *American Journal of Orthopsychiatry, 53*(1), 110–115.

Miley, K. K., O'Melia, M., & DuBois, B. L. (1995). *Generalist social work practice: An empowering approach.* Boston: Allyn and Bacon.

Miller, D. (1981). Alternative paradigms available for research on American Indian families: Implications for research and training. In J. R. Red Horse, A. Shattuck, & F. Hoffman (Eds.), *The American Indian family: Stresses and strengths* (pp. 79–91). Proceedings of the Conference on Research Issues, Phoenix, AZ, April 1980. Isleta, NM: American Indian Social Research and Development Associates.

Miller, D., & Moore, C. D. (1979). The Native American family: The urban way. In *Families today: A research sampler on families and children,* (1). Washington, DC: Government Printing Office. (National Institute of Mental Health Science Monographs).

Minkler, M. (1996). Critical perspectives on ageing: New challenges for gerontology. *Ageing and Society, 16,* 467–487.

Morgan, J., & O'Connell, J. C. (1987). The rehabilitation of disabled Americans. *International Journal of Rehabilitation Research, 10,* 139–149.

National Indian Council on Aging. (1984). Indian and Alaska Natives. In E. B. Palmore (Ed.), *Handbook on the aged in the United States* (pp. 269–276). Westport, CT: Greenwood Press.

National Indian Council on Aging. (1988). *American Indian elderly: A demographic profile.* Albuquerque, NM: Author.

Novak, M. (1997). *Issues in aging: An introduction to gerontology*. New York: Longman.

Oakland, L., & Kane, R. L. (1973). The working mother and child neglect on the Navajo reservation. *Pediatrics, 51*(5), 849–853.

O'Brien, S. (1989). *American Indian tribal governments*. Norman, OK: University of Oklahoma Press.

O'Brien, S. (1993, September). *Politics and American Indians*. Paper presented at the University of Wisconsin-Madison symposium Leading Issues in American Indian Studies, Madison, WI.

Olson, J. S., & Wilson, R. (1984). *Native Americans in the twentieth century*. Chicago: University of Illinois Press.

Pevar, S. L. (1992). *The rights of Indians and tribes: The basic ACLU guide to Indian and Tribal rights* (2nd ed.). Carbondale, IL: Southern Illinois University Press.

Pillemer, K. A. (1986). Risk factors in elder abuse: Results from a case-control study. In K. A. Pillemer & R. S. Wolf (Eds.), *Elder abuse: Conflict in the family* (pp. 239–263). Dover, MA: Auburn House Pub. Co.

Pillemer, K. A., & Finkelhor, D. (1988). The prevalance of elder abuse: A random sample survey. *The Gerontologist, 28*(1), 51–57.

Price, J. (1976). North American Indian families. In C. Mindel & R. Habenstein (Eds.), *Ethnic families in America* (pp. 248–270). New York: Elsevier.

Quinn, M. J., & Tomita, S. K. (1986). *Elder abuse and neglect: Causes, diagnosis, and intervention strategies*. New York: Springer Pub. Co.

Red Horse, J., Lewis, R., Feit, M., & Decker, J. (1978). Family behavior of urban American Indians. *Social Casework, 59*(2), 67–72.

Red Horse, J. R. (1980). Family structure and value orientation in American Indians. *Social Casework, 61*(8), 462–467.

Red Horse, J. R. (1981). American Indian families: Research perspectives. In J. R. Red Horse, A. Shattuck, & F. Hoffman (Eds.), *The American Indian family: Stresses and strengths* (pp. 1–11). Proceedings of the Conference on Research Issues, Phoenix, Arizona, April, 1980. Isleta, NM: American Indian Social Research and Development Associates.

Robbins, S. P. (1984). Anglo concepts and Indian reality: A study of juvenile delinquency. *Social Casework, 65*(4), 235–241.

Ryan, R. A. (1981). Strengths of the American Indian family: State of the art. In J. R. Red Horse, A. Shattuck, & F. Hoffman (Eds.), *The American Indian family: Stresses and strengths* (pp. 25–43). Proceedings of the Conference on Research Issues, Phoenix, Arizona, April, 1980. Isleta, NM: American Indian Social Research and Development Associates.

Sandefur, G. D., & Sakamoto, A. (1988). American Indian household structure and income. *Demography, 25*(1), 71–80.

Saravanabhavan, R. C., & Marshall, C. A. (1994). The older Native American Indian with disabilities: Implications for providers of health care and human services. *Journal of Multicultural Counseling and Development, 22*, 182–194.

Schweitzer, M. M. (1983). The elders: Cultural dimensions of aging in two American Indian communities. In J. Sokolovsky (Ed.), *Growing old in different societies: Cross-cultural perspectives* (pp. 168–178). Belmont, CA: Wadsworth Pub. Co.

Shomaker, D. (1990). Health care, cultural expectations and frail elderly Navajo grandmothers. *Journal of Cross-Cultural Gerontology, 5*, 21–34.

Snipp, C. M. (1989). *American Indians: The first of this land*. New York: Russell Sage Foundation.

Stanford, E. P., & Du Bois, B. C. (1992). Gender and ethnicity patterns. In J. E. Birren, R. B. Sloane, & G. D. Cohen (Eds.), *Handbook of mental health and aging* (2nd ed.) (pp. 99–117). New York: Academic Press.

Staples, R., & Mirande, A. (1980). Racial and cultural variations among American families: A decennial review of the literature on minority families. *Journal of Marriage and the Family, 42*, 887–903.

Stauss, J. (1986). The study of American families: Implications for applied research. *Family Perspective, 20*(4), 337–350.

Stauss, J. (1988). Native-American families: Myth and reality for educators. In H. B. Williams (Ed.), *Empowerment through difference: Multicultural awareness in education* (pp. 289–306). Peoria, IL: Glencoe.

Steinmetz, S. K. (1988). *Duty bound: Elder abuse and family care.* Newbury Park, CA: Sage.

Stuart, P., & Rathbone-McCuan, E. (1988). Indian elderly in the United States. In E. Rathbone–McCuan & B. Havens (Eds.), *North American elders: United States and Canadian perspectives* (pp. 236–254). New York: Greenwood.

United States Bureau of the Census. (1992). *United States summary: Census of population and housing.* [Summary Tape 1C, CD-ROM]. Washington, DC: Author.

United States Senate Hearing 100–981 (1988). *The American Indian elderly: The forgotten population.* Hearing before the Special Committee on Aging, United States Senate, 100–98, Pine Ridge, South Dakota, July 21, Serial No. 100–25.

Weibel-Orlando, J. (1990). Grand parenting styles: Native American perspectives. In J. Sokolovsky (Ed.), *The cultural context of aging: Worldwide perspectives* (pp. 109–125). New York: Bergin & Garvey Pub.

Williams, G. C. (1980). Warriors no more: A study of the American Indian elderly. In C. L. Fry (Ed.), *Aging in culture and society* (pp. 101–111). Brooklyn, NY: J. F. Bergin Pub., Inc.

Wolf, R. S. (1989). Statement, Hearing, Subcommittee on Human Services. In House of Representatives, Select Committee on Aging (Ed.), *Elder abuse: An assessment of the Federal response.* Washington, DC: Com. Pub. No. 101–719.

Wolf, R. S., & Pillemer, K. A. (1989). *Helping elderly victims: The reality of elder abuse.* New York: Columbia University Press.

Yates, A. (1987). Current status and future directions of research on the American Indian child. *American Journal of Psychiatry, 144*(9), 1135–1142.

Yellowbird, M., & Snipp, C. M. (1994). Native American families. In R. L. Taylor (Ed.), *Minority families in the United States: A multicultural perspective* (pp. 179–201). Englewood Cliffs, NJ: Prentice-Hall.

Part Five

Elder Abuse in Multicultural Perspective: Theory and Practice

Chapter 12

Elder Abuse:
Its Meaning to Caucasians,
African Americans,
and Native Americans[1]

Margaret F. Hudson & John R. Carlson

In 1983, Phillips raised two questions about elder mistreatment that are still relevant: What is it? Who says so? This chapter, like our program of research, focuses on these two important questions. Specifically, our aims are to identify clues to various groups' perceptions of elder abuse and elder neglect, which can form the basis for a standard definition of each concept that is sensitive to both expert and public perspectives. In this chapter, the perceptions of elder abuse held by three racial subgroups of the population are presented.

BACKGROUND

Although research on elder mistreatment (which includes both elder neglect and elder abuse) began in the late 1970s, researchers have repeatedly expressed concern about the lack of precision and consistency in definitions of both elder abuse and elder neglect (Bookin & Dunkle, 1985; Gelles & Cornell, 1985; Giordano & Giordano, 1984; Hudson, 1986, 1989; Hudson & Johnson, 1986; Johnson, 1986; Pedrick-Cornell & Gelles, 1982; Pillemer & Suitor, 1988; Salend, Kane, Satz, & Pynoos, 1984: Thobaben & Anderson, 1985; Valentine & Cash, 1986; Wolf, 1988). Definitions of phenomena are important because "ultimately they shape total response to the question" (Callahan, 1988, p. 454). Yet according to Wolf (1988), "From the very beginning of scientific investigation into the nature and causes of elder abuse, definitions have been a major issue" (p. 758).

[1]This study was funded by the National Institute on Aging, Grant # R01 AG12575-01. The authors wish to thank Elizabeth Tornquist for her editorial assistance and the Design & Education Center at the School of Nursing, the University of North Carolina at Chapel Hill, for production of the figures and tables.

The lack of precise and consistent definitions of the main variables of interest in the field has limited the usefulness of the research conducted. Because of the variety of definitions used by individual researchers and the 50 state adult-abuse laws, what is considered to be elder abuse (or elder neglect) by one researcher or in one state may not be abuse to another researcher or in another state. This has prevented comparison of research findings and the development of a national database, and has impeded detection, instrument development, the exploration of causal theory and the assessment of incidence and prevalence (Department of Health and Human Services, 1992; Giordano & Giordano, 1984; Hudson & Johnson, 1986; Pedrick-Cornell & Gelles, 1982; Wolf, 1988). As a result, reliable findings have been the exception rather than the rule (Hudson, 1986; Pedrick-Cornell & Gelles, 1982; Pillemer & Suitor, 1988), hindering the development of intervention and prevention programs (Wolf, 1988).

Clinicians are left without guidelines as to what constitutes abuse or neglect. Schene and Ward (1988) note that "[o]nly if definitions are standardized at the national level can there be national standards for identification, reporting and remediation" (p. 19). Without them, clinicians make ineffective attempts at diagnosis and resolution (Hudson & Johnson, 1986) and, at times, an escalation of the mistreatment occurs if professionals are not sensitive to the varying perceptions of acceptable behavior among different population groups (Long, 1986).

A classification system that includes precise, conceptually distinct, and measurable definitions of the main concepts of interest is clearly essential to progress in the elder-mistreatment field (Hudson, 1989, 1991; Pedrick-Cornell & Gelles, 1982).

Our program of research was begun as an effort to address the lack of definitional precision, consistency, and standardization. In 1988, using a three-round Delphi technique, a nationwide panel of elder-mistreatment experts from a variety of disciplines inductively developed a five-level taxonomy of elder mistreatment and theoretical definitions of 11 categorical concepts specified, including elder abuse and elder neglect (Hudson, 1988, 1991). However, although the experts' taxonomy and definitions provide a sound beginning for achieving standard definitions of specific elder mistreatment concepts, they do not include the public's perceptions or the understanding that comes from "the lived experience," and, by and large, they reflect a White, middle-class perspective.

Clearly, the multiple perspectives of the diverse populations of Americans, including those with abuse experience, need to be included in the process of classifying and defining elder mistreatment concepts (Hudson, 1988, 1991; Pillemer & Suitor, 1988), yet public perceptions have not been sought purposely until recently (Gebotys, O'Connor, & Mair, 1992; Hudson, 1994; Hudson & Carlson, 1994; Moon & Williams, 1993; Peretti & Majecen, 1991). This has been an important gap in this process. Indeed, because professionals and lay persons play different but equally important roles in prevention, detection, and treatment of mistreatment, any classification or definition is inadequate without the public's perceptions (Giovannoni & Becerra, 1979). Further, without public input, definitions may be ethically and pragmatically insensitive to the public that they are intended to serve. Finally, definitions need to include the meaning of the experience for participants and persons at risk for mistreatment. Incorporation of the lived experience is important because the meaning of elder abuse (or elder neglect) may differ depending on whether one's perception is based on intellectual understanding or observed or lived experiences.

In addition, different subgroups may view these phenomena differently. Yet research that addresses elder mistreatment in minority groups has until recently been nonexistent (Brown, 1989; Griffin, 1994; Hudson, 1994; Longres, 1992; Maxwell & Maxwell, 1992; Moon & Williams, 1993). Neglect and abuse are socially defined phenomena that reflect a society's distinction between acceptable and unacceptable interpersonal behaviors. Such distinctions tend to emerge as norms, which vary from society to society, from culture to culture, and between and even within racial or cultural groups. Within complex societies such as the United States, in which one culture dominates, there are nevertheless multiple subgroups of the population. Thus, perceptions of acceptable behaviors can vary. Until the public's perceptions of elder abuse (and elder neglect) and any similarities and differences among population groups' perceptions are known, any definition proposed cannot serve the people it is intended to serve in a manner that is genuinely helpful.

STUDY METHODS

Design

The study presented here built on the 1988 Delphi study described earlier (Hudson, 1988, 1991) by using the expert panel's taxonomy and definition of elder abuse as "starting points." Elder abuse rather than elder neglect was chosen for study because the public is likely to have had more exposure through mass media to the concept of abuse than to neglect. Because the expert panel members were almost exclusively White, middle-class, well-educated, and articulate professionals, their classification and definition of elder abuse served as the stimulus for responses by a more diverse group of persons, including those who might have been at risk for or have actually had abuse experience, as either abusers or abused. This approach allowed the experts' theoretical perspectives to be tested by the "real world" perspectives of a wider range and larger number of people representing some of the major racial and cultural groups in society.

Because little research had previously been conducted on the topic, an exploratory, descriptive design was used. The study was guided by six aims:

1 Examine the perceptions of elder abuse held by middle-aged and older adults residing in six culturally diverse counties of North Carolina.

2 Identify the demographic variables that show significant correlation with specific population groups' definition of elder abuse, including experience with abuse as an abused and/or abuser.

    3 Compare the types of elder abuse that the public recognizes with those in the experts' taxonomy.

    4 Identify the types of abusive behavior that the public believes warrant professional intervention.

    5 Develop a taxonomy of elder abuse that incorporates the public's and experts' perceptions of its components.

    6 Develop a definition of elder abuse that incorporates the public's and experts' perceptions of its essential characteristics.

The results that pertain to the three racial groups' perceptions of elder abuse are presented in this chapter. In the study, race was self-ascribed and used as an attempt to delineate groups with more shared than different cultural heritages.

Sampling Procedure

The goal was to get a heterogeneous sample of approximately 950 people that reflected the distinct regions, races, and ethnic groups of North Carolina so that diverse views on elder abuse would be included. The six counties selected for data collection incorporated the main races and cultural/ethnic groups in North Carolina: Caucasian, African American, and Native American. Participants had to represent one of these racial groups; be 40 years of age or older; be community-dwelling; be able to understand and speak English; have functional vision, hearing, and cognition; and be willing to participate. A stratified, clustered random sample based on the three main variables of age (middle-aged or older adult), gender, and race (Caucasian, African American, or Native American) was recruited using census group blocks.

Instruments and Data Collection

All participants were interviewed to ascertain their perceptions of the meaning and types of elder abuse. The intent was to tap their perceptions using both closed- and open-ended questions, and both behavioral and theoretical approaches. As there were no established instruments relevant to the goals of the study, two instruments based on the experts' 1988 taxonomy and definition of elder abuse were developed and pilot tested (Hudson, 1994; Hudson & Carlson, 1994). These two scales composed the first two parts of the interview schedule. Three versions of the schedule were developed and used so that the random order of the statements that were read to the participants was varied and thus did not affect their evaluation of the items.

    The formal interview schedule began with the Elder Abuse Vignette Scale (EAVS), which explores the types and meaning of elder abuse through behavioral examples. The goal is to identify the range of behavioral interactions that the public believes are included in the concept of elder abuse (Hudson & Carlson, 1994). The scale is composed of 37 vignettes (Figure 12.1) that are evaluated using five sets of bipolar adjectives each with seven response options, ranging from *very nonabusive* to *very abusive* (Hudson & Carlson, 1994). The intent of the

*1. The elder feels helpless and afraid because the caregiver repeatedly threatens to put the elder in a nursing home if the elder does not behave.

*2. The elder briefly felt some pain and heard a loud ringing when the friend pushed the hearing aid into the elder's ear and said, "You are going to wear this because I am tired of having to yell so you can hear me."

*3. The elder has a bruised back and hip and a broken back bone because the home health aide pushed the elder across the room, then shoved the elder, who fell across the foot of the bed.

-4. The elder felt mixed-up, for when the elder angrily said that the relative was late, the relative calmly replied that they would not be late for the doctor's appointment, the elder was just mistaken about the time.

5. In rushing past elder, the neighbor bumped the elder who fell down the steps, breaking a wrist.

6. The elder is angry because when the elder refused to take the usual three o'clock pill, the relative began crying and angrily said, "You are so stubborn that it is impossible to take care of you. Now take this pill like you are supposed to."

*7. During an argument the relative began yelling and swearing at the elder who became frightened and turned quickly to leave, falling and breaking an arm.

8. The elder feels angry and resentful because, without talking to the elder about it, the doctor told the elder's relatives to sell the elder's car and not let the elder drive anymore.

*9. The elder has many bruises, internal injuries and a broken arm because the relative beat the elder with punches and kicks.

-10. The elder has a large bruise on the arm because when the elder started to fall down, the nurse grabbed the elder by the arm.

*11. The elder was surprised and has a cut lip because during an argument the relative slapped the elder's face and said, "Shut up!"

12. The elder wonders why the relative suddenly stomped out of the room, slamming the door, after the elder refused to change out of dirty clothes.

*13. The elder is angry and feels cheated because the druggist has again given the elder fewer pills than were ordered and paid for.

*14. The elder was startled when the caregiver grabbed the elder's shoulders and shook the elder while saying, "Now stop that!"

*15. Because the elder spills things, the caregiver keeps the elder in a small bedroom all the time, and now the elder is becoming depressed and confused.

*16. The elder is very upset and has cuts and tears in the private area because the caregiver forced the elder to have sex.

-17. When the elder couldn't think of the name of a friend, the caregiver said, "Now take your time and the name will come back to you."

18. When the neighbor who took the elder to the grocery store kept telling the elder to hurry up, the elder became flustered and stumbled.

19. The elder is ashamed and hurt because, while working together to fix a cabinet, the relative said, "Can't you do anything right anymore? I asked you to push and you pulled!"

*20. The elder is afraid and the urinary problem is getting worse because the caregiver threatened to "beat the hell out of" the elder if the elder did not quit wetting the bed.

*21. Now the elder is quiet, withdrawn and confused because the doctor ordered a pill to stop the elder from bothering the nurses by ringing the bell frequently.

Figure 12.1 EAVS Items

*22.   The elder feels childish and belittled because the caregiver spanked the elder's bottom and said, "Now stop that or you'll hurt yourself."

*23.   The elder's body is covered with large and painful scrapes and burns because the caregiver put the elder in hot water and scrubbed the elder with harsh soap and a brush.

*24.   The elder was tense and the pain shot hurt because the nurse grabbed the elder's arm and leg, and roughly turned the elder over before giving the medicine.

*25.   The elder has a large bruise and a cracked rib because when the elder would not lend any money, the relative got angry and threw a glass ashtray, hitting the elder in the chest.

 26.   The elder is ashamed and anxious because the caregiver threatened to put diapers on the elder "just like a baby" if the elder does not quit wetting everything.

*27.   The elder has a black eye and two loose teeth and is afraid because the relative hit the elder in the face with a fist.

*28.   The elder is angry and hurt, and feels trapped because the relative charges the elder $20 to drive the elder to every doctor's appointment.

*29.   The elder is uncomfortable and cannot take a deep breath because the nursing home aide puts the vest restraint on too tightly.

 30.   When calling the elder, the relative usually does not let the phone ring long enough before hanging up, thus in rushing to answer the phone the elder tripped and fell.

*31.   The elder feels helpless and lonely because the caregiver refuses to let any of the elder's friends visit, giving the excuse that visits upset the elder.

-32.   The elder was excited and happy when the relative took the elder for a ride to visit the elder's old home place.

#33.   The elder feels insulted upon hearing the nurse say, "I just love caring for these old folks. They are all such sweet, cute little 'ole things."

#34.   The elder is a bit disgusted because while talking with a friend, the elder got sprayed in the face with some spit.

*35.   When the relative slashed at the elder with a kitchen knife, barely missing the elder, the elder was terrified and left home to stay with a neighbor.

*36.   The elder started to cry when caregiver slapped the elder's hand and said, "Stop playing with your food and eat."

*37.   The elder was surprised when the home health aide pinched the elder's arm to get the elder's attention.

* abusive; – not abusive; # neutral.

Figure 12.1   EAVS Items (Continued)

scale is to identify examples of elder abuse that have general applicability, rather than specific types of abuse that apply only to such contexts as abuse of disabled elders or abuse between elderly spouses or institutional elder abuse or elder abuse by adult-child caregivers. Another intent is to identify which behaviors are consistently seen as abusive, which are seen as nonabusive, and which are considered borderline behaviors, so that the boundaries of elder abuse can be determined.

The second part of the interview focused on types of elder abuse and the theoretical meaning of the concept "elder abuse" using the Elements of Elder Abuse Scale (EEAS). This scale was designed to identify those components of the experts' elder abuse definition and taxonomy with which the public agreed, so as to develop a definition and a taxonomy of elder abuse that would incorporate the areas of agreement of experts and the public (Hudson & Carlson, 1994). The EEAS

1. Physically forcing an elder to do something that he/she does not want to do is a form of elder abuse.

2. Verbally forcing (coercing) an elder to do something that he/she does not want to do is a form of elder abuse.

3. Yelling and swearing at an elder need to occur more than once in order to be called elder abuse.

4. In contrast to pain after surgery, for example, elder abuse results in unnecessary suffering for the elderly person.

5. Elders are at risk for abuse because they are seen as being physically weaker than when they were younger.

6. When an elder is harmed unnecessarily, it is elder abuse whether or not the person intended to harm the elder.

7. Some elder abuse is committed by relatives—husbands, wives, sons, daughters, grandchildren, nieces, etc.

8. Elder abuse can cause physical, emotional, social and/or financial harm to an elder.

9. Healthy elders can be abused.

10. Slapping an elder once is elder abuse.

11. Elder abuse always includes some form of harm for the elder, such as pain, loss, injury, suffering, etc.

12. Elder abuse does not decrease the elder's quality of life.

13. Elder ABUSE is doing something to an elder that harms the elder, while elder NEGLECT is the failure to do someting one should do to help the elder.

14. The use of physical force, such as slapping, hitting, or kicking, is one form of elder abuse.

15. The use of verbal force, such as yelling or swearing at or belittling an elder, is not a form of elder abuse.

16. Elder abuse is mistreatment because the behavior involved harms the elder.

17. Some elder abuse is committed by friends and neighbors.

18. Threatening to harm an elder is a form of elder abuse.

19. Behavior that prevents the basic social needs of an elder from being met, such as keeping the elder in one room all the time, is a form of elder abuse.

20. In order to be abused, the elder has to be dependent on the person who does the abuse.

21. A person can abuse another without meaning to do so.

22. Some elder abuse is committed by formal caregivers, such as nurse's aides, nurses, orderlies, doctors, etc.

23. In contrast to street crime by strangers, elder abuse is committed by a person the elder knows and SHOULD be able to trust.

24. Repeatedly preventing an elder's close friends from visiting without good reason is a form of elder abuse.

25. Hitting an elder only one time is not elder abuse.

26. Stealing an elder's money or property is a form of elder abuse.

Figure 12.2   EEAS Items

is composed of 26 statements about elder abuse (Figure 12.2), each reflecting a single component of the experts' definition or taxonomy (Hudson, 1988, 1991). The five response categories range from *strongly agree* to *strongly disagree*.

The third part of the interview schedule contained questions on participant characteristics and aging and abuse experience. Specifically, it examined partici-

Table 12.1   Subgroups of the Sample Based on Race, Age, and Gender

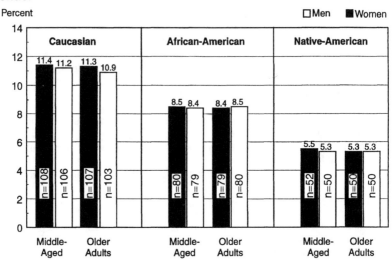

pants' knowledge of and experience with older adults, abuse in general, and elder abuse. These closed-ended questions were followed by five open-ended questions that elicited perceptions of elder abuse (Hudson & Carlson, 1994).

Descriptive statistics and multiple regressions were calculated on the responses to the closed-ended questions, and content analysis was conducted on the responses to the open-ended questions. Statistical testing for racial category differences in responses to the EAVS and the EEAS was part of a test of a more general modeling process that considered the main and interactive effects of racial category, age group, gender, educational level, and abuse experience. The effects of racial category reported here are net effects not attributable to the other variables. Because the sampling design was complex, statistical tests appropriate for the sample design were generated using the SUDAAN statistical analysis package (Shah, Barnwell, & Bieler, 1995).

Sample Characteristics

The total sample was composed of 944 North Carolina adults: 424 Caucasians, 318 African Americans, and 202 Native Americans. Their ages ranged from 40 to 93 years with a mean age of 61.8 years. All ages except 92 years were represented. Approximately half of the sample were middle-aged adults (40 to 64 years, $n = 475$, 50.3%) and half were older adults (65 years and older, $n = 469$, 49.7%); half were females ($n = 476$, 50.4%) and half were males ($n = 468$, 49.6%). In Table 12.1 a breakdown of the sample based on age, gender, and race is presented.

The sample's level of education ranged from 1 to 23 years with every number of years between these two extremes represented. The mean level of education was 12.14 years. In Table 12.2 the sample's educational levels are presented. The yearly incomes ranged from less than $10,000 per year to more than $100,000 per

Table 12.2   Educational Levels of the Sample

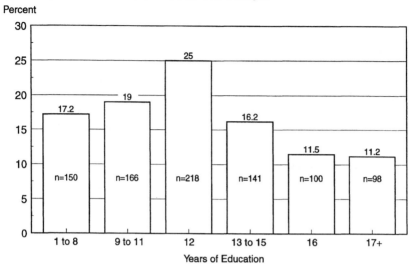

year. Approximately half ($n = 459$, 48.9%) were still working; half ($n = 480$, 51.1%) were not. Most were married ($n = 614$, 65.2%) Protestants ($n = 871$, 92.8%) who grew up in rural areas ($n = 570$, 60.7%).

Most of the respondents had heard the term elder abuse prior to being interviewed (92.4%) and almost half (47.1%) personally knew of an elder abuse situation. Further, 178 of the respondents (19.1% of the 930 who answered the question) said they had been abused at some time in their lives; 34 of the older adults (7.5% of the 452 who answered the question) reported that they had been abused since turning 65 years of age; and 57 respondents (6.2% of the 917 who answered the question) reported that they had abused someone at some time; 19 of these reported that they had abused an elder. Most of the abused (89.2%) and abusers (77.8%) reported that the abuse had involved more than one episode.

RESULTS

Areas of Agreement

Overall, the total sample and its three racial subgroups had similar perceptions of elder abuse. Their responses to the EEAS items, which presented each aspect of the experts' taxonomy and definition of elder abuse for consideration, indicated support of all aspects of the taxonomy, and all aspects of the definition with one exception. They believed that yelling or swearing at and slapping or hitting an elder *once* is enough to call it elder abuse. Of the 37 EAVS items, all the racial groups perceived 23 items as abusive (indicated by an asterisk on Figure 12.1), 4 items as not abusive (indicated by a minus sign), and 2 items as neutral (indicated by a number sign). The other eight items were rated differently by the three groups. The African Americans rated three additional items (items 18, 19, and 30) as abusive; the Native Americans rated not only these three but four additional items (items 5, 6, 8, and 26) as abusive.

Racial Differences in EAVS Results

In general, based on group means a pattern was found: The Native Americans ranked more items as abusive and 22 items at a higher level of abuse severity than did the African Americans, who in turn rated more items as abusive and 15 at a higher level of severity than did the Caucasians. These findings are presented in Table 12.3.

Table 12.3   Main Effects of Race on EAVS Items

Item #	Beta coefficients		$^*p$	
	NA vs C	AA vs C	NA vs C	AA vs C
1	0.8262*	0.4523*	.0000	.0326
5	0.8759*	0.4805*	.0000	.0141
6	1.1262*	0.3366	.0000	
7	0.6752*	0.5358*	.0000	.0006
8	0.8990*	0.2029	.0001	
10	−0.5931*	0.2741	.0082	
11	0.1022	0.2093*		.0064
12	0.9323*	0.4547	.0000	
13	1.0485*	0.2711	.0000	
14	0.7657*	0.5898*	.0001	.0215
15	0.6108*	0.3698	.0029	
18	1.1632*	0.8105*	.0000	.0005
19	0.7687*	0.6438*	.0000	.0013
20	0.3175*	0.2530*	.0020	.0116
21	0.4833*	0.2448	.0333	
22	0.5322*	0.5593*	.0111	.0378
23	0.1534*	0.1046*	.0000	.0031
24	0.3051	0.3459*		.0296
26	0.9424*	−0.2069	.0000	
27	−0.1367*	0.0187	.0283	
29	0.8404*	0.7450*	.0001	.0000
30	0.7485*	0.3104	.0008	
31	0.7087*	0.4285*	.0001	.0125
32	−0.0995*	0.0248	.0158	
33	0.5588*	0.1096	.0202	
34	0.3326	0.8120*		.0018
36	0.4787*	0.3661	.0260	
37	0.7902*	0.7624*	.0011	.0002

AA = African Americans; C = Caucasians; NA = Native Americans.
No significant differences were found for the item numbers that are not listed.
When the coefficient under any of the columns is positive, the first racial category named in the column heading had a higher mean than the second category. A negative sign indicates that the first group had a lower mean.

The Native Americans as a group rated 20 of the 24 items that the total sample ranked in the midrange (neutral to moderately abusive) on the not-abusive to abusive scale and two of the severely abusive items at a higher level of abusiveness than did the Caucasians. They also rated two of the nonabusive items at a higher level of nonabusiveness. In contrast, the item in which the relative hits the elder in the face with a fist (which the total sample rated as severely abusive), the Native Americans rated as severely abusive but as less severely abusive than did the other two groups. Similarly, the African Americans as a group rated 12 of the midrange items and 3 of the severely abusive items at a higher level of abusiveness than did the Caucasians, and three items higher than did the Native Americans.

Racial Differences in EEAS Results

The participants' responses on the EEAS also indicated significant differences in their perceptions based on race. Table 12.4 reports the results of comparing each pair of racial categories. The Native Americans and African Americans were more likely than Caucasians to strongly agree that physically forcing an elder to do something that he or she does not want to do is a form of elder abuse. The Native Americans were more likely than the other two groups to strongly agree that verbally forcing an elder is elder abuse and that some elder abuse is committed by relatives. They were also more likely than the other two groups to disagree that yelling and swearing at an elder needs to occur more than once in order to be called elder abuse, and that the use of verbal force, such as yelling or

Table 12.4   Main Effects of Race on EEAS Items

Item #	Beta coefficients		*p	
	NA vs C	AA vs C	NA vs C	AA vs C
1	1.1724*	0.7736*	.0069	.0248
2	1.0951*	0.4347	.0015	
3	−0.7133*	0.1268	.0004	
5	−1.1942*	−0.3406	.0019	
6	0.3989	0.6613*		.0027
7	5.5744*	0.4670	.0000	
9	−1.5392*	−0.6589	.0133	
11	0.1452	0.5282*		.0377
15	−0.9828*	0.1005	.0099	
16	−1.0493*	−0.6626	.0125	
19	0.3660	1.7915*		.0040
21	−0.4269	−0.6059*		.0223

AA = African Americans; C = Caucasians; NA = Native Americans.
No significant differences were found for the item numbers that are not listed.
When the coefficient under any of the columns is positive, the first racial category named in the column heading had a higher likelihood of agreeing than the second category.
A negative sign indicates that the first group had a lower likelihood of agreeing.

Table 12.5 Interaction Effects of Race, Age, and Gender on EAVS Items

Item #	Variables	Effects
10	Race and Gender $p = .0033$	NA men rated the item less abusive than NA women. This difference was less pronounced in C men and women and reversed in AA men and women.
13	Race and Gender $p = .0181$	NA & AA men rated the item more abusive than did the women, while C women rated it more abusive than C men.
18	Race and Gender $p = .0266$	Among C the women rated the item as more abusive than men, while among AA & NA men and women there was little difference.
21	Race and Age $p = .0095$	Among C & AA, the middle-aged rated the item more abusive than did older adults, while the reverse was true among the NA.
22	Race and Gender $p = .0007$	Among AA & NA, men rated the item as more abusive than did women, while the reverse was true among C men and women.
24	Race and Gender $p = .0361$	C women rated the item more abusive than did C men, while AA men & women rated it nearly the same, and NA women rated it less abusive than NA men.
28	Race and Age $p = .0042$	Older adults rated the item more abusive than did the middle-aged, but the difference was more pronounced among AA than NA & C.
	Race and Gender $p = .0000$	Among AA, men rated the item more abusive than women, while among C & NA the reverse was true and the difference smaller.
33	Race and Age $p = .0242$	Among all 3 groups the middle-aged rated the item as more abusive, but the difference was more pronounced in the C group and least in the NA group.
35	Race and Age $p = .0364$	Among the C, the middle-aged rated the item more abusive than did the older adults, while the ratings were close in the AA & NA groups.
37	Race and Gender $p = .0206$	Women rated the item more abusive in all 3 groups, but the difference was most pronounced in the C group.

AA = African Americans; C = Caucasians; NA = Native Americans.

swearing at or belittling an elder, is not a form of elder abuse. In addition, they were less likely than the other groups to agree that elders are at risk for abuse because they are seen as physically weaker than when they were younger; healthy elders can be abused; and elder abuse is mistreatment because the behavior harms the elder.

African Americans were more likely than the other groups to agree that when an elder is harmed unnecessarily, it is elder abuse whether or not the person intended to harm the elder; elder abuse always includes some form of harm for the elder; and behavior that prevents the basic social needs of an elder from being met is a form of elder abuse. This group was less likely than the Caucasian group to agree that a person can abuse another without meaning to do so.

Interactive Effects of the Variables

Although the main effects accurately indicate differences in perceptions of certain EAVS and EEAS items based on the respondents' race, analyses of the interactive effects (Tables 12.5 and 12.6) clearly indicate that for some of the EAVS and EEAS items the effects of race are better understood in combination with age and gender. Our analyses show that although one or two of the main variables (race, age, gender, educational level, and abuse experience) accounted for some of the variance in respondents' perceptions of certain items, none was consistently correlated with respondents' ratings of the items. In fact, on certain items Native Americans or African Americans within a specific gender or age group rated an item like Caucasians did. Therefore, predicting a respondent's perceptions based

Table 12.6   Interaction Effects of Race, Age, and Gender on EEAS Items

Item #	Variables	Effects
1	Race and Age $p = .0364$	A difference in agreement was observed between NA and C middle-aged & older adults, while almost none existed between the two AA age groups.
9	Race and Age $p = .0016$	Among older adults, the AA & NA were more likely to agree than were middle-aged, while among the C the reverse was true.
15	Race and Age $p = .0218$	Among AA & NA the older adults were more likely to agree than the middle-aged, while there was little difference in agreement between the 2 C age groups.
25	Race and Gender $p = .0354$	C & NA women were more likely to agree with the item than men, while among AA the men were more likely to agree.

AA = African Americans; C = Caucasians; NA = Native Americans.

on his or her race or age or gender, alone or in combination, could be quite erroneous. Further, the predictive ability of age plus gender plus race was quite low; these three variables plus educational level and abuse experience accounted for only 5% to 13% of the variance in the rating of the various EAVS and EEAS items.

DISCUSSION

The finding of the public respondents' high degree of agreement with both the types and definitional components of elder abuse indicates strong support for most aspects of the experts' taxonomy and definition of elder abuse. The public's one area of disagreement with the experts pertains to the frequency with which harmful behaviors have to occur in order to be elder abuse. This public sample indicated that both harmful and potentially harmful interactions with elders are not acceptable and that one incidence of such interactions is abusive.

In contrast to our findings, which were based on the public's perceptions of physical, psychological, financial, and social elder abuse, Gebotys, O'Connor, and Mair (1992) found that what professionals define as physical abuse may differ from the view of the public. This difference in findings may be due to the differences in elder abuse definitions used in the two studies, their small, mainly White, middle-class sample that was not randomized, and differences in the data collection methods used in the studies.

In another study, Peretti and Majecen (1991) identified some of the various behaviors that are perceived by older adults to equal emotional abuse. The findings of their study are not comparable to ours because of differences in definitions of emotional elder abuse, the fact that their very small sample was not randomized, and a data collection approach that allowed neglectful behaviors to be included with abusive behaviors. However, their respondents perceived some behaviors as emotionally abusive that also were included in our EAVS and EEAS, and were perceived as abusive by our respondents, such as confinement, demeaning commentary to an elder, and threats of violence.

It would be useful to further investigate the public's versus professionals' and experts' perceptions of elder abuse using large random samples in order to more completely delineate areas of agreement and disagreement. It also would be helpful to determine the reasons for any areas of disagreement found.

Our findings of some differences in perceptions of elder abuse based on respondents' racial groups are useful in understanding their unique perspectives. The Native Americans included more EAVS items in their concept of elder abuse than did African Americans, who in turn included more than Caucasians. This pattern also was seen in the three groups' ratings of the severity of items. These findings may be due to differences in the racial groups' respect for elders and differences in group norms about acceptable versus unacceptable behaviors. Yet other factors could also affect persons' perceptions of abuse. Therefore, these findings warrant further investigation. Because there is tremendous diversity among Native

Americans and African Americans (Carson, 1995; Cazenave, 1983) and our study only included members from two tribes and African Americans from four counties within one state, the findings may be different with different tribes of Native Americans and different groups of African Americans. There are some indications that the norm of respect for the aged is changing within some Native American groups, and that this change, along with other factors, may be increasing elder Native Americans' risk for mistreatment (Brown, 1989; Carson, 1995; Maxwell & Maxwell, 1992). If risk is increasing, protective norms may be changing.

Although Native Americans have not been included in related studies, African Americans have been included in two. Using a nonprobability sampling method, Moon and Williams (1993) interviewed 90 older adults, 30 in each of three racial groups (Caucasian Americans, African Americans, and Korean Americans), to examine how various potentially abusive situations were perceived. One of their findings was quite similar to ours: A higher percentage of the African American respondents than Caucasian or Korean Americans perceived elder abuse in 6 of the 13 scenarios; the Korean Americans perceived abuse in only two. In another study, Griffin (1994) conducted interviews with a purposive sample of 10 elder abuse victims and 6 perpetrators to explore the subtleties of abuse and abusive relationships among rural elderly African Americans. She found that physically abusing elders was particularly unacceptable among rural African Americans. Our findings support hers and further suggest that all four types of elder abuse are not acceptable to either African Americans or Native Americans.

However, because our study only included representatives from three racial groups, all from one Southern state, it would be useful to seek further information on these findings with additional large random samples of the public, including the racial groups represented in our sample and others. It also would be useful to address respondents' perceptions of the meaning of elder abuse using similar and different approaches.

IMPLICATIONS

Our findings have clear implications for research, practice, education, and policy. First and foremost, there was a high degree of agreement among the public and its subgroups in their perceptions of elder abuse, as well as a clear indication that elder abuse is unacceptable. Further, all three racial groups indicated a significant amount of support for the experts' taxonomy and definition of elder abuse. This indicates that with further research on this topic, it could well become possible to develop a taxonomy and definition of elder abuse with which the majority of experts and various groups who make up the public agree, and thus to arrive at a standard definition that could be used as a national guideline.

The areas of disagreement, specifically the fact that Native Americans rated more of the EAVS items as abusive than did African Americans and Caucasians, and that African Americans rated more as abusive than did Caucasians, may indicate that the two minority groups continue to hold on to their norms of respect and caring for elders (Carson, 1995; Kivett, 1993; Marino, 1988) and that they may be more sensitive to the abuse of power through their experiences with racism. Further, the Native American respondents' rating of more items as abusive and rating them higher on the level of abusiveness is congruent with the "harmony ethic" held by some Native Americans. This ethic encourages believers to maintain harmonious interpersonal relationships by not giving offense and by sharing one's self and possessions with others (Loftin, 1983).

Knowledge of minority groups' norms and unique perceptions of elder abuse are important issues to share through education. They are also important issues to keep in mind when assessing suspected abuse situations. What may not be perceived as abuse by a professional who represents one racial group may well be perceived as such by the abuse participants who represent another racial group. The reverse also may be true. A study in which the perceptions of elder abuse held by victims are compared with those of professionals who detect the abuse could be quite helpful in identifying important similarities and differences and the reasons for them.

The areas of agreement and disagreement are indications of the willingness of minority group members to share their perceptions and the importance of including them in studies that address the issue of elder abuse. Their perspectives add breadth and richness to the data and allow us to have a more accurate sense of the unique perspectives of subgroups within the population. This is especially important because so little is known about minority groups' experiences with or perceptions of elder abuse or elder neglect. Additional research should be done in this area.

The findings from the interactive effects of age, race, and gender on the EAVS items indicate that predicting a person's perceptions of elder abuse based on that person's age, gender, or race would likely be erroneous. Although these variables did affect respondents' perceptions of elder abuse, they did not produce an additive model in predicting perceptions, but a multiplicative model with different variables having a different degree of simple and interactive effects for different items. Further, the variables only accounted for 5% to 13% of the variance in respondents' perceptions. Some other unknown variables account for the much larger, missing percentage. It may well be that one's total life experiences and personal norms of unacceptable interpersonal behavior are important variables in the perception of elder abuse.

Thus, stereotyping of or making assumptions about persons' perceptions of elder abuse based on their race, gender, or age, alone or in combination, could be erroneous. For clinicians working with cases of suspected elder abuse, it would be wise to ask the elder if he or she feels abused. Researchers need to be especially careful to remember that racial, gender, and age groups are in fact very heterogeneous, not homogeneous; and they must therefore look carefully for between- and within-groups similarities and differences. Further, the variable of "race" is often an imprecise measure (Jones, Snider, & Warren, 1996; Krieger, 1996), both of people's racial heritage and of group norms. Many Americans are of mixed racial, cultural heritage or both. These issues, as well as the similarities and differences found by researchers among groups, need to be addressed cautiously and sensitively in both the educational and policymaking arenas.

REFERENCES

Bookin, D., & Dunkle, R. E. (1985). Elder abuse: Issues for the practitioner. *The Journal of Contemporary Social Work, 66,* 3–12.

Brown, A. S. (1989). A survey on elder abuse at one Native American Tribe. *Journal of Elder Abuse & Neglect, 1*(2), 17–37.

Callahan, J. J. (1988). Elder abuse: Some questions for policy-makers. *The Gerontologist, 28*(4), 453–458.

Carson, D. K. (1995). American Indian elder abuse: Risk and protective factors among the oldest Americans. *Journal of Elder Abuse & Neglect, 7*(1), 17–39.

Cazenave, N. A. (1983). Elder abuse and Black Americans: Incidence, correlates, treatment and prevention. In J. I. Kosberg, (Ed.), *Abuse and maltreatment of the elderly: Causes and interventions* (pp. 187–203). Boston: Wright PSG.

Department of Health and Human Services. (1992). *Report from the Secretary's task force on elder abuse.* Bethesda, MD: Author.

Gebotys, R. J., O'Connor, D., & Mair, K. J. (1992). Public perceptions of elder physical mistreatment. *Journal of Elder Abuse & Neglect, 4*(1/2), 151–171.

Gelles, R. J., & Cornell, C. P. (1985). *Intimate violence in families.* Newbury Park, CA: Sage.

Giordano, N. H., & Giordano, J. A. (1984). *Individual and family correlates of elder abuse.* Unpublished manuscript.

Giovannoni, J. M., & Becerra, R. M. (1979). *Defining child abuse.* New York: The Free Press.

Griffin, L. W. (1994). Elder maltreatment among rural African Americans. *Journal of Elder Abuse & Neglect, 6*(1), 1–27.

Hudson, M. F. (1986). Elder neglect and abuse: Current research. In K. A. Pillemer & R. S. Wolf (Eds.), *Elder abuse: Conflict in the family* (pp. 125–166). Dover, MA: Auburn House.

Hudson, M. F. (1988). A Delphi study of elder mistreatment: Theoretical definitions, empirical referents and taxonomy. *Dissertation Abstracts International,* Vol. 50, UMI PUZ8909673.

Hudson, M. F. (1989). Analyses of the concepts of elder mistreatment: Abuse and neglect. *Journal of Elder Abuse & Neglect, 1*(1), 5–25.

Hudson, M. F. (1991). Elder mistreatment: A taxonomy with definitions by Delphi. *Journal of Elder Abuse & Neglect, 3*(2), 1–20.

Hudson, M. F. (1994). Elder abuse: Its meaning to middle-aged and older adults, Part II: Pilot results. *Journal of Elder Abuse & Neglect, 6*(1), 55–81.

Hudson, M. F., & Carlson, J. R. (1994). Elder abuse: Its meaning to middle-aged and older adults, Part I: Instrument development. *Journal of Elder Abuse & Neglect, 6*(1), 29–54.

Hudson, M. F., & Johnson, T. F. (1986). Elder neglect and abuse: A review of the literature. In C. Eisdorfer (Ed.), *The annual review of gerontology and geriatrics* (pp. 81–134). New York: Springer.

Johnson, T. F. (1986). Critical issues in the definition of elder mistreatment. In K. A. Pillemer & R. S. Wolf (Eds.), *Elder abuse: Conflict in the family* (pp. 167–196). Dover, MA: Auburn House.

Jones, W. K., Snider, D. E., & Warren, R. C. (1996). Deciphering the data: Race, ethnicity, and gender as critical variables. *Journal of the American Medical Women's Association, 51*(4), 137–140.

Kivett, V. R. (1993). Informal supports among older rural minorities. In C. N. Bull (Ed.), *Aging in rural America* (pp. 204–215), Newbury Park, CA: Sage.

Krieger, N. (1996). Inequality, diversity, and health: Thoughts on "race/ethnicity" and "gender." *Journal of the American Medical Women's Association, 51*(4), 133–136.

Loftin, J. D. (1983). The "harmony ethic" of the conservative eastern Cherokees: A religious interpre-
    tation. *Journal of Cherokee Studies, 8*(1), 40–43.
Long, K. A. (1986). Cultural considerations in the assessment and treatment of intrafamilial abuse.
    American Journal of Orthopsychiatry, 56(1), 131–136.
Longres, J. F. (1992). Race and type of maltreatment in elder abuse systems. *Journal of Elder Abuse
    & Neglect, 4*(3), 61–83.
Marino, C. (1988). Honor the elders: Symbolic associations with old age in traditional eastern Chero-
    kee culture. *Journal of Cherokee Studies, 13*, 3–18.
Maxwell, E. K., & Maxwell, R. J. (1992). Insults to the body civil: Mistreatment of elderly in two
    Plains Indian tribes. *Journal of Cross-Cultural Gerontology, 7*, 3–23.
Moon, A., & Williams, O. (1993). Perceptions of elder abuse and help-seeking patterns among
    African American, Caucasian-American, and Korean-American elderly women. *The Gerontolo-
    gist, 33*(3), 386–395.
Pedrick-Cornell, C., & Gelles, R. J. (1982). Elder abuse: The status of current knowledge. *Family
    Relations, 31*, 457–465.
Peretti, P. O., & Majecen, K. G. (1991). Emotional abuse among the elderly: Affecting behavioral
    variables. *Social Behavior & Personality, 19*(4), 255–261.
Phillips, L. R. (1983). Elder abuse: What is it? Who says so? *Geriatric Nursing*, May/June, 167–170.
Pillemer, K. A., & Suitor, J. J. (1988). Elder abuse. In V. B. Hasselt, R. L. Morrison, & M. Hersen
    (Eds.), *Handbook of family violence* (pp. 247–270). New York: Plenum Press.
Salend, E., Kane, R., Satz, M., & Pynoos, J. (1984). Elder abuse reporting: Limitations of statutes.
    The Gerontologist, 24(1), 61–69.
Schene, P., & Ward, S. F. (1988). The vexing problem of elder abuse: The relevance of the child
    protection experience. *Public Welfare, 46*(2), 14–21.
Shah, B. V., Barnwell, B. G., & Bieler, G. S. (1995). *SUDAAN user's manual: Software for analysis
    of correlated data*, Release 6.40. Research Triangle Park, NC: Research Triangle Institute.
Thobaben, M., & Anderson, L. (1985). Report elder abuse: It's the law. *American Journal of Nursing*,
    April, 371–374.
Valentine, D., & Cash, T. (1986). A definitional discussion of elder mistreatment. *Journal of Geronto-
    logical Social Work, 9*(3), 17–28.
Wolf, R. S. (1988). The evolution of policy: A 10-year retrospective. *Public Welfare, 46*(2), 7–13.

Chapter 13

Culturally Specific Outreach in Elder Abuse

Lisa Nerenberg[1]

INTRODUCTION AND BACKGROUND

Professionals and researchers in the field of elder-abuse prevention increasingly have come to recognize the significant extent to which culture determines the way in which elder abuse is manifested and perceived. The likelihood that victims will seek out or accept protective services and the type of services that they find acceptable or helpful to a great extent also are determined culturally. Cultural attitudes and expectations define family roles and responsibilities, determine how resources are distributed within families, and dictate how families cope with stress. If service providers are going to be effective in reducing vulnerability and victimization among members of diverse communities, they need to understand the nature and interplay of those cultural factors that affect the risk of abuse, helpseeking behavior, and families' service needs.

This chapter focuses on culturally specific outreach, or outreach programs that are designed to extend protective or preventive services to specific cultural communities. It begins by presenting the experiences of the San Francisco Consortium for Elder Abuse Prevention in attempting to improve access to services. The next section describes general approaches to outreach that have been used in San Francisco and other communities and presents specific techniques or strategies for extending access to underserved groups. The section that follows draws from these experiences in defining some of the special considerations and challenges that are inherent in designing culturally specific outreach programs. The final section formulates these considerations into principles that can provide guidance and direction to other communities in designing culturally specific outreach programs.

[1]The author wishes to gratefully acknowledge the following individuals whose knowledge, insights, and perceptions contributed to this chapter: The members of the We Are Family Leadership Group, including Betty Hardy, Tress Stewart, Eugenia Burfict, Josephine Shaw, Doriane Miller, Cynthia Alexis, Agnes Morton, Sylvia Jones, and Malene Njeri; Veronica Rodriguez, Carmen Mendieta, Greta Glugoski, Maria Guillen, Yolanda Sanchez, and Donna Benton.

History of the San Francisco Consortium's Culturally Specific Outreach Efforts

The San Francisco Consortium for Elder Abuse Prevention was organized in the early 1980s to improve the city's professional response to abuse. The program model was designed by a citywide task force of professionals after surveying local agencies about their experiences in handling abuse cases and soliciting their input about the service needs of victims and their families. With the information it collected from the survey, the task force went on to design a plan for service delivery. One of the fundamental challenges that the task force faced was to meet the needs of San Francisco's extremely diverse elderly population.

With limited public resources for protective services, the program planners chose to take maximum advantage of San Francisco's relatively extensive network of private, not-for-profit agencies that serve particular geographic and cultural communities. After many months of discussion and deliberation, the task force designed the consortium model that is still in operation today. The plan called for one agency to organize a network of health and human-service agencies and provide them with the information, training, and on-going technical support that they needed to effectively serve their own clients who were victims of, or at risk for, elder abuse. The Goldman Institute on Aging (previously Mount Zion Hospital) was selected to coordinate the program. Since its inception, the Consortium's membership has grown to 78 public and private agencies.

The decision to enhance the ability of community agencies to work with their own clients who were being victimized, rather than funneling all cases to a single agency, was based on the assumption that agencies that were well established in the communities they served, and that had established trust and credibility, would be more effective in dealing with the complex problem of elder abuse. These community agencies also would be better equipped to address the social and cultural factors associated with abuse and would be more accessible geographically.

To better serve its member agencies, the Consortium has continually organized forums, events, and special projects to generate and share information about how elder abuse is manifested and perceived in different cultural and ethnic communities. Working with member agencies, the Consortium's leadership has explored a variety of avenues to reaching diverse groups to better understand their needs and to extend services and information. Several of these efforts and their outcomes are described in the following section.

GENERAL APPROACHES TO OUTREACH

A Conference to Explore Abuse in the Asian Community

In 1985, Consortium staff began working with representatives from Self Help for the Elderly (SHE), a multiservice agency that serves primarily Chinese seniors, to explore elder abuse in the Chinese community. To initiate the effort, the two organizations cosponsored a conference. Because it was felt that there would be parallels between the issues faced by Chinese families and members of other Asian communities, the two organizations decided to expand the scope of the conference to include discussion about abuse in the Japanese, Vietnamese, Filipino, and Korean communities as well. A planning committee, which included mental-health workers, program administrators, medical professionals, and direct service providers from each of these groups, was assembled to plan the event.

During the early planning meetings, many members of the committee observed that they were not seeing cases of elder abuse among the clients they served. They were, however, interested in exploring the issue further and determining whether abuse was not, in fact, a problem in their communities or if, as some expected, it simply was not being reported to agencies. The planning sessions became a forum for candid discussion about the status of the elderly in the various communities, sharing experiences about the challenges inherent in providing services to elderly Asians, and speculation about the social, economic, legal, and cultural factors that contributed to, or mitigated, the risk of elder abuse.

The format for the conference, which was held in May of 1985, included a general introduction to the issue of elder abuse and the San Francisco Consortium, followed by a presentation on legal remedies. The remainder of the day was devoted to panel discussions during which representatives from the participating communities described the status of their elderly members. Specific topics that were addressed included each group's patterns of immigration; the immigration status of seniors and their eligibility for public benefits; the role of the elderly in their families (both in their countries of origin and in the United States); stresses that were affecting family life; patterns of service utilization; obstacles to services; and cultural factors that may contribute to or deter abuse.

A variety of themes emerged in the discussions. Although each community represented was distinct in terms of its history, experiences, economic status, conventions, and many other factors, there were many commonalties. Foremost among the problems faced by Asian seniors that were identified was the intense isolation that many seniors were experiencing as a result of language and cultural barriers that distanced them from their families, particularly from their grand-children. For many, geographic barriers further separated them from formal and informal support networks. The fact that many older Asians looked after their grandchildren during the daytime while their children were at work further increased their isolation and reduced their access to formal and informal supports. Although these childcare responsibilities were generally viewed as a positive and fulfilling role for Asian seniors, service providers felt that in some families, the level of childcare that seniors were providing was clearly burdensome and exploitive. Another form of mistreatment that was identified by participants involved immigrant families in which younger members had come to the United States first and later sent for elderly family members. To sponsor an elderly family member, these families were required to pledge that they would provide financial support to the newcomers, which disqualified the older person from receiving public benefits. Some families were failing to follow through on their promises to provide financial support, leaving the older person with neither family nor public support.

Members of the planning committee also identified a variety of obstacles that discouraged or prevented seniors from benefiting from existing services. These included cultural taboos and sanctions against airing family matters in public, which was viewed as bringing shame to the family. It was repeatedly suggested that Eastern religious beliefs encouraged people to accept their fates in life, thereby discouraging them from taking steps to end their victimization.

The conference, which was well attended and favorably evaluated by the participants, also served as a springboard for future work in the Chinese community. Subsequent to the event, SHE was successful in securing funding for a part-time case manager to work with victims of abuse, and the agency's caseload of abuse cases has continued to grow since that time. The agency has remained active in the Consortium through its participation on the program's Steering Committee and Multidisciplinary Team, and by participating in Consortium training events. Through this participation, SHE staff stay abreast of current developments in the field of elder abuse, are familiar with effective methods and approaches, and share their experiences with the broader service network. The organization also has continued to sponsor training and skills-building programs for professionals and outreach events for seniors. It recently conducted a community forum on elder abuse during which agency staff performed skits to demonstrate the various types of abuse and stimulate discussion. The skits were followed by a panel discussion by experts who provided information about local services and responded to questions from the audience. The event generated a significant amount of coverage in the Chinese media.

It can be assumed that SHE's ongoing commitment to elder-abuse prevention, the resources that it has devoted to providing direct services to victims, and the visibility that the program has achieved in the community have contributed to the agency's success in sustaining an active abuse-prevention program. The other organizations that participated in the conference, however, did not develop ongoing service or outreach programs.

Outreach in San Francisco's Latino Community

Several months after the conference on abuse in the Asian community, Consortium staff began working with another member agency that serves San Francisco's Mission District, a neighborhood that includes Central and South American, Mexican, Puerto Rican, and Cuban families. The organizations decided to plan a conference patterned after the one conducted in the Asian community. The planning process for the event proceeded in much the same fashion with representatives from community agencies coming together to explore the status of the elderly in their communities and identify cultural factors that might contribute to or deter abuse and obstacles to services. The format for the event also was patterned after the conference on abuse in the Asian community. Although the conference itself was well attended and favorably evaluated, it did not succeed in stimulating on-going or sustained programs of outreach or services.

In subsequent years, Consortium staff participated in, or hosted, several discussion groups that focused on elder abuse in the Latino community. Among these was a series of meetings that the Consortium cohosted with San Francisco SAFE, a crime-prevention program. SAFE had received a grant to conduct a campaign of outreach in the Mission District aimed at raising awareness about elder abuse. The group met for several months to assess the community's need for abuse-prevention services and information.

During these meetings, service providers who worked in the community indicated that they were observing abuse but that victims were unwilling or reluctant to report cases to public agencies. They feared that reporting abuse could jeopardize their immigration status or that of their children or lead to deportation if they were undocumented. This issue became the topic of several meetings, during which representatives from the city's department of social services, the police, and the sheriff's office presented their agencies' policies with regard to confidentiality. These discussions, however, were not successful in allaying participants' apprehensions about reporting. Developments that occurred at the time that the group was meeting, including the passage of state policy (Proposition 187) that restricts access to benefits and social services by immigrants, further undermined trust toward public agencies by the community. It can be assumed that "welfare reform" will further reduce access to services, intensify strains on families, and perpetuate greater secrecy about family problems. In the face of these trends and uncertainties, agencies that serve the Latino community have been reluctant to engage in activities aimed at case-finding or reporting.

Outreach to African American Seniors

Efforts to improve service delivery to African American seniors in San Francisco followed a different route. When members of the Consortium's Steering Committee (the group that oversees the Consortium's program) observed that African American seniors were not accessing protective services, it prompted the Steering Committee and Consortium staff to initiate a series of dialogues with other service providers, seniors, and clergy to explore the scope and nature of elder abuse in the African American community. The findings and ideas generated by these discussions were integrated into a plan for conducting outreach in the African American community that called for enlisting churches to help raise awareness about abuse and improve access to services. A small seed grant was secured from a local foundation to launch the outreach program. The grant enabled the Consortium to hire a member of the Steering Committee, who is African American, to devote several hours a week to organize the effort and to produce outreach materials.

The original project plan called for recruiting a small group of volunteers from churches that serve primarily African American seniors, including "church mothers," members of missionary groups, or other natural leaders. According to

the plan, the volunteers would receive information about elder abuse and available services at informal gatherings and would then serve as liaisons between the
churches and the social service network.

Shortly after the project began, a Leadership Group of African American service providers was organized to oversee the project. The original membership of
the Leadership Group included a public-health nurse who is also on the faculty
of a local college, the director of a substance-abuse prevention program, and a
physician who directs a public-health center and is also the cofounder of an organization that provides support and advocacy services to grandparents who are primary caregivers to their grandchildren. Later, several additional members joined
the group including another public-health nurse, a caseworker from the public
guardian's office, an information and referral specialist, an outreach worker from
a consumer-advocacy organization, a victim advocate from the district attorney's
office, and the coordinator of an emergency medical response program. In addition to having extensive professional experience and expertise, several Leadership
Group members were actively involved in churches and had extensive experience
in conducting culturally specific outreach.

During its early meetings, the Leadership Group made significant revisions
in the original outreach plan. One of the group's first decisions was to develop
a positive theme for the campaign. The group felt that placing the emphasis of
outreach efforts on exposing abusers would be demoralizing and divisive to the
community. Leadership Group members also felt that a great deal of the abuse that
they were seeing in their work was the result of families being overextended and
trying to cope with untenable economic conditions and caregiving demands. For
that reason, they decided to choose a theme that would acknowledge the difficulties that families were experiencing and look for approaches that offered support
and encouragement. The group also wanted a theme that would promote positive
images of family life and acknowledge the enduring strengths of African American families. The group chose the name *We Are Family* for the project to reinforce
this positive emphasis on families.

In subsequent months, the group articulated a set of principles for the outreach project. These principles called for acknowledging the unique circumstances of African American seniors, building upon the strengths of the African
American community, extending the point of access to services into the community, providing opportunities for seniors to meet service providers in settings that
were familiar and "safe," using preferred styles of communication, and enlisting
the help of trusted members of the community to endorse programs or vouch for
the integrity of service agencies. The group also emphasized the need for agencies
to actively solicit feedback from seniors and respond to problems or obstacles that
the seniors encountered in seeking services.

Drawing from these principles, the group decided to focus on the problem of
seniors losing their homes through foreclosure, because home loss was a problem that was particularly acute within the African American community. It was
observed that "equity-rich and income-poor" seniors, in particular, were being

targeted by lenders and family members and pressured or coerced into taking out home-equity loans. When family members pressured seniors into taking out the loans, it was often to use the money for their own needs or purposes. For a variety of reasons, including fraudulent or misleading practices by lenders, family members failing to return money borrowed from the loans, or seniors not understanding the terms of the loans, many seniors were defaulting on the loans and losing their homes. We Are Family's approach to addressing this problem was to try to prevent home loss by discouraging seniors from taking out risky loans in the first place and directing them to alternative resources for meeting urgent cash needs. Several community events were held, during which seniors were not only warned about the risks of home equity loans but also provided with information about other ways of stretching their resources such as seniors' discounts and programs that offered special services for seniors. Service providers representing a wide range of agencies and services also were invited to talk to seniors about their services and provide them with written materials. The events also included entertainment and cultural presentations including an African American storyteller, a poet, and theatrical readings.

Although We Are Family had hoped to work closely with churches in conducting outreach activities, the participation of clergy and church-affiliated groups has been limited. Although a few churches hosted events, few clergy attended or encouraged congregants to attend educational programs.

DESIGNING CULTURALLY SPECIFIC OUTREACH

Issues Involved in Developing Culturally Specific Outreach

San Francisco's experiences in developing the outreach projects described have shed light on some of the issues, challenges, and obstacles involved in providing culturally specific outreach and suggest the need for further exploration into promising approaches. To further flesh out these issues, the Consortium hosted two informal round-table discussions of service providers and researchers. One group, which included members of We Are Family's Leadership Group and Donna M. Benton of the University of Southern California, discussed elder abuse and culturally specific outreach in the African American community. A second session, which included San Francisco service providers and Yolanda Sanchez of the University of Nevada-Reno, discussed elder abuse and outreach in the Latino community. During the sessions, participants were asked to describe the types of abuse that they were seeing in their communities, their perceptions about community needs with respect to abuse-prevention services, and obstacles or challenges to service delivery. The following section summarizes several of the themes that emerged in the group discussions. Excerpts from the discussions are included.

Common Types of Abuse

Although group members reported that they were encountering all types of abuse (physical, psychological, financial, and neglect) among the clients that they served, both groups emphasized the high prevalence of neglect, which they attributed to the fact that families were trying to cope with highly demanding or untenable situations with inadequate resources. Cases were cited by members of the African American group in which individual, working family members were providing support or care to several generations of children, grandchildren, in-laws, and parents. In some families, seniors were providing support and care to impaired or unemployed adult children, or to grandchildren whose parents were unavailable because of substance abuse, incarceration, or mental illness. Members of the Latino group noted that it was common for families who discovered that elderly members in their native countries were in failing health to bring the elderly relative to the United States so that they could provide needed care. This often was done in crisis situations without regard to whether the older person was eligible for medical or social services, or without fully understanding the nature of the older person's condition, its progression, or the extent of the older person's care needs. As a result, these families often found themselves caring for severely impaired family members with little or no outside resources or support.

Financial abuse also was viewed as a pervasive problem by members of both groups. In some situations, financial abuse escalated to physical abuse when abusers were denied money or a place to live. As described in the previous section, another type of financial abuse that is particularly prevalent in the African American community involves elderly homeowners who are pressured or coerced by lenders, family members, or others, to take out home-equity loans and turn over the cash to abusive family members. Frequently, the seniors are unable to repay the loans, resulting in foreclosure and the loss of the home.

Perceptions of Abuse

In discussing these situations, members of both groups described significant differences in how abuse was perceived within their communities and by outsiders. It was noted, for example, that struggling or impoverished families tended to reject the notion that one family member's income or resources should be used exclusively for that person if other family members were also in need. Examples were cited in which older family members who had pensions or public benefits shared their resources with others or allowed other family members to live in their homes without contributing to household expenses. In some situations, elderly members were unable to meet their own needs for food, medication, or other necessities because they were sharing resources with others in their homes.

> In the African American community, diabetes is a big problem. Some seniors who
> have a lot of other family members in their homes can't cover the rent or house pay-

ments, pay all the other bills, and still eat the way they should. So they get into trouble with their blood sugar levels and they wind up in hospital emergency rooms.[2]

Although these situations may be viewed as exploitive by outsiders, the families, including the older persons whose needs are not being met, often do not see it that way. Older members may feel that providing for their family's needs is an obligation or necessity to preserve the family. They may see their families' difficulties as stemming from societal problems and economic conditions rather than malevolence on the part of individual family members. If workers come in and suggest that it is exploitive for other family members to use an older person's resources, they often find that the family does not agree that there is a problem.

I was working with a woman whose grown daughter, son-in-law, and three or four grandchildren came to live with her in her home. She felt that it was her responsibility to provide for them all. She came to our agency because her water bill was so astronomical that she could not afford to pay it and they were getting ready to turn off the water. She didn't see it as abuse. To her, the problem was the water company.

Clearly, we're dealing with a generation that has different notions about obligation. Seniors believe in holding families together at all costs, even if it means sacrificing themselves. This is very prevalent in the African American community.

Even when elderly parents see their children's behavior as abusive, many refuse to do anything about it. One explanation for parents' tolerance of abuse that was suggested by group members was that elderly parents are more accepting of their children's behavior because they feel that they (the children) routinely confront extreme and unfair hardships in their lives. Parents who see their children experience exclusion and brutality sometimes react with a sense of protectiveness and are less likely to hold them accountable for their behavior.

Parents try to find ways to compensate for the fact that they can't make the racism go away. So they don't hold their children accountable. They are trying to protect them.

Cultural Barriers to Services

Cultural prohibitions against exposing family problems to outsiders also was cited as a formidable deterrent to seniors seeking out needed services. Both groups discussed intense cultural pressures against revealing family problems to outsiders.

Seniors want so much to live like they used to. They don't want to take their business out of the house. In the African American community, you didn't take anything out of the house. Everything was dealt with in the family. Seniors think they can still do this. They're afraid of betraying their families.

[2] All quoted extracts were taken from two informal round-table discussions hosted by the San Francisco Consortium for Elder Abuse Prevention.

Owing to cultural expectations that children care for their elderly parents, families that are unable to do so experience high levels of shame and embarrassment, which further discourages disclosure of abuse. The parents themselves may be ashamed of their children's abusive behavior.

> In the Latino culture, elders take a lot of pride in the accomplishments of their children, so it is very difficult for them to admit that a child is abusing them. They don't want to say "look at how my son treats me."

The whole notion of looking to outsiders for help in family matters is also alien to some families. Members of both groups cited a tendency for families to respond to crises by getting directly involved, rather than contacting agencies for help, even if it resulted in family caregivers overextending themselves. The extent to which this tendency is the result of a lack of information about services, distrust of the system, or the belief that appealing to the formal service network is an indication of failure is unclear.

Systems Barriers

Some of the reluctance by seniors and their families to avail themselves of services stems from the fact that the methods and approaches that the service system employs are not viewed as helpful or appropriate. Traditional approaches to abuse fail to acknowledge the broader context in which abuse occurs and are likely to be viewed as divisive to families, or overly simplistic. For example, abuse has been attributed to pathological relationships between abusers and victims. In light of the intense pressures that families are experiencing, it may be unrealistic to address elder abuse as a separate and distinct problem that can be addressed in isolation. Pervasive stressors include high rates of unemployment, drug abuse, the preying upon communities by unscrupulous businesses (including insurance vendors, home-repair companies, and mortgage companies), and pervasive anti-immigrant and racist sentiments. This observation suggests that more holistic approaches to outreach and service delivery that address the multiple and interrelated needs of families are needed.

Relations between service providers and family members often are strained by damaging misperceptions and unrealistic expectations that impede their ability to work together. Members of the Latino group, for example, observed that Anglo service providers hold the stereotype that all Latinos have extended family networks that provide (or should provide) needed care to elderly members when, very often, this is not the case. If workers' judgments are clouded by these stereotypes, they may fail to provide or authorize needed services.

> There's this myth that we are "taking care of our own." But the reality is that we can't always take care of our own. It's not that we don't want to. It's that sometimes, we

can't. We have children to take care of and are struggling to get by. But nobody wants to admit that they can't take care of their own.

Even in cases in which family members are available to help, culturally prescribed roles and expectations may prevent them from doing so or restrict their ability to intervene effectively. For this reason, family members may look to the service community to help them.

> In the Latino community, the elderly, especially elderly women, have a special role in the family and are treated with great respect. I worked with two brothers whose mother was becoming increasingly demented. We told the sons that it was really time to look at placement. But when they asked their mother if she was willing to move, she said "no." They knew that she really needed to be placed, but they weren't going to be the ones to make the decision. They wanted someone else to decide. That's what eventually happened. There was a crisis and someone in the community intervened.

It was also observed that family members have a tendency to "pull out" or abandon elderly relatives if agencies become involved, perhaps believing that their continued involvement will jeopardize the services. These observations suggest that service providers need to build partnerships and negotiate roles with families so that their involvement enhances, rather than undermines, the families' involvement.

Distrust of the service network also was cited repeatedly as a barrier to seniors seeking help from agencies. This distrust is attributed to negative experiences with the social-service system and social policies that have been damaging to family life.

> There is a basis for this mistrust. You need to look at it from the historical context. People who received public assistance early on had their lives disrupted. Authorities turned their homes upside down. Men would pretend they didn't live with their families if it would jeopardize the families' benefits.

Within the Latino community, the fear that social-service agencies will discriminate against immigrants and report undocumented persons to the Immigration and Naturalization Service is pervasive. Negative perceptions of law enforcement also are particularly pronounced among members of minorities who are disproportionately represented in the criminal-justice system. Group members speculated that California's recently enacted "three strikes, you're out" law (which requires mandatory extended sentences for anyone who is convicted of three felonies) will make victims even less likely to report abuse to law enforcement.

> To do outreach, we need to address this mistrust. We need to acknowledge how racism has played itself out in the community and how it has created this distrust.

DISCUSSION

Approaches to Outreach

Surprisingly few elder-abuse prevention programs across the country have developed outreach campaigns that are specifically designed to encourage members of underserved groups to seek out needed services. With a few exceptions, those that have been conducted have not been evaluated to assess their impact. Consequently, conclusions about the effectiveness of different approaches to outreach are largely anecdotal and speculative. Members of the two discussion groups shared their experiences, ideas, perceptions, and suggestions about outreach. Donna Benton, who participated in the group that discussed abuse in the African American community, also presented information about culturally specific outreach campaigns that she had identified in other communities to lay the groundwork for discussion. This section summarizes these discussions, highlighting various approaches and techniques that had been used by group members and in other communities.

Outreach programs that have been designed to raise awareness about elder abuse and encourage victims, witnesses, and others to report it tend to fall within one of two categories, which can be conceptualized as "direct" versus "nondirect" approaches. The City of New York's "That's Abuse" campaign is an example of the direct approach. Posters and billboards, on which abuse is depicted with photographs (e.g., someone taking money out of an older woman's purse), are used to define abuse. The text on the posters reads, "That's abuse," and directs readers to report situations to protective service agencies. Several variations of the posters have been designed portraying members of various ethnic groups. Preliminary outcome evaluations have demonstrated that the campaign has significantly increased abuse reports by members of the groups being featured. The project also is using the posters in public housing projects that have high concentrations of members of the targeted groups.

Other projects, including San Francisco's We Are Family, have de-emphasized abuse, choosing instead to highlight the positive contributions of extended family networks and focusing on measures to support families. A similar approach is being used by the Pennsylvania Department of Aging in its "Honor and Respect" campaign, which targets African American, Hispanic, and rural seniors. The campaign stresses community action, promotes preventive interventions, and positions area agencies on aging as friends rather than enforcers.

There seems to be widespread agreement among those who are experienced with outreach campaigns that the manner in which the topic of abuse is presented to seniors significantly affects their receptivity to the information and the likelihood that they will respond favorably to the outreach message. It was noted that the use of value-laden labels such as *victim, perpetrator*, and *abuse* is viewed by many as stigmatizing and tends to alienate victims. Seniors are likely to believe that seeking help is a sign of personal failure or defeat; reframing the issue to emphasize that seeking help is an indicator of strength is one way of eliminating this barrier.

> We need to emphasize that it takes strength to reach out. Help won't come unless you ask for it.

Other ways of reducing shame include emphasizing to vulnerable seniors that their abusive children or grandchildren need help, which they will get only if the older person refuses to let the abuse continue. Focusing on the positive aspects of the older person's relationship with the abuser also may reduce defensiveness and increase his or her receptivity to interventions.

> I know of a case in which a son brought his mother to this country to live with him but was then abusive to her. It was not a good situation, but he was connected enough to her to want to have her with him and for her to be part of his life. That was positive and needed to be emphasized.

Creating opportunities to "self-recognize" the problem is another way to avoid stigmatizing or casting shame upon individuals who have been victimized. An approach that has been used by group workers if they suspect that individuals in a group setting are experiencing abuse is to bring in service providers to make general presentations to the group about the problem and available services. In this way, the vulnerable person receives the information about needed services without having to disclose the abuse to the other members of the group.

Another approach to avoid stigmatizing victims is to ask groups or individuals if they know of anyone who is being abused. In addition to encouraging them to think about others they know who may be at risk, it provides an opportunity for them to ask questions or take written materials without disclosing whether the information is for themselves or others.

> If you act like abuse is happening to an older person, a wall goes up. So we need to couch the outreach message as "this may be happening to someone you know. Keep this information and give it to a friend."

If victims are willing to discuss abuse with their peers, the support and encouragement they receive can be very helpful. Abuse is a frequent topic at meetings of support groups for primary caregivers of grandchildren in the African American community. In this setting, the grandmothers share their experiences, describe what they have done under similar circumstances, and offer encouragement to those in need. This process also occurs spontaneously in settings in which seniors congregate, such as adult day health centers or housing projects.

A recurrent theme in discussions about culturally specific outreach is the need for building trust. Service providers who want to encourage seniors to accept services may need to establish high levels of trust and credibility if they are going to be effective. It may take many weeks or months for seniors to disclose that they have been victimized. Once a relationship has been established, however, it is much more likely that the older person will be willing to accept the service providers' suggestions for what they can do to end their victimization. Conducting routine visits, even short visits, and performing small services for the older person can help to build the relationship. If victims are introduced to protective-service providers by third parties with whom the older person has a trusting relationship, it tends to facilitate this trust building process.

> Clients come to us and say 'I have no food in my house.' So, we find some way to get them food. And then, when they come back for something else, we may start asking about where their money is going, what's really going on. And then we find that there's a family member living with the older person who is on drugs and pressuring the older person for money.

Enlisting the Support of Churches in Outreach

Because the church has traditionally been the foundation of family and community life in the African American and Latino communities, several elder abuse prevention outreach programs have attempted to enlist church support in outreach activities. The experiences of some, like San Francisco's We Are Family, have been disappointing. Suggested explanations for churches' reticence to get involved include the fact that clergy are being inundated with requests to become involved in social issues and lack the time to participate. Many ministers hold other daytime jobs and minister to their congregations in the evening or on weekends. Many churches lack support staff who can respond to calls or letters from agencies. With increasing demands and diminished resources, even the traditional practice of checking in with members of the congregation who stop coming to church has been abandoned by some churches, reducing the churches' ability to detect and respond to problems. It also has been suggested that clergy may be reluctant to become involved in issues like elder abuse that traditionally have placed the blame for abuse on family members for mistreating others, perceiving that it places them in the position of taking sides in family issues.

Despite these experiences, group members expressed optimism about future collaboration with churches. It was observed, for example, that within the African American community, churches are in a period of renewal or revitalization, which is accompanied by an emphasis on family life and personal responsibility. This trend has resulted in noticeable increases in attendance at church by men and younger people.

Some service providers have found that appealing to clients' spiritual beliefs and values is an extremely powerful force in helping them through traumatic life events or situations. It instills hope and optimism that can increase the likelihood that they will change their situations.

> I had one client, who was one of my hardest cases. Her son was abusing her on all levels. She had been evicted because of her son, didn't have any money, and couldn't

walk up stairs. When we started to talk about the Virgin of Guadelupe, you could see her spirits rise. It increased her faith that things would get better.

Challenges to Successful Outreach

Several themes have consistently resonated through discussions about culturally specific outreach. One message is that if outreach is to be effective, those organizations and agencies that sponsor programs must be willing to reassess traditional practices and, in some cases, discard or abandon old ways of doing business. An obvious example is that traditional approaches to providing protective services require that clients come forward and request services or agree to accept services that are offered to them by protective-service workers. In the latter instances, contacts typically occur if agency personnel have received abuse reports from third parties who have witnessed the abuse. In these situations, the workers are unknown to the seniors and are strictly limited by their agencies' policies with regard to the amount of time that they can spend with clients and the number of visits they are authorized to make.

In light of the evidence emerging from successful outreach programs, it appears that for agencies to succeed in reaching underserved groups, they need to develop mechanisms for offering services to clients in settings that are familiar, accessible, and acceptable to them, and they should allow workers greater flexibility in the amount of time they devote to clients. Experience has shown that on-going and sustained contact may be needed to encourage some seniors to accept help. This suggests that to be effective, workers may need to make routine visits or meet informally with seniors at community centers or at churches over a period of time to establish themselves, gain trust and credibility, and be available to vulnerable seniors. They may need to offer informal services that their agencies have not historically provided. If it is not possible to station outreach workers in targeted communities, agencies must, at a minimum, work closely with organizations or churches that are trusted in the community and that can assist in identifying abuse and facilitating referrals. Because these activities may not fit within an agency's traditional program guidelines, its policies may need to be reassessed.

Some of the specific methods or practices that have been found to be effective in reaching underserved groups may be incompatible with Western tenets of professionalism. For example, it is generally considered unprofessional for service providers to talk about themselves, accept gifts, or discuss issues as personal as spiritual beliefs. However, failure to relate to clients on a personal level may prevent workers from establishing trusting relationships with those they are trying to reach. Refusal to establish personal and reciprocal relationships may cast workers as aloof or suspect. Cultural and professional practices related to privacy and confidentiality also may be in conflict, restricting workers' effectiveness. The common practice of separating suspected victims and abusers so that they can be interviewed privately, for example, may be offensive to families, arouse suspicion, or alienate family members who may otherwise be available to help.

To overcome obstacles that are inherent in culturally specific outreach and ensure the success of outreach efforts, it is essential that all members of the sponsoring organization, from line staff to the board of directors, clearly understand what the agency is trying to achieve and its methods for doing so. This includes staff who are not directly involved in outreach as well as those who are. Although service providers who engage in outreach typically find it enriching and challenging, if they do not have the firm support, commitment, and understanding of their agencies and coworkers they can be placed in compromising or distressing situations. Coworkers may resent the fact that they use unconventional techniques or they may view outreach workers as unprofessional in their approaches. They may have negative views toward the outreach workers' focus on a particular cultural group or see it as favoritism. If an outreach worker succeeds in encouraging an older person to come to his or her agency for services and the older person does not receive the services that they have been promised, or if they are not treated sensitively by other members of the organization, it can seriously damage the outreach worker's credibility and effectiveness with the community. To overcome these potential obstacles, outreach workers cannot work in isolation. The agencies they represent must have a strong commitment to improving access, a willingness to invest time and resources in the outreach effort, and an openness to modifying policies and procedures to support the outreach effort.

Funding agencies, too, must become familiar with the approaches and techniques used in culturally specific outreach and committed to the outreach goals. A recurrent frustration voiced by outreach workers is that outreach to underserved groups is often considered to be "ancillary" and, therefore, expendable. If overall agency or program funding is reduced, outreach is often the first activity to be suspended. Abruptly terminating outreach can irreparably damage relationships within a community that have taken extended periods of time to establish and can perpetuate distrust and negative attitudes toward the service-delivery system.

Finally, the impact of culturally specific outreach is difficult to evaluate. Traditionally, the effectiveness of outreach campaigns has been measured by the number of reported cases that can be attributed to outreach activities. This indicator of success may not be appropriate if clients are reluctant to make reports to public agencies. In these cases, it may be more effective for outreach workers to provide advice, support, and assistance to other community agencies that are directly involved with clients without actually working directly with the older people. Outreach campaigns also may be assessed in terms of the units of service that the outreach agency provides. Traditional definitions and categories of service may need to be modified to better reflect the approaches, strategies, and tasks employed in culturally specific outreach, and to accurately measure their success in achieving goals and objectives. Funding agencies need to work with outreach providers and members of underserved communities in developing criteria for evaluating programs that are realistic and that capture the intent of the outreach effort.

Chapter 14

A Synthesis of Current Knowledge on Minority Elder Abuse

Margaret Rittman, Lisa B. Kuzmeskus, & Mary A. Flum

Elder abuse probably has occurred for centuries, but awareness and recognition of the problem is relatively new. In the United States, elder abuse was not recognized as a serious social problem until the early 1970s, when adult protective service laws were established in several states and researchers began studying the problem. Today, most states have enacted some type of elder-abuse legislation addressing domestic elder abuse, have voluntary or mandatory reporting requirements, and have developed prevention and treatment programs to meet the needs of the elderly and their families. Although progress has been made in treating and preventing elder abuse, research efforts on the nature of elder abuse have lagged farther behind. As we begin to better understand elder abuse, in general, we need to continue making more extensive forays into researching and understanding the possible differences in cultural perceptions and treatment of elder abuse in different minority communities.

This chapter presents a synthesis of research intending to provide an overview of the research conducted thus far on elder abuse among minority populations in the United States. This chapter is divided into four sections that cover the major ethnic minorities in this country. The first section delves into the subject of elder abuse in the Black community, reviewing the literature on the incidence of elder abuse, the characteristics of the victims and perpetrators of abuse, and the causal factors. The second section provides an overview of elder abuse among the Hispanic population and talks about the characteristics of Hispanic elders and their families, abuse and neglect of Hispanic elders, and the cultural issues that need to be considered when working with Hispanic elders. The next section discusses elder abuse among American Indians and covers the empirical research and causal factors and provides a discussion of the definition of elder abuse among American Indians. The fourth and final section covers elder abuse among Asian American populations and reviews the empirical research, the concept of filial piety, the notion of suffering as a part of life, and the issue of privacy of families and concludes with a discussion of intervention recommendations.

ELDER ABUSE WITHIN THE BLACK COMMUNITY

Research on elder abuse in the Black population is extremely limited given the size of the population and its recent demographic trends. It is expected that the growth of the Black elderly population will exceed the rate of growth of the White elderly population by the year 2000 (Harel, McKinncy, & Williams, 1990). Furthermore, the empirical research that has been conducted is often contradictory, making conclusive findings across the literature difficult to reach. The following is a review of findings from research conducted thus far concerning elder abuse in the Black community.

Studies on Elder Abuse Among Blacks

The true incidence of elder abuse in the Black population is unknown. However, several researchers have conducted empirical research in this community that suggests that elder abuse may be a growing problem. However, according to Cazenave (1981) and Crystal (1987), recent studies about elder abuse, which included Blacks as part of the samples, have not had sufficient numbers of Black elderly persons and have not explored the qualitative details of Black life or the lives of the Black elderly. Additionally, inclusion of any specific questions about Black people in research studies has been limited and received very little attention (Griffin & Williams, 1992). Furthermore, results from the incidence studies that have been conducted show inconsistent and contradictory findings.

Steinmetz (1990) argues that the findings from several studies seem to predict higher elder-abuse rates among Blacks compared with Whites. And Steinmetz and Pellicciaro (1986) predicted that based on knowledge of abusive families, Black elderly women are at greater risk for being abused than are White. Conflictingly, Cazenave and Straus (1979) found that Black elderly were much less likely to be abused by a relative than were White elderly. The findings from these studies demonstrate that the relationship between race and elder abuse is uncertain (Cazenave, 1981).

Longres, Raymond, and Kimmel (1991) found that people who allegedly maltreated Blacks were invariably Black themselves and were likely to be 50 years of age or younger, females, and, if they were family members, daughters. Although this was a small study and not representative of the Black population, it has been supported by another study of elder maltreatment (Longres, 1992). In addition, this second study found that perpetrators were not likely to be either living with the older adult or providing care but were likely to have substance-abuse problems. Furthermore, it has been learned that in order to increase the accuracy of information about elder abuse among the Black population, it is important to include sufficient numbers of minority-group members in the sample and to consider the characteristics that influence minority experiences (Williams and Griffin, 1991).

Discussion

When examining the etiology of Black family abuse, societal experiences of some Blacks who abuse may be likened to those of victims of abuse, who in turn become abusers themselves (Steinmetz, 1988). Such societal experiences of Blacks may include their history of slavery, poverty, racism, and lack of access to quality education, employment, housing, and health and social services. Staples (1976) also suggests that the explanation for higher rates of violence among Blacks may be their social predicament in American society, especially in the southern region of the United States, which historically has reacted violently to Black quests for social equity.

Williams and Griffin (1991) suggest that elder abuse among Blacks may be a result of familial exposure to violence, male socialization to violence, long-standing familial conflicts, or stress on the primary caretaker due to the needs of the frail elderly family member. Societal influences direct the patterns of behavior among Blacks and shape the Black experience in this country, and it is this background that has influenced how and why Blacks' lives and family configurations are different from those of Whites (Williams & Griffin, 1991). Although these unjust life experiences do not justify violent behavior, Cazenave (1981), Hare (1979), and Asbury (1987) note that violence may be a way of reacting to the lack of options available to meet definitions of success generated by society, which are controlled by the majority race. Cazenave (1981) adds that when societal, family–kin–community, individual, and precipitating factors are considered, it becomes clear that although some countervailing forces may exist against the abuse of the Black aged, generally the social conditions under which they live suggest that many Black Americans are at a potentially higher risk than other groups for the occurrence of elder abuse. Certainly there are factors that cannot and must not be ignored. The oppressive behaviors that reduce or prevent options of Black elders may be seen as a violation of individuals' rights, which can be one form of abuse (Griffin & Williams, 1992). Any further studies on elder abuse in the Black population should take into account the sociological history of Blacks in this country.

ELDER ABUSE IN THE HISPANIC COMMUNITY

Although the dearth of studies on elder abuse among Hispanic persons is widely acknowledged, a greater number of studies have been done on the characteristics of the Hispanic elderly population. This information can be extremely helpful in discussing possible elder abuse in this country. This section examines the usefulness and limitations of the data from available studies, and what these findings imply. The dynamic nature of an ethnic group's acculturation into a society, however, suggests that the implications of these current studies may change as the Hispanic population ages. This may occur because younger Hispanics, who probably will reside in the United States for a longer time period than their older, foreign-born relatives, may change and adapt their approach to family issues, such as the care of aging parents, as they age and assimilate their families in this country.

In examining social-service issues, an important factor to consider is the diversity and breadth of the Hispanic group. The Hispanic population in this country includes those from Mexico, Puerto Rico, Cuba, and Central and South America, with each country or region having its own cultural traditions. In the literature examined for this chapter, research typically focused only on one specific cultural group in the United States, such as Mexican Americans; some research addressed issues that were more generalizable to the entire spectrum of Hispanic groups. Research encompassing both specific and general Hispanic groups is examined here. Additionally, it is important to heed the warning of Boyajian (1990), who cautions that authors' comments should not be considered the "final word" in understanding other cultures but should be seen as a starting point to help us go beyond our own cultural biases.

Characteristics of Hispanic Elderly and Their Families

The Hispanic family is typically considered to be part of a tight, intimate network involving an extended, multigenerational family that includes friends and godparents, who have "joined the family" and who provide lifelong support for family members. Hispanics, more than almost any other cultural group, are credited with having familial relationships in which each person looks out for the other's welfare and interests. Brenes Jette and Remien (1988) examined relationship factors that contributed to the Hispanic family's success in keeping its cohesiveness among members of different generations and found several cultural factors were important, particularly to the elderly. These included

> "confianza," the value of trust... "personalismo," trust in the immediate person, not the secondary institution... "respeto," the value of respect intrinsically owed to other persons, particularly elders... and "verguenza and orgullo," the sense of shame to be avoided at all costs and the value of pride to be upheld in all aspects of one's life. (p. 355)

These factors are important because they illustrate that Hispanic elders typically want to have problems addressed only by the family, not by outsiders, and that the family does not want the outside world to know about any problems, such as abuse, that the family may be experiencing. The importance of family togetherness contributes to the fact that Hispanic elderly do not ask for help outside the family, even if assistance from the family is unavailable or not forthcoming. In a survey of elder-abuse research among minority groups, Stein (1991) found that family loyalty makes it very difficult to identify cases of abuse and neglect in Hispanic families. The prominence of "filial responsibility," whereby adult children are responsible for the care and support of the elderly, also figures prominently in Hispanic families' thinking and may influence the elder's decision against using outside social services (Applewhite & Daley, 1988). A study of Mexican Americans (Farias & Handley, 1990) found that the family is very important because it is a refuge for those who are discriminated against and who start at the "bottom of the economic ladder." The family becomes the source of strength for bettering dismal living conditions. Because of the importance of the family for the survival of the individual, any outsider who threatens this cohesive family unit will find that the members typically become uncommunicative.

In a study of low-income elderly in California, Lubben and Becerra (1987) found that cultural values, economic need, and the poor health of aging parents may prompt adult children in Mexican and Chinese families to share housing and help their elderly parents more often than other ethnic groups (although the study found that the level of help the elderly received in low-income White and Black families also was extensive). Census reports consistently show that Hispanics have the highest poverty rate of any ethnic group. In 1995, of persons of Hispanic origin, 30.3% lived in poverty, slightly more than the 29.3% of Blacks who did, and much greater than the poverty rates of 11.2% for Whites and 14.6% for Asians and Pacific Islanders (Baugher & Lamison-White, 1996).

In conclusion, although some say that Hispanic families are close-knit because of their structure, others disagree and say it is primarily based on economic need. Although it appears that Hispanic elderly are well respected by their families, little research has been done on this issue. One researcher presents an alternative theory that suggests that Hispanic families must live together because of economic need and that Hispanic elders typically are not treated well by family members. Trevino (1988) also emphasizes that a common misconception exists that Hispanic elderly are taken care of by the extended family. Hispanic elderly in different cultural groups may be living in isolation and rejection, even though the extended family is in place, Trevino asserts.

Research Findings on Abuse and Neglect of Hispanic Elders

In one of the first elder-abuse studies that included Hispanics, Hall (1987) found in looking at 126 cases of elder maltreatment in minority families (Blacks and Hispanics) and 161 cases in nonminority families in Texas that there were no striking differences between the two groups. Overall, many families were living in poverty. Looking at differences within the minority cases, Hall found that compared with Blacks, Hispanics may have a less-developed social-support system, such as a caregiver and an identified source of medical care (a physician, clinic, or emergency room), although the majority of people of all racial groups had no support system. Fifty-eight percent of Black elderly persons had no known caregiver; 79% of Hispanics did not have a caregiver (nonminorities had 76% with no known caregiver). However, 80% of Blacks had a known source of medical care, compared with only 59% of Hispanics. Hall cautions, however, that the data are based on a sample for Hispanics that was almost 50% smaller than that of Blacks, and thus the Hispanic percentages may be inflated.

One study on elder abuse found that Puerto Rican respondents revere their elderly and elder abuse was anathema to this group. Anetzberger, Korbin, & Tomita (1996) found that in focus groups with Puerto Ricans, who were either 60 years of age or older or who were "baby boomers," the elderly were

> so important to family tradition and functioning that actions directed against elders other than the most positive ones of love and respect had a tendency to be regarded as unacceptable at best and abusive at worst. (p. 206)

Research on Cultural Issues to Consider When Working with Hispanic Elderly Persons

According to Brenes Jette and Remien (1988), research has shown that a client's cultural background is an important consideration in the development of treatment modalities. For professionals working with Hispanic elders on issues about abuse, researchers have found that adapting factors important to the family's cohesiveness may help in establishing rapport with the elderly. To increase effectiveness with the elderly, caseworkers should establish and work on the following factors: *personalismo*, knowing the Hispanic elder as a total person before addressing important personal matters or tasks; *dignidad*, establishing a personal working relationship that reflects dignity and self-worth; *respeto*, respect between the professional and the Hispanic client; and *confianza*, trust between the two parties (Applewhite & Daley, 1988). The time spent in establishing a good relationship with an Hispanic elderly person may encourage the person to work with the adult protective service staff or caseworker.

Applewhite and Daley (1988) also cite extensive research literature on access and utilization to social services by Hispanic elderly which shows that many barriers or factors influence this group's typical underutilization of social services. These factors include an inability or unwillingness to travel beyond familiar neighborhoods to access services, a lack of knowledge about services, a strong preference for ethnic providers or helpers instead of the dominant culture's arrangements, and, in a study of Mexican Americans, the absence of bilingual and bicultural therapists. Addressing these barriers by providing accessible neighborhood outreach services and therapists and providers proficient in the Hispanic language and Hispanic cultural ways would be important in helping Hispanics to begin utilizing social services.

ELDER ABUSE WITHIN THE AMERICAN INDIAN[1] COMMUNITY

Although the reported rate of elder abuse is very low among American Indians, elder abuse does exist. However, the key to understanding elder abuse within the American Indian community is in examining the unique dynamic of its culture. According to the National Center on Elder Abuse, in 1996 there were 293,000 reports nationwide of elder abuse, neglect, and exploitation. However, the reports of elder abuse pertaining to American Indians represent only a small fraction of all the reports received. According to 1996 data less than 1% of all domestic elder-abuse reports received by mandated state report-receiving agencies were on elders who are American Indian (Tatara & Kuzmeskus, 1997). Although the number of elder-abuse reports received on American Indians is very small, it is believed that there are a larger number of unreported incidents of abuse, neglect, and exploitation of American Indians.

A possible reason for the low number of reports may be the American Indians' unique value system, which may inhibit the detection of elder abuse. Their culture is one that "grants dignity and authority to its elders" (Coles, 1989) and one in which the families of American Indians have traditionally cared for their elders within their own homes (Smith, 1993). Elder abuse is a problem to which American Indians do not wish to admit, for it works against the complex grain of their value systems, which may vary by tribal affiliation (Carson, 1995; Danaan, 1990). Furthermore, American Indians do not want the help of "outsiders" in identifying elder abuse, and it is a problem that American Indians wish to use their own internal systems to address (Danaan, 1990; National Aging Resource Center on Elder Abuse, 1989; Rogers & Gallion, 1978; Stein, 1991).

The few empirical studies conducted on the subject of elder abuse among American Indians show that abuse occurs both on and off the reservation, and these studies have consistent findings (Brown, 1989; Maxwell & Maxwell, 1992; Yakima Indian Nation, 1987). One finding shows that of the different types of elder maltreatment, neglect has consistently been found to be the most prevalent among American Indians. The reasons for this are many and have been documented not only in the empirical research but also in the qualitative discussions of several authors (Carson, 1995; Stein, 1991).

Empirical Research Findings

The Yakima Indian Nation (1987) conducted a needs assessment survey of 162 tribal individuals 55 years of age or older. This assessment found that 34% of the elders surveyed had suffered some type of abuse. Furthermore, it was found that abuse was most severe in areas of rural isolation in which the elders frequently

---

[1]The terms *American Indian* and *Native American* often are used interchangeably to refer to the same community. For the purpose of this chapter, because *Native American* also includes the Aleut and Eskimo population, the term *American Indian* will be used to refer to this population.

were neglected. Secondary to neglect, elders were exploited "through the practice of leaving grandchildren or other young family members with elders for lengthy periods of time. In many cases elders are not capable, physically, emotionally and financially to properly care for these young children" (Yakima Indian Nation, 1987, p. 5). Overall this needs-assessment survey documented a need for elder-abuse education and prevention among the Yakima Indian Nation.

Brown (1989), in a study of 37 elderly Navajo, also found neglect to be the most prevalent form of abuse, accounting for 45.9% of the elder abuse. Verbal or psychological abuse accounted for 21.6% of the elder abuse in this study, and financial exploitation also was 21.6% of the abuse cases. Physical abuse was found to be the least prevalent form of abuse (16.2%). This study also addressed the issue of perpetrators of abuse. Brown found that the perpetrators of abuse "were equally divided between those who were members of respondents' immediate families (i.e., spouses, children, and grandchildren) and others (i.e., neighbors)" (p. 24). Interestingly, these findings on the types of abuse are consistent with the other empirical research conducted on American Indians by the Yakima Indian Nation (1987) and Maxwell and Maxwell (1992).

Maxwell and Maxwell (1992) conducted a study of elder maltreatment among two Plains Indians Tribes. The findings of this study, although consistent with those of Brown and the Yakima Nation, further document the complexity of elder abuse. Maxwell and Maxwell found wide variations in the frequencies and types of abuse and neglect. The study focused on elder maltreatment on two reservations, for the purpose of this study identified as the "Lone Mountain Reservation" and the "Abundant Land Reservation." Maxwell and Maxwell reviewed the archives of the Indian Health Services, which specified the hospital use rate of the elders on the reservation, and they conducted a series of interviews and discussions with the tribal elders, their families, and community leaders. Maxwell and Maxwell found that elder abuse did exist on both reservations but that the definition of elder abuse was different from how it had typically been defined. Furthermore, these researchers found that the types and frequencies of abuse and neglect varied between the two reservations. Physical abuse and neglect were common on the Lone Mountain Reservation. However, on the Abundant Land Reservation neglect was common but physical abuse was claimed to not exist. On both reservations elder abuse was not defined as a problem of the individual but rather it was believed to be a problem of the community.

Causal Factors for Elder Abuse Among American Indians

Several researchers have attempted to investigate the causal factors related to elder abuse. Three significant studies discussed in this section found that there are factors, both risk and protective, that may contribute to the likelihood of abuse and neglect of the elderly.

Brown (1989) investigated the causes of elder abuse by concentrating on family characteristics, in particular on the caregiver relationship. Brown found that abuse of the elderly was associated with the suddenness of dependency, mental problems, and problems with caregivers—either personal problems or the caregivers being unprepared for their responsibilities. Carson (1995) identified risk factors for abuse as poverty, changes in family relationships, and the poor health status of elderly American Indians.

Maxwell and Maxwell (1992) found that elder abuse was inextricably linked with the "indicators of community disorganization" (p. 3). These indicators included unemployment, substance abuse, limited economic resources, and geographic location. Brown (1989) concurs with this assessment in his finding of the meaning of economic exploitation. Although financial and material exploitation were prevalent among the Navajos in his study, they were defined as a cultural privilege and duty to help their family, not as abuse.

American Indians and Their Concept of Elder Abuse

Although many researchers have found elder abuse to be present among American Indians, American Indians themselves often do not believe that they have been abused (Brown, 1989; Carson, 1995; Danaan, 1990; Stein, 1991). Carson states that "this [belief] may be partially due to the strong loyalty that elders have to their families (and vice versa) which influence their perceptions of mistreatment" (p. 29). What is defined as abuse by the majority population often may be construed to be the norm by the minority population. For example, in an incident of financial exploitation, the use of an elder's money for the well-being of the family supersedes the use of the money for the elder's own well-being. An elder will go without needed medication to feed or clothe his or her family. Danaan (1990) states that "Native Americans value individual autonomy within a well-defined social structure" that emphasizes the stability of the group and that "some degree of role conformity, cooperation, and group welfare will be placed above individual welfare" (p. 5-3), and Nerenberg (1995) concurs when she states that the "Native American culture provides a well-defined social structure that places prime importance upon group survival" (p. 3). Furthermore, research has found that some American Indian elders feel that elder abuse is a problem of society, not a problem of the individual, and believe that it should be treated as a societal ill (Carson, 1995; Maxwell & Maxwell, 1992).

In summary, the literature on elder abuse among American Indians is minimal and at best provides only a cursory picture of the problem. The literature supports the notion that although elder abuse is a problem facing American Indians, it is one that must be addressed through the use of culturally specific definitions and actions.

ELDER ABUSE IN THE ASIAN AMERICAN COMMUNITY

As with other minority groups, little research has been published on mistreatment of elders in the Asian American community. However, a thorough review of studies in this subject group found more information available on Asian Americans than most ethnic groups. This section looks at available literature in all areas of Asian American elder abuse and neglect, as well as studies and literature on other cultural factors relating to the attitudes of the Asian American elderly toward receiving needed services from outside their families. These attitudes can figure prominently in whether or not an elderly person receives or refuses to receive needed services; the latter may predispose them to abuse or neglect. This section examines cultural groups in the Asian American community for which there is published information, particularly the Japanese, Vietnamese, and Korean American populations. One weakness of most of the published studies conducted with elderly Asian Americans, which should be noted, is the small sample size.

Studies on Elder Abuse Among Asian Americans

Several studies on Asian American elder abuse have established the existence of at least a few different types of abuse, particularly psychological and financial abuse. In the Japanese culture Kaneko and Yamada (1990) found that mistreatment of mothers-in-law by their daughters-in-law commonly consisted of the daughters-in-law not speaking to the mothers-in-law or ignoring them and making rude statements about them to others. This type of emotional abuse can be seriously harmful to the elderly woman. A study by Anetzberger, Korbin, and Tomita (1996) found that Japanese American elders identified "rough treatment," physical and psychological abuse, as the worst thing family members can do to the elderly. In another recent analysis, Tomita (1998) presented information that showed that elderly Japanese American interviewees believed their culture protected its community by not discussing any problems with "outsiders," problems that could make Japanese people appear dishonorable. The Japanese American culture typically "supports being unpleasant at home but not in public," one elderly interviewee said in the study. Tomita's research (1994) also showed the role of male dominance in the Japanese American society, with elderly female interviewees reporting instances of physical and verbal abuse by males. The concept of the "group" being more important than the individual, coupled with the acceptance of male superiority, and the covering up of any unpleasant behaviors by those in the Japanese American culture may cause elderly women to disregard the fact that they have been abused, Tomita found.

In a small ($n = 12$) study by Le (1996), it was shown that emotional abuse was the most typical form of elder abuse in a Vietnamese American community, followed by verbal abuse, with financial and physical abuse nonexistent. Chang and Moon (In press), in interviews with 100 elderly Korean Americans, found that of the 46 abuse cases respondents reported, financial abuse was most frequent, followed by psychological abuse. Moon and Williams (1993) discovered large differences among ethnic groups, particularly Korean Americans, regarding their perceptions of elder abuse. Overall, Korean Americans were less sensitive to, or more tolerant of, potentially abusive situations than were Caucasians or African Americans. When elderly women were presented with 13 possible elder-abuse situations, Korean American women defined fewer of these as elder abuse than did women in the other ethnic groups. Across all groups, the study suggests, elderly respondents looked at three major factors in deciding if a scenario was an elder abuse risk: the intention of the person involved, the circumstantial factors, and the specific nature of the behavioral act. Korean American elderly women were inclined to define elder abuse in a more narrow context and were significantly less likely to seek help compared with other groups. Moon and William's study raises the question of whether there should be two classification systems of elder abuse, one that is universally applicable to all groups and another that is culturally appropriate for each ethnic group. To what degree should potential cultural differences in perception and help-seeking behavior be considered in recognizing elder-abuse cases and fashioning appropriate intervention strategies?

In looking at elder abuse, one author suggested that we must look beyond our common definitions of abuse for the majority population and see that other behaviors, such as the use of "aggressive and cruel silence" among the Japanese Americans to punish others (Tomita, 1994, p. 46), are devastatingly abusive, although this behavior certainly is not limited to Japanese Americans or any minority group.

Several factors may contribute to the reluctance of Asian American elderly to involve those outside the family in elder abuse cases. These reasons include filial piety; the idea of suffering as part of Buddhist, Confucian, and other religious philosophies of life; the propensity to value privacy in family life; and the idea that family takes precedence over the individual. The next sections examine each of these concepts, citing research on family attributes and studies on elder abuse that illustrate these ideas.

Cultural Factors Affecting Elder Abuse in Asian American Communities

Filial Piety Asian cultures often adhere to the Buddhist and Confucian practices of filial piety and respect for elders (Braun, Takamura, & Mougeot, 1996; Tomita, 1994). Elders may believe they are being abused if their adult children do not act in the expected, traditional ways of deference to the elderly (Chang & Moon, 1997).

Chang and Moon (1997) found that most elderly Korean American respondents identified elder abuse in terms of "abrogation of filial piety," which suggests the centrality of children, even adult children, in the lives and well-being of elderly Korean Americans. In a 1996 study, Moon found that elders' subjective intimacy with their grown children, even if they were not living together, was critical for life satisfaction for elderly Koreans living in the United States. Filial piety, termed *hyo* in Korean, dictates the parent–child relationship and necessitates that children respect, obey, and interact with their parents in a polite and respectable fashion. In Korean society there is special emphasis on the filial piety of adult sons, who traditionally enjoy exclusive inheritance rights and are expected to care for all of their elderly parents' needs. Because of this precedent of the adult sons' entitlement to the family's money and property, it may be easier for the sons to exploit the elders' finances, which was the most commonly reported type of abuse in Chang and Moon's study. Typically, the son confiscated the parents' Supplemental Security Income checks but failed to take care of the parents.

Pang (1996) also examined filial piety, among other attributes of Korean immigrants, such as respecting seniority, etiquette, and demeanor as a form of self-cultivated mental and behavioral discipline, which is important for keeping peace both with oneself and with others. Many of the Korean elders in Pang's study resented babysitting, cooking, and cleaning house for adult children, as they had performed these tasks when they were parents and questioned why they had to do these tasks again. These experiences may result in feelings of betrayal in the Korean elderly; however, the elders may not consider discussion and negotiation of family relationships regarding these problems to be appropriate (Pang, 1996), so these situations may not improve.

In the Vietnamese American community, immigrants also typically believe that there should be deep affection and responsibility between parents and children. This concept of filial piety is extremely important in Vietnamese society. To emphasize this importance of family life in their Asian culture, Vietnamese members of a focus group (Braun et al., 1996) recited a poem from their homeland extolling filial piety when they were asked about their families:

> Therefore in our hearts we will always worship, obey, and respect our parents. To fulfill filial piety is to be a pious child. (p. 221)

Lee (1987) cautioned against accepting the false assumption that all Asian families extend support to all their members. Extended families may not be free of conflicts, Lee warns, and even if Asian families can help their elderly members, this assistance may be inadequate. Asian elders should have the chance to access social workers and needed services outside the family, without the social worker's presumption that the family can provide for all needs, Lee writes.

Suffering as Part of Life   Buddhist and Confucian ideals profess that suffering is to be an expected part of life, and this philosophy extends to many Asian cultures in which Buddhist and Confucian philosophies are practiced (Tomita, 1994; Pang, 1996). In this context elders may view suffering as their fate and may think it cannot or should not be changed but simply should be endured. In fact, elderly Koreans may tolerate suffering to create harmonious interpersonal relationships, and if they or people close to them deviate from moral standards or expectations, the elders may become sad and depressed. Instead of readily discussing these issues, the elders try to hide these emotions from others (Pang, 1996). Tomita (1998) found that elderly Japanese American women in unhappy domestic situations would accept situations as being "their fate," partially because of their Buddhist beliefs, and tended to believe that most things are determined by fate and predestination.

These attitudes of the acceptance of suffering may hamper an elderly Asian person in acknowledging that he or she has been subjected to abuse. Without acknowledgment, treatment is obviously difficult to initiate.

Privacy of Families   One recent study (Anetzberger et al., 1996) examining how four ethnic groups, including Japanese Americans, define and identify elder abuse provides important cultural information that also relates to other Asian American groups. When presented with a case example in which an elderly person was mistreated by a family member, Japanese Americans said they would first take action by talking to family or friends about the abuse; the other three ethnic groups (European Americans, African Americans, and Puerto Ricans) said that they would contact the proper authorities or agencies serving elders. This information illustrates the closed nature of communication in Japanese American families and, in general, in many Asian American families, and the difficulties that case workers (particularly those of non-Japanese or non-Asian backgrounds) may have in obtaining information on possible elder abuse or neglect cases. Interestingly, the study, which used a focus-group methodology for guided small-group discussions, showed that only Japanese Americans rated psychological abuse as the worst type of abuse (over psychological neglect, physical neglect, or exploitation) (Anetzberger et al., 1996).

Lee (1987) found that many Asian American elderly prefer to remain within their own cultural communities and do not like to turn to social workers for assistance because it goes against their ethnic values of self-reliance and pride. These elders also said that they did contact social workers because of other problems such as "dehumanizing life experiences, language barriers, and cultural differences." However, Lee (1987) believes that these situations for the elderly may be changing as Asian Americans realize that some problems cannot be solved in the family. One recent study showed that Vietnamese immigrants in Honolulu were very willing to use needed social and economic services (Braun et al., 1996).

Family Takes Precedence Over the Individual   Vietnamese families adhere to a cultural norm whereby family is more important than the individual and elders are deferred to, even if they are cantankerous (Braun et al., 1996). This study also found that Vietnamese American members of a focus group expressed great regard for family cohesiveness and obligation. These family members have strong reasons to follow cultural norms, however:

> Key informants also confirmed the strong mediating role of family in Vietnamese culture, noting that punishment for family members who deviate can be disownment by the family. This carries tremendous shame and embarrassment, if not stigma, inasmuch as the deviant's moral identity is forever damaged. (p. 220)

Applying this information to an elder-abuse situation, elders may not want to turn in abusive family members, as the family could be stigmatized and the perpetrator could be disowned. This obviously could weigh heavily on the mind of a Vietnamese American elderly person, or one of his or her friends or relatives, if he or she were thinking about seeking services needed to deal with an abusive situation.

The family's survival also may take precedence over the individual in Japanese society, and that could result in abuse for the elderly person. A little known Japanese and Asian cultural "tradition" may be an age-old practice of abandoning older persons to preserve the family's resources; a more modern adaptation of that may be the failure to provide medically, socially, or materially for an elderly person (Tomita, 1994).

Tomita (1998) also reports that the group's worth is valued over self-worth in Japanese American communities, and this can cause the elderly, particularly women, to not acknowledge their abuse, as they believe they are secondary to the family. "In a self-denying society, the potential for exploitation is great," Tomita writes (1994, p. 45).

Intervention Recommendations for Working with Asian American Elders

Chang and Moon (In press) suggest employing the concept of filial piety in finding solutions to Korean American elder abuse, as some incidents of psychological abuse are culturally specific to Korean American elders, who may believe that their adult children or daughters-in-law do not show proper respect, care, and sensitivity for their feelings and needs. Using this information, practitioners may use social intervention by placing themselves as mediators between the elderly and their children and by helping all family members understand and share their problems, misunderstandings, and expectations. Having everyone involved realistically evaluate their situations and develop plans to improve or change conditions for all parties can make mediation a success and improve the quality of life for an elderly Korean American family member. Chang and Moon promulgate the idea that the entire Korean American community, including churches, social-service agencies, and social clubs may prevent elder abuse and neglect and help stop it if it occurs by starting family programs that work on interactions and improve relationships between the different generations.

In working with Japanese American elderly, it may be good to ask the mistreated elders to focus on the family or child's needs as well as their needs (Tomita, 1994), because of the Japanese emphasis on the common good. This may elicit a better response from elder-abuse victims than asking them to focus only on themselves, which would be a foreign concept. An elderly person also may be conditioned culturally not to ask for anything, and if the younger Americanized generation takes this at face value, problems may ensue (Tomita, 1994). These differences could be broached by the social worker to let the adult children know that the parents may need more than what they are able to ask for. Discussion with the caseworker or professional and the family about these issues may be invaluable.

Japanese typically like to use an intuitive communication approach to downplay differences, maintain harmony, and strengthen group loyalty, in contrast to Americans, who typically like to maximize differences and use confrontation and compromise approaches in conversation, as well as intellectual sparring (Tomita, 1994). These differences in styles should be acknowledged and this information used in designing strategies for elder-abuse intervention and prevention in Japanese American populations. Because of the strong group identity and often the denial of one's unique self in the Japanese population, practice standards in the United States should include developing methods to treat the "we-self" instead of the "I-self," Tomita concludes (1998).

SUMMARY AND RECOMMENDATIONS

The collected research on elder abuse in different minority communities across the United States has only begun to examine the problem of elder abuse in minority communities. Although the existence of elder abuse has been documented in many ethnic groups, the small sample sizes in most of these studies present the drawback of not being statistically generalizable from the sample to entire minority populations. However, the difficulty in finding sample populations should not be underestimated, and the samples, although small, appear to be very illustrative of the types of abuses occurring in different communities. The research findings, thus far, suggest that whether in majority or minority communities, elder abuse is a complex phenomena that is not easily attributed to any one characteristic. In particular, we recommend that future research should better explore socioeconomic factors in elder abuse cases. We need to examine whether poverty is a prime causal factor and stressor in many elder-abuse cases, instead of typically focusing only on a racial or cultural explanation. Elder abuse does exist across all socioeconomic groups, and it is important to understand how this may be manifested. Although it may be easy to document elder abuse in an economically disadvantaged minority family in which a drug-using adult child steals an elderly parent's Social Security check, it may be more difficult to recognize abuse in an advantaged, majority family that forces an elder into a nursing home so as not to unduly deplete a future inheritance. Thus, it is apparent that we need to more closely examine elder abuse in all strata of society, not merely among those who fall under the purview of adult-protective services, typically the poor and disadvantaged.

We also need to consider each culture's definition of elder abuse and to add that to our general definitions of elder abuse, which are generally applied to the majority community. This follows the suggestion of Moon and Williams (1993), who raise the idea of having both a universally applicable definition of elder abuse and one that is culturally appropriate for each ethnic group. For example, we need to examine the strength in many minority communities of their focus on the community as being more important than the individual. Because this has not been the view of the majority of the population in the United States, this apparent "cultural bias" may lead us to inaccurate conclusions about the existence of abuse. However, we also need to work with minority communities who solely emphasize the importance of the community over the needs of the individual. We need to encourage an examination of the worth and needs of individuals in all communities. This can be seen as particularly necessary in cases in which an elderly person is miserable in his or her environment because he or she has subverted his or her needs completely to the group's or family's needs. Finally, we hope that future research will continue to shed light on the complex interplay of the characteristics or factors that place families at risk of committing elder abuse.

REFERENCES

Anetzberger, G. J., Korbin, J. E., & Tomita, S. K. (1996). Defining elder mistreatment in four ethnic groups across two generations. *Journal of Cross-Cultural Gerontology, 11*, 187–212.

Applewhite, S. R., & Daley, J. M. (1988). Cross-cultural understanding of social work practice with the Hispanic elderly. In S. Applewhite (Ed.), *Hispanic elderly in transition* (pp. 3–16). New York: Greenwood Press.

Asbury, J. (1987). African-American women in violent relationships: An exploration of cultural differences. In R. L. Hampton (Ed.), *Violence in black families: Correlates and consequences*. Lexington, MA: Lexington Books.

Baugher, E., & Lamison-White, L. (1996). *Poverty in the United States: 1995*. U.S. Bureau of the Census. Current Population Reports, Series P60–194. Washington, DC: U.S. Government Printing Office.

Boyajian, J. (1990) Cross-cultural considerations in professional decision-making: Beyond generalizations. In J. Boyajian (ed.) *Adult protective services practice guide* (pp. 5-1–5-2). St. Paul, MN: Minnesota Department of Human Services.

Braun, K. L., Takamura, J. C., & Mougeot, T. (1996). Perceptions of dementia, caregiving, and help-seeking among recent Vietnamese immigrants. *Journal of Cross-Cultural Gerontology, 11*, 213–228.

Brenes Jette, C., & Remien, R. (1988). Hispanic geriatric residents in a long-term care setting. *The Journal of Applied Gerontology, 7*(3), 350–366.

Brown, A. S. (1989). A survey of elder abuse on one native American tribe. *Journal of Elder Abuse and Neglect, 1*(2), 17–37.

Carson, D. K. (1995). American Indian elder abuse: Risk and protective factors among the oldest Americans. *Journal of Elder Abuse and Neglect, 7*(1), 17–39.

Cazenave, N. A. (1981, October). *Elder abuse and Black Americans: Incidence, correlates, treatment and prevention*. Paper presented at the annual meeting of the National Council on Family Relations, Milwaukee, WI.

Cazenave, N. A., & Straus, M. (1979). Race, class, network embeddedness and family violence: A search for potent support systems. *Journal of Comparative Family Studies*, 10(3), 281–300.

Chang, J., & Moon, A. (1997) Korean American elderly's knowledge and perceptions of elder abuse: a qualitative analysis of cultural factors. *Journal of Multicultural Social Work*, 6(121–2), 139–155.

Coles, R. (1989). Full-moon wisdom (treatment of the elderly in Hispanic and Indian cultures). *New Choices for the Best Years*, 29, 94–96.

Crystal, S. (1987). Elder abuse: The latest "crisis." *The Public Interest*, 88, 56–66.

Danaan, A. (1990). Working with Native Americans: Some common themes. In J. Boyajian (Ed.), *Adult Protective Services Practice Guide*. St. Paul, MN: Minnesota Department of Human Services.

Farias, L., & Handley, J. (1990). Protective services issues and Hispanic clients: Mexican-Americans as example. In J. Boyajian (Ed.), *Adult Protective Services Practice Guide*. St. Paul, MN: Minnesota Department of Human Services.

Griffin, L. W., & Williams, O. J. (1992). Abuse among African-American elderly. *Journal of Family Violence*, 7(1), 19–35.

Hall, P. A. (1987). Minority elder maltreatment: Ethnicity, gender, age and poverty. *Ethnicity and Gerontological Social Work*, 9(4), 81–93.

Hare, N. (1979). The relative psychosocial economic suppression of the Black male. In W. D. Smith (Ed.), *Reflection of Black psychology*. Washington, DC: University Press.

Harel, Z., McKinney, E., & Williams, M. (1990). Introduction. In Z. Harel, E. McKinney, & M. Williams (Eds.), *Black aged*. (pp. 131–145). Newbury Park, CA: Sage Publications, Inc.

Kaneko, Y., & Yamada, Y. (1990) Wives and mothers-in-law: Potential for family conflict in post-war Japan. *Journal of Elder Abuse and Neglect*, 2, 87–99.

Le, Q. K. (1996). Assessment of relationships among Vietnamese elders and their families. An unpublished research report for completion of a Master of Science degree in the gerontology program at San Jose State University, CA.

Lee, J. (1987) Asian American elderly: A newly neglected minority group. *Ethnicity and Gerontological Social Work*, 9(4), 103–116.

Longres, J. F. (1992). Race and type of maltreatment in an elder abuse system. *Journal of Elder Abuse & Neglect*, 4(3), 61–83.

Longres, J. F., Raymond, J. A., & Kimmel, M. S. (1991). *Black and White clients in an elder abuse system*. In T. Tatara, M. Rittman, & K. J Flores (Eds.), *Findings of five elder abuse studies* (pp. 53–80). Washington, DC: National Center on Elder Abuse.

Lubben, J., & Becerra, R. (1987). Social support among Black, Mexican, and Chinese elderly. In D. E. Gelfand & C. M. Barresi (Eds.), *Research and ethnic dimensions of aging* (pp. 130–144). New York: Springer Publishing Co.

Maxwell, E. K., & Maxwell, R. J. (1992). Insults to the body civil: Mistreatment of elderly in two plains Indian tribes. *Journal of Cross-Cultural Gerontology*, 7, 3–23.

Moon, A. (1996). Predictors of morale among Korean immigrant elderly in the United States. *Journal of Cross-Cultural Gerontology*, 11, 351–367.

Moon, A., & Williams, O. (1993) Perceptions of elder abuse and help-seeking behavior among African American, Caucasian American, and Korean American elderly women, *The Gerontologist*, 33(3), 386–395.

National Aging Resource Center on Elder Abuse. (1989). *American Indians and elder abuse: Exploring the problem*. Washington, DC: Author.

Nerenberg, L. (1995). To reach beyond our grasp: A community outreach guide for professionals in the field of elder abuse. San Francisco Consortium for Elder Abuse Prevention, San Francisco, CA. This manual was prepared pursuant to the U.S. Department of Health and Human Services, Grant No. 90-AM-0660.

Pang, K. Y. C. (1996). Self-care strategy of elderly Korean immigrants in the Washington DC metropolitan community. *Journal of Cross-Cultural Gerontology*, 11, 229–254.

Rogers, C. J., & Gallion, T. E. (1978). Characteristics of elderly pueblo Indians in New Mexico. *The Gerontologist*, 18(5), 482–7.

Smith, T. D. (1993). The elderly Native American: 'Forgotten again.' *Aging, 365,* 50–51.

Staples, R. (1976). Race and family violence: The internal colonialism perspective. In L. E. Gary & L. P. Brown (Eds.), *Crime and its impact on the Black community.* Washington, DC: Howard University, Institute for Urban Development Center.

Stein, K. F. (1991). *Working with abused and neglected elders in minority populations: A synthesis of research.* Washington, DC: National Aging Resource Center on Elder Abuse.

Steinmetz, S. K. (1988). *Duty bound: Elder abuse and family care.* Newbury Park, CA: Sage Publications, Inc.

Steinmetz, S. K. (1990). Elder abuse: Myth and reality. In T. H. Brubaker (Ed.), *Family relationships in later life.* Newbury Park, CA: Sage Publications, Inc.

Steinmetz, S. K., & Pelliccario, J. (1986). Women, ethnicity, and family violence: Implications for social policy. In W. A. VanHorne (Ed.), *Ethnicity and woman.* Madison, WI: University of Wisconsin System.

Tatara, T., & Kuzmeskus, L. B. (1997). *Summaries of the statistical data on elder abuse for FY 95 and FY 96.* Washington, DC: National Center on Elder Abuse.

Tomita, S. K. (1994). The consideration of cultural factors in the research of elder mistreatment with an in-depth look at the Japanese. *Journal of Cross-Cultural Gerontology, 9,* 39–52.

Tomita, S. K. (1998). Exploration of elder maltreatment among the Japanese. In T. Tatara (Ed.) *Understanding elder abuse in minority populations* (pp. 119–139). Philadelphia: Brunner/Mazel.

Trevino, M. (1988). A comparative analysis of need, access, and utilization of health and human services. In S. Applewhite (Ed.), *Hispanic elderly in transition* (pp. 61–71). New York: Greenwood Press.

Williams, O. J., & Griffin, L. (1991). Elder abuse in the Black family. In R. L. Hampton (Ed.), *Black family violence: Current research and theory* (pp. 117–127). Lexington, MA: Lexington Books.

Yakima Indian Nation. (1987). Don't wound my spirit: Yakima Indian nation's guide to protecting elders from abuse, neglect and exploitation. This guide was prepared pursuant to U.S. Dept. of Health and Human Service Administration on Aging, Grant No. 90A0214.

Concluding Remarks

Toshio Tatara

Three of the forty-some resolutions adopted by the official delegation of the 1995 White House Conference on Aging prominently recognized elder abuse as a serious social problem that needs to be addressed at the national level (1995 White House Conference on Aging). This was considered a victory for all those who had advocated greater public awareness of elder abuse. Because the purpose of the Conference was to set forth a national policy agenda on aging issues for the next decade, the delegates concerned with elder abuse fought particularly hard to try to convince other delegates (all of whom were participating in the Conference on behalf of some groups or "causes") that elder abuse should be included in the major resolutions to be adopted at the Conference. The result was remarkable, given that only a small number of the delegates represented the interest of the elder-abuse community at the Conference. I was one such delegate and found the accomplishments of elder-abuse advocates at the Conference gratifying. It was unfortunate that the staff office for the 1995 White House Conference on Aging was subsequently defunded by Congress and was dissolved before any substantive follow-up activities could be planned for the resolutions adopted by the official delegates.

What was amazing about the discussions on elder abuse at the Conference was the fact that there was little or no recognition of minority elders. Minority elders' unique circumstances in elder maltreatment were seldom mentioned even by minority experts (whose presence was barely felt because of their small number). After observing this situation firsthand, I decided to do something to change it. My decision, motivated by a desire to help others understand the importance of minority elders with respect to elder abuse, eventually led to the realization of three projects of national significance. One of them now manifests itself as this book, thanks to Taylor & Francis and their staff. The other two projects are the convening of a National Conference on Understanding and Combating Elder Abuse in Minority Populations and the publication of a report of conference proceedings, and the launching of the Multicultural Study of the Attitudes Toward Maltreatment and Reporting.

The national conference focusing on elder abuse in minority populations, held on board the Queen Mary in Long Beach, California, from June 24 through June 27, 1997, was an unprecedented event, in which many of the nation's leading minority researchers and practicing professionals concerned with elder abuse gathered together to discuss ways to understand and combat elder abuse in minority communities. The Archstone Foundation in Long Beach made this conference (which was attended by nearly 300 people) possible by awarding a grant to the National Center on Elder Abuse (NCEA), which planned and managed the conference. Most of the authors of the chapters in this book participated in the conference and played leading roles. The Archstone Foundation, which changed its name from the FHP Foundation in 1997 and started to support mostly aging projects, assisted NCEA in organizing the Long Beach conference and was totally responsible for compiling and disseminating the conference proceedings. The Archstone Foundation came forward to fund NCEA's proposal on the conference when only a few people were concerned with looking at elder abuse in minority populations.

Next, it is well accepted in the elder-abuse research community that the perception of what are abusive behaviors toward elders varies from one culture to another. Previous studies were concerned with comparing among a small number of racial and ethnic groups (Moon & Williams, 1993; Anetzberger, Korbin, & Tomita, 1996), but I decided to test this notion, using a larger number of cultural groups (i.e., minority populations) in the United States and abroad. Thus, the main objective of the study was to learn how the perceptions and attitudes of elderly people toward maltreatment differ from one population to another. It was fortunate that most of this country's leading minority researchers in elder abuse were able to take part in the multicultural study. As a result, the study covered a total of six racial/ethnic populations: Black, Hispanic, American Indian, Japanese American, Korean American, and White American. One of the unique features of the study was the fact that three Hispanic researchers participating in the study were able to design one standardized Spanish-language survey tool that was subsequently used for Mexican American elders in Texas, elders in Puerto Rico, and a sample of Latino elders residing in New Mexico. In addition to these racial/ethnic groups in the United States, we were able to collect data for the study in Finland, Japan, and Korea, using the survey tools translated into the languages of these countries and the assistance of researchers who are native to these countries. At the time when these concluding remarks were prepared, data collected from different groups were still being analyzed at the University of California at Los Angeles research facility, which worked closely with NCEA.

Finally, this book project has become the largest of the projects on minority elder abuse that I started a few years ago. With the book project soon coming to an end, I would like to reflect on the significance of the project one last time. This book, *Understanding Elder Abuse in Minority Populations*, examines the problems of abuse, neglect, and exploitation in the Black, Hispanic, Asian American, and Native American communities. Almost every one of the authors is native to the culture on which he or she has written a chapter. Additionally, all of the authors are recognized experts in elder abuse, either as researchers or practicing professionals. Specifically, three chapters address elder abuse among Blacks, with Hall (Chapter 2) and Griffin (Chapter 3) providing insight into the Black communities mainly based on their work experiences, and Benton (Chapter 4) discussing research on risk factors for abuse among Black elders. Next, three other chapters focus on elder abuse in the Hispanic communities, starting with Yolanda Sanchez (Chapter 5) elaborating on reasons for the lack of elder abuse research in the Latino community. Then, Mitchell et al. (Chapter 6) examine findings of an extensive study of elder mistreatment in the Mexican American community in Texas, and Carmen Sanchez (Chapter 7) describes elder-abuse problems and programs serving the elderly in Puerto Rico. Two more chapters are devoted to discussing the issue of elder abuse in the Asian American communities, with Moon (Chapter 8) reviewing her research of the Korean community in Los Angeles, and Tomita (Chapter 9) presenting her work among Japanese American elders. Finally, the book includes two chapters that address elder abuse in the Native American community, with Brown (Chapter 10) providing summaries of his extensive studies with Native American elders and Carson and Hand (Chapter 11) examining a range of issues that pertain to elder abuse in the Native American community.

In addition to these 10 chapters addressing elder abuse in specific racial/ethnic populations, the book also included two chapters that discussed elder abuse in cross-cultural perspectives. One of these papers (Chapter 12) focused on findings from a multicultural study of perceptions of elder abuse; the other (Chapter 13) described ways to design culturally specific elder-abuse outreach programs. Finally, inclusion of a chapter that offered an in-depth review of the elder-abuse research literature pertaining to minority elders (Chapter 14) in this book represents a valuable contribution to the field of elder abuse. The review, which involved an extensive computer-assisted search of materials, focuses on elder-abuse research pertaining to the Black, Hispanic, American Indian, and Asian American communities.

The publication of this book clearly is a significant event, not only because its contents have not been addressed previously, but because of a number of other reasons. First, thanks to the publisher's desire to examine the issue thoroughly, more than one chapter was sought for each ethnic/racial group. This decision allowed the inclusion of papers with different (sometimes contrasting) viewpoints for each group. For example, Hall (Chapter 2), Griffin (Chapter 3), and Benton (Chapter 4) are all African American professionals, but their perspectives are quite different. The chapters on Hispanics are somewhat different from the chapters on Blacks because their authors were concerned with three different Hispanic communities. For example, the research interest of Yolanda Sanchez (Chapter 5) is the Spanish-speaking population in New Mexico; Mitchell and her colleagues (Chapter 6) are exclusively concerned with Mexican Americans in Texas for the purpose of this book. Similarly, Carmen Sanchez (Chapter 7) focuses only on Puerto Rican elders. The chapters on each of the other racial/ethnic populations also provide diverse viewpoints similar to the chapters on Black and Hispanic elders, although only two chapters were set aside for each group.

Second, the book covered both research findings and professional-practice issues, and this approach should prove effective in gaining a broader readership of the book. Research on minority elder abuse is a relatively new discipline and is still evolving. However, research interest in both minority elders and elder abuse are growing among professionals concerned with aging issues, as evidenced by the recent increase in the number of workshops on these topics at major national aging conferences and by the increased quantity of research publications addressing these topics. Given these trends, it will only be a matter of time before more researchers focus on elder abuse in minority populations. However, adult protective service professionals already are seeing minority elders being disproportionately overrepresented among the victims of elder abuse. Yet, as pointed out by many authors of this book, resources with which these professionals can consult are totally lacking at the present time. That being the case, it is likely that both the proceedings of the Long Beach conference and this book will be included in the resources on which practicing professionals serving minority elders can depend.

In the final analysis, I am convinced that the release of this book is very timely, because the interest of thousands of people (including researchers and practitioners) in minority elders is becoming heightened. I hope they will find, as I have, the material in this book informative. Finally, I also hope that this book, along with other publications on the mistreatment of minority elders, will result in many more people joining in efforts to strengthen the field of research and practice addressing elder abuse in minority populations.

REFERENCES

Anetzberger, G., Korbin, J., & Tomita, S. K. (1996). Defining elder mistreatment in four ethnic groups across two generations. *Journal of Cross-Cultural Gerontology, 11,* 187–212.

Moon, A., & Williams, O. (1993). Perception of Elder Abuse and Help-Seeking Patterns Among African American, Caucasian American, and Korean American Elderly Women. *The Gerontologist, 33,* 386–395.

White House Conference on Aging (1995). *The road to an aging policy for the 21st century.* Washington, DC: Author.

Index

243